AF505426

The European Union and culture

Manchester University Press

European Policy Research Unit Series

Series Editors: *Simon Bulmer, Peter Humphreys* and *Mick Moran*

The European Policy Research Unit Series aims to provide advanced textbooks and thematic studies of key public policy issues in Europe. They concentrate, in particular, on comparing patterns of national policy content, but pay due attention to the European Union dimension. The thematic studies are guided by the character of the policy issue under examination.

The European Policy Research Unit (EPRU) was set up in 1989 within the University of Manchester's Department of Government to promote research on European politics and public policy. The series is part of EPRU's effort to facilitate intellectual exchange and substantive debate on the key policy issues confronting the European states and the European Union.

Titles in the series also include:

Globalisation and policy-making in the European Union Ian Bartle

Creating a transatlantic marketplace Michelle P. Egan (ed.)

The politics of health in Europe Richard Freeman

Immigration and European integration Andrew Geddes

Agricultural policy in Europe Alan Greer

The European Union and the regulation of media markets Alison Harcourt

Mass media and media policy in Western Europe Peter Humphreys

The politics of fisheries in the European Union Christian Lequesne

Sports law and policy in the European Union Richard Parrish

The Eurogroup Uwe Puetter

EU pharmaceutical regulation Govin Permanand

Regulatory quality in Europe: Concepts, measures and policy processes Claudio M. Radaelli and Fabrizio de Francesco

Extending European cooperation Alasdair R. Young

Regulatory politics in the enlarging European Union Alasdair Young and Helen Wallace

The European Union and culture

Between economic regulation and European cultural policy

Annabelle Littoz-Monnet

Manchester University Press

Manchester and New York

distributed exclusively in the USA by Palgrave

Published by Manchester University Press
Oxford Road, Manchester M13 9NR, UK
and Room 400, 175 Fifth Avenue, New York, NY 10010, USA
www.manchesteruniversitypress.co.uk

Distributed exclusively in the USA by
Palgrave, 175 Fifth Avenue, New York,
NY 10010, USA

Distributed exclusively in Canada by
UBC Press, University of British Columbia, 2029 West Mall,
Vancouver, BC, Canada V6T 1Z2

British Library Cataloguing-in-Publication Data
A catalogue record for this book is available from the British Library

Library of Congress Cataloging-in-Publication Data applied for

ISBN 978 0 7190 7435 6 *hardback*

First published 2007

16 15 14 13 12 11 10 09 08 07   10 9 8 7 6 5 4 3 2 1

Typeset in Sabon
by Action Publishing Technology Ltd, Gloucester
Printed in Great Britain
by Biddles Ltd, King's Lynn

Contents

Acknowledgements

Writing this book would not have been possible without the support of a number of people and institutions. First, special thanks go to Jeremy Richardson at Oxford University. He provided me not only with invaluable intellectual and academic guidance while I was in the course of conducting my research but also with the encouragement and the enthusiasm that were necessary to pursue the project to its end. I am also grateful to Sonia Mazey at Oxford University for her feedback on the theoretical aspects of my work. Among my colleagues, I would like to thank Jürgen Neyer for his very helpful feedback on the theoretical and conceptual aspects of my research, Edward Gray for his time (reading early versions of the manuscript in their entirety …) and his enlightening comments on my work, and Flemming Splidsboel Hansen for his good suggestions too. I am also very grateful to the two anonymous referees from Manchester University Press, who provided very detailed and valuable comments on the manuscript. In connection with my field work, I would like to thank Monsieur le Ministre Jack Lang, former Minister of Culture and Minister of Education in France, who generously agreed to discuss the construction process of European cultural policy during an interview set up in Paris in December 1999, and also gave me access to a considerable amount of archival documentation from the French Ministry of Culture. I also express my great gratitude to the EU, French and UK officials, interest group representatives and members of the European Parliament, who gave their time to answer my questions. Special thanks go to Patrick Olivier, from the French Ministry of Culture, and David Levy, from the BBC, who both agreed to read a substantial part of the earlier versions of my case studies. In financial terms, the project could not have been conducted without the support of the British Economic and Social Research Council (ESRC), which granted me a three-year research award, and St Hilda's College at Oxford, which granted funding for research trips and conferences on various occasions. Last but not least, my family and friends provided me with invaluable advice and moral support.

Abbreviations

AIDAA	International Association of Audiovisual Writers and Directors
BBC	British Broadcasting Corporation
CDU/CSU	Christlich Demokratischen Union (Christian Democratic Union)
CICCE	Comité des Industries Cinématographiques Européennes
CLT	Compagnie Luxembourgeoise de Télédiffusion
CNC	Centre National de la Cinématographie
DBS	Direct Broadcasting Satellite
DCMS	Department of Culture, Media and Sport (UK)
DG	Directorate General
DLL	Direction du Livre et de la Lecture (France)
EAT	European Advertising Tripartite
EBU	European Broadcasting Union
EC	European Community
ECJ	European Court of Justice
EP	European Parliament
EPP	European People's Party
ETNO	European Telecommunications Network Operators' Association
EU	European Union
FEP	Federation of European Publishers
FERA	Fédération Européenne des Réalisateurs Audiovisuels
FNAC	Fédération Nationale d'Achat des Cadres
GATS	General Agreement on Trade in Services
GATT	General Agreement on Tariffs and Trade
GEMA	Gesellschaft für Musikalische Aufführungs (German copyright society)
GESAC	Groupement Européen de Sociétés d'Auteurs et de Compositeurs
HDTV	High Definition Television
IFPI	International Federation of the Phonographic Industry

IT	Information Technology
ITC	Independent Television Commission (UK)
MEPs	Members of the European Parliament
MFN	Most-favoured nation
NBA	Net Book Agreement
QMV	Qualified Majority Voting
RTL	Radio Télévision Luxembourg
SACEM	Société des Auteurs Compositeurs Editeurs de Musique
SGCI	Secrétariat Général du Comité Interministériel pour les questions économiques Européennes
SPD	Sozialdemokratische Partei Deutschlands
TF1	Télévision Française 1
TWF	Television Without Frontiers
UEF	Union Européenne des Fédéralistes
UK	United Kingdom
US	United States
WIPO	World Intellectual Property Organization
WTO	World Trade Organization

1

Cultural policy as a contested area

The trajectory of Communitarisation, the process by which European level policies are developed and the sector's governance (at least in terms of policy-making) takes place in Brussels, varies significantly across policy sectors. Most EU policies found a basis in the Treaty of Rome. Yet some policy sectors were Communitarised in the absence of a Treaty basis for Community intervention. Community policies were created in the telecommunications and environment fields, for instance, although the original Treaty made no mention of a Community role in these sectors. In the same way, no formal competence on cultural policy appeared in the original Treaty[1] – the first legal basis for a very narrowly defined EU competence on culture appeared with the Maastricht Treaty reform in 1992. Yet the Communitarisation of domestic policies in the cultural sector *has* occurred. European institutions have extensively intervened in the realm of audio-visual, book, copyright and cultural heritage matters, to name only those sectors where EU intervention has been the most substantial. As early as the 1970s, the European Court of Justice (ECJ) issued various rulings related to audio-visual, copyright, works of art, national treasures or book trade issues. ECJ cases examined the compatibility between the regulatory aspects of member states' cultural policies and EU competition rules and also, perhaps even more crucially, gave a legal basis for the European Community (EC) to intervene in the cultural sector. At the same time, the European Parliament (EP) issued resolutions drawing attention to the need for EU-level cultural policies and the European Commission published its first policy proposals for EU intervention in the field. Concrete policy developments soon followed. The 'Television Without Frontiers' Directive (89/552/EEC), which established the principle of free flow for television programmes within the EU, as well as minimal harmonised rules for television programmes, was issued in 1989. In the field of intellectual property, five directives were adopted in the 1980s and 1990s, which harmonise copyright legislation within the EU. Besides the regulatory aspects of EU intervention, various support mechanisms intended to promote the European audio-visual industry, encourage artistic creation, foster exchanges and cooperation between artists from different EU states, and ensure the preservation of European heritage were also initiated. Symbolic initiatives, such as the 'European City of Culture' event, the European Year of Cinema, and the setting up of European awards for artists, to mention only a few, were initiated in the 1980s. These developments are wide-ranging.

This is particularly striking since the cultural sector is an especially critical case of integration. As mentioned, there was no Treaty basis for Community intervention in the field before 1992. Even since then, Community intervention is meant to comply with a strictly defined principle of subsidiarity, which states that the Community should take action only if and in so far as the objectives of the proposed action cannot be sufficiently achieved by the member states. Culture has indeed traditionally been considered the domain of national sovereignty and member states are particularly disinclined to transfer their competence in this area. Along with the sheer fact that culture has been perceived as the domain of national competence, stark differences in member states' own conceptions of cultural policy abound (Sallois *et al.* 1993; Zetterholm 1994). Culture is an area where diversities between member states are particularly obvious – not only are peoples' cultures, in an anthropological sense, very different, but institutional forms of managing this area are also specific to each country – and anchored in national cultural styles. In the UK, cultural concerns were brought together under the responsibility of the Secretary of State for National Heritage in 1991, whereas in France a state minister has been in charge of cultural affairs since 1959 (Sallois *et al.* 1993). The British Secretary of State for Culture, Media and Sport is not only responsible for museums, libraries, music and film, but also for the press, historic buildings, tourism and sport. These differences among EU countries raise very basic questions concerning the nature of the cultural policy that the EU is entitled to implement.

Cultural policy is indeed a rather 'unsettled universe' that encompasses such varied issues as patronage, national heritage, artists' rights and intellectual property, the cultural industries, public education, pornography and censorship, entertainment markets, and cultural tourism. What pertains to the field of 'cultural policy' often reflects *political choices* made by national – or supranational, as will be seen here – governments. To take only one example, copyright issues are dealt with by the national ministries of culture in Spain, France, Norway, Italy, the Czech Republic, Poland, Portugal, Denmark, Finland and Greece. In other countries, a governmental department deals specifically with intellectual property issues; this is the case in the UK (the 'Patents Office', which has a copyright subdivision), in Hungary and in the Netherlands for instance. Finally, intellectual property is under the remit of the ministry of justice in Sweden and in Germany, the Department of Enterprise, Trade and Employment in Ireland, and the Ministry of Economy in Luxembourg.

Yet despite the 'difficult' nature of cultural policy as a field of integration, the governance of the policy sector has increasingly shifted towards the European level. Perhaps even more surprisingly yet, EU-level intervention in the cultural sector has essentially initiated the liberalisation of cultural industries' markets. Even when legislative solutions were agreed upon by member states, the latter essentially furthered the economic liberalisation of the cultural sector and imposed only minimal common standards. EU support programmes have only had a limited impact upon the art sector in Europe. Such an outcome goes against the widely spread belief that European cultural policy[2] was a 'French creation', which reflected French policy preferences (Littoz-Monnet 2003).[3] Given the highly publicised nature of France's endeavours in promoting the 'cultural exception' theme in international arenas, the common assumption is indeed that if one regulatory model was to be adopted at the EU level in the cultural sector, it would be the French one. This book highlights, instead, that not only were France's initiatives often a *reaction* to supranational developments that were already under way but also that once the process of EU policy formation was entrenched, France was not successful in 'locking in' its own policy model during EU policy negotiations.

The book seeks to explain this 'unexpected' policy outcome. Several alternative policy options were indeed available in the cultural field. In addition to the question of the appropriate level of governance for cultural matters, there was a debate over the objectives that EU cultural policy was meant to be fulfilling. Should a negative or a positive type of integration be promoted? Should EU policy-makers in fact apply economic principles to the cultural sector, in order to promote the liberalisation of cultural markets, or instead develop *dirigiste*[4] policies acknowledging the 'specificity' of the cultural field? Finding out why certain policies were opted for – in the event a market liberalisation strategy of the sector – in a policy sector where the choice of policy options is a 'non-obvious' enterprise, given the unsettled nature of the policy area, will shed light on essential aspects of the inherent dynamics of the EU decision-making and policy-making process.

Cultural policy: whose responsibility? Which objectives? Explaining integration dynamics and policy outcomes

In the book, the term 'Europeanisation' is used when referring to the penetration of the European dimension in national arenas of politics and policy (Börzel 1999), while the term 'Communitarisation' refers to the emergence and development at the European level of distinct structures of governance.[5] Attending to cultural policy makes it clear that both of these stages (Europeanisation/Communitarisation), in the process of 'governance shift' from the national to the supranational level, need to be considered. The argument goes thus. From the 1970s onwards, the ECJ and the Directorate General (DG) Competition, making use of their judicial and regulatory powers, initiated a negative type of integration, which essentially consists of eliminating trade barriers, while positive integration aims to harmonise national legislation and set up common forms of administration. Negative integration seems indeed to be particularly effective in areas where economic integration can be advanced by applying fairly explicit prohibitions in the treaties against national policies constituting barriers to the free mobility of goods, services, capital and persons or distortions of free competition (Scharpf 2000: 15). In this mode of governance (the 'hierarchical decision' mode), competencies were centralised at the European level and exercised by supranational actors without the participation of member governments. These functions are performed by the ECJ as well as the European Commission when it is acting as a guardian of the Treaty in infringement procedures against national governments (Scharpf 2000: 14). The process of negative integration, which did not involve the creation of a distinct supranational policy in the cultural sector, nevertheless had a strong impact on domestic policies. The policy sector was 'Europeanised' in the sense that the European dimension penetrated national arenas of politics, and member governments had to adapt their legislative and policy traditions to EU-level developments.

From this first 'Europeanisation phase', which occurred in the audio-visual, book and copyright policy sectors in the 1970s and 1980s, ensued a process leading to the formation of distinct policies and structures of governance at the EU level ('Communitarisation'). This Communitarisation phase resulted, essentially, from an attempt of *dirigiste* states to lock in their favoured policy models at the EU level. In reaction to the wave of negative integration promoted by the Court and the Commission from the 1970s onwards, those member states whose legislative and policy traditions were at odds with the liberalisation strategies developed by supranational structures attempted to develop their own initiatives. In particular, France, where a *dirigiste* policy model was in place in the cultural sector, attempted to lock in its favoured policy model at the EU level. *Dirigiste* states hoped that by pulling the decision-making process towards a 'joint decision' mode (Scharpf 2000: 18), in which aspects of intergovernmental negotiations and supranational centralisation are combined, they would be better able to further their policy preferences at the EU level. In the face of EU institutions' *de facto* intervention in the cultural sector, reorienting the policy debate at the EU level seemed to be the best available strategy.

Thus, two coalitions of actors were in the 'game', trying to gain – or preserve – control over policy. In this conflict, the portrayal of the policy problems at stake was a key weapon. The *dirigiste* or cultural coalition,[6] led by France and the cultural lobby, attempted to define culture as an area where 'special laws' should be applied. In the *dirigistes'* view, a so-called cultural specificity justifies the exemption of the cultural sector from market mechanisms. The 'liberals', led by the UK and DG Competition within the Commission, defended an economic definition of the cultural sector, which justified, on the contrary, the application of EU competition law. In fact, allied to tensions between levels of governance were tensions between conflicting ways of addressing the policy problems at stake. Framing policy problems in one specific way was a means, for policy actors, to gain control over policy. Thus, the policy-making process was characterised by the continuous adjustment between two coalitions of actors and their competing fashions of framing the policy problems. Yet, EU-level policy outcomes have not just been a balanced compromise between the preferences of the *dirigistes* and the liberals.

Essentially, the French attempt to 'rescue' cultural policy at the EU level failed. The *dirigistes* could not, once the locus of governance had shifted towards the European level, change the way policy problems were tackled. Why was that? The book's explanation goes thus. Because cultural policies were initially Communitarised as a result of the *de facto* intervention of EU institutions, which were applying economic principles to cultural matters by making use of their judicial and regulatory powers, *dirigiste* states' room for manoeuvre was restrained at the stage of policy negotiations. EU institutions were indeed successful in making the nature of the status quo (the situation without any EU-level common solution agreed upon by member states) less desirable for *dirigiste* member states. Even without formally accepting the delegation of their competence in specific cultural policy sectors, member states were subject to the enforce-ment of EU competition rules by the ECJ and DG Competition within the Commission. Technological developments were also putting pressure on domestic legislative and regulatory arrangements. Thus, when member states negotiated over possible common solutions within the Council of Ministers – the only way through which the *dirigistes* could have tried to impose a market-correcting mechanism in order to counter the propensity of the ECJ and the Commission to apply economic principles without the participation of member governments – *dirigiste* states were in a weak position. They were indeed unlikely to oppose even non-satisfactory EU-level solutions agreed upon by a majority of member governments, since the default situation was not favourable to their preferences either.

The dynamics of policy formation (the selection of policy options at the EU level), once the dynamics of Communitarisation have already taken place, are therefore directly connected to the factors that provoke Communitarisation itself. By looking at these two phenomena together, one can grasp a better understanding of both EU integration and EU 'policy outcomes'. Dividing the study of 'the nature of the beast' and that of 'integration' is counterproductive if one accepts that the two variables under examination are closely connected – and even more, interdependent.

Understanding how this 'unlikely' process of Communitarisation has occurred, and why, despite the widespread assumption that EU cultural policy was 'exported' by the French, another regulatory model was in fact adopted at the EU level, is highly relevant to explaining European integration dynamics, formal and informal processes of decision-making in the EU and broader debates on evolving forms of governance in the context of economic and technological globalisation.

Theorising policy-building at the EU level

Departing from the conventional theoretical debate
The process of European integration has been the object of continuing controversies between 'intergovernmental' and 'supranational' or 'neo-functionalist' perspectives. The latest version of the intergovernmental explanation of the EU is provided by Moravcsik (1993, 1999), who assumes that states are rational actors who play 'two-level games' (Putnam 1988). Intergovernmentalist theories of European integration argue that major choices in favour of Europe reflect the preferences of member states, which aim to further their economic interests (see also Garett 1992; Hoffman 1966). The outcomes of negotiations are seen as the result of the bargaining power of the states. Functionalist approaches see European integration as the product of growing international interdependence. Haas (1964) emphasises the importance in the integration process of supranational institutions and their propensity to maximise their powers. He recognises the continuing importance of national political elites, but explains that in response to new policies at the EU level, shifts in the expectations and activities of individuals are expected to emerge via 'political spill-over'. Shifts in loyalty increase the dynamic towards the development of a new political community. Haas also recognises the importance of 'functional spill-over', a process by which cooperation in one sector engenders cooperation in another, previously unrelated, sector. Standholtz and Stone Sweet (1997, 1998), in their 'supranational governance' model, also explain that integration is driven by private transnational actors who perceive an interest in the implementation of European rules. Thus, scholars have been successful in demonstrating that non-member state actors have been able to exercise considerable influence in the determination of policy outcomes at both the sub-national and supranational levels. However, neither intergovernmentalism nor theories drawn from neo-functionalist insights have

convincingly proven their ability to deal with *multi-level interactions*. Puchala (1999) argues that competing approaches explain different phenomena that have been occurring in the experience of the EU. And that distinguishing what institutionalism/neofunctionalism and intergovernmentalism respectively explain, and what they 'respectively do not explain' (1999: 330) is crucial to our understanding of European integration.

The case of cultural policy lends credence to his statement. Intergovernmentalist theories cannot account for the way in which supranational institutions developed autonomous agendas or for the role played by private actors in by-passing member governments in order to further their preferences. As for functionalist theories, while they provide useful insights into the mechanisms which promote the Communitarisation of public policies, they do not analyse the way in which member states seek to maximise their perceived interests by developing goal-oriented strategies; nor do they provide a theoretical framework that could explain the conditions under which national policy actors are successful or not in imposing their policy preferences at the EU level. The supranational governance framework does recognise that member states react to supranational entrepreneurship strategies and try to shape EU-level policy orientations. However, supranational governance theory neither accounts for the way member states aim to pull back the decision-making process into a more intergovernmental mode, nor does it provide insight into the strategies states use in order to push integration in directions favourable to their interests.

Even more problematic is the failure of 'grand theories' to shed light on the *interactions* between developments taking place at distinct levels of governance. It is this perceived failing in both that has largely inspired the multi-level governance model (Hooghe and Marks 2001), which sheds light on the 'multi-actorness' of the policy-making process. However, the multi-level governance model does not attempt to explain the mechanisms of Communitarisation – the phenomena by which governance in given policy sectors increasingly takes place at the EU level. It is a static model which only describes the EU policy-making process once EU policies are already in place. Yet developments initiated by actors at one given level of governance can *induce* policy developments from other actors at other levels of governance, thus provoking a shift in the locus of governance from the national towards the European level.

Another shortcoming in the existing literature on European integration is the lack of examination of the role played by policy ideas in explaining 'locus of governance shifts'. The cultural policy case makes it clear that policy ideas are a crucial component of the dynamics of European integration. If ideas are not easily separated from the interests of the actors that support them, they nevertheless are means through which actors can *successfully* achieve their strategies. The role of agenda-definition in policy-making has however been examined by comparative politics approaches. A growing number of studies in the field of public policy and more specifically in the area of agenda definition (Baumgartner and Jones 1993; Baumgartner and Jones 1994; Bosso 1994; Rochefort and Cobb 1994) conceive public debate as a specific realm where conflict among policy actors is manifest. Whether disputes are seen in terms of conflict to define what will become the dominant 'policy image' (Baumgartner and Jones 1993), or of the 'politics of problem definition' (Rochefort and Cobb 1994), or of clashes among the 'interpretative packages' (Gamson and Modigliani 1989) that constitute the culture of a public matter, the definition of policy problems looms as an important phenomenon in the processing of political activities. Yet these studies confine themselves to examining the role of agenda/problem definition in the policy-making process at one given level of governance, i.e. within a state. The dynamics of European integration, by contrast, have mainly been examined through the lenses of International Relations theories. Public policy approaches, when applied to the study of the EU, have been used to explain certain aspects of its 'daily politics'. Using the insights of agenda-definition approaches to explain EU integration dynamics will, therefore, allow us to capture under-researched aspects of the 'locus of governance' shift process in the EU.

Towards a dynamic multi-level model
It will be proposed here to use a dynamic framework able to capture how interactions between multiple actors at different governance levels, and the policy ideas they sponsor, can result in a) a 'locus of governance shift' between the national towards the supranational level and b) the selection of certain policy outcomes over others at the EU level. By contrast with the classic 'multi-level governance' model (Hooghe and Marks 2001), the model proposed aims to capture how multi-level interactions between actors provoke 'locus of governance' shifts – rather than characterising the EU policy-making process once these dynamics have already taken place. It is a 'dynamic' multi-level governance model, which explains how interactions between different levels induce integration dynamics. The model developed here also includes a *time dimension*. Rather than picturing interactions between actors at different levels of governance at a given n moment, it looks at how action from policy actors at a given level of governance at time x can provoke/induce action by other policy actors at another level of governance at time y.

The theoretical framework proposed draws upon the 'image and venue' approach developed by Baumgartner and Jones (1991, 1993). Initially applied to civilian nuclear policy in the US, the 'image and venue' approach examines the interaction of beliefs and values concerning a particular policy with the existing set of political institutions. By looking at tensions between 'venues' – different jurisdictions – and conflicting 'policy images' – defined as 'the interaction of beliefs and values concerning a particular policy' (Baumgartner and Jones 1991: 1045), it allows us to capture interrelated processes of interaction between *competing governance levels*, on the one hand, and *opposing policy preferences* on the other.

An actor-based approach   Baumgartner and Jones (1991, 1993) treat political actors as capable of strategic action within given institutional structures; thus structures and the individual strategies of 'policy entrepreneurs' both play important roles (1991: 1045). In their model, actors are also capable of using policy ideas in an instrumental manner in order to further their interests and control policy. Yet the book does not take a general stance on the primacy of ideas versus interests as explanatory variables of actors' preferences – and it is not the main object of the book either to try evaluating the respective impact of both in the policy process. Rather, the book would accept that policy ideas are not always purely instrumental tools but can also define the political discourse and eventually limit the number of solutions available to actors (Rein and Schön 1991; Campbell 1998; Sabatier 1998). Ideas and interests are often interpenetrated, and distinguishing the relative explanatory power of each is a difficult endeavour.[7] As Jacobsen argues (1995: 286), in order to explain the independent power of ideas, the latter 'must be shown to exert influence untainted by the interests that they have just been shown to interpenetrate'; thus highlighting the impracticality of separating the two variables.

The book deals with this issue by 'sequencing' the policy process. It shows that at the stage of preference formation both ideas and interests pulled their weight in the way actors defined their positions. While the impact of policy ideas resulted in some policy models being seen as more 'appropriate' than others by policy actors, economic or institutional interests were sometimes also in the picture. Thus, the book argues that ideas and interests are entwined in an intractable manner at the stage of policy formation. Yet at the stage of policy negotiations, when several actors were competing in order to impose their policy preferences – once formed – actors essentially *used* policy ideas in order to further their – perceived – interests and control policy, as proposed by the 'image and venue' approach.[8] Thus, while bearing shortcomings, 'sequencing' the policy-making process can, to some extent, provide a way of combining interest-based and ideational explanations of the policy-making process: ideas can shape actors' perceptions of their interests, at the stage of preference formation, and be used as instrumental tools to further these perceived interests, at the stage of policy formulation.

Images and institutional venues   Baumgartner and Jones shed light on the connection between policy images and institutional venues. They argue that each venue carries with it a decisional bias, because both participants and decision-making routines differ from one venue to another. Thus, they argue that in a given pluralist political system, subsystems can be created that are highly favourable to, for instance, a given industry. As a result, 'when the venue of a public policy changes, as often occurs over time, those who previously dominated the policy process may find themselves in the minority, and erstwhile losers may be transformed into winners' (1991: 1047). Thus, 'as venues change, images may change as well' and reciprocally 'as the image of a policy changes, venue changes become more likely' (1991: 1047).

But change can occur, since there always remain other institutional venues that can serve as avenues of appeal for the 'losers' in a given subsystem. Baumgartner and Jones (1991) argue, in essence, that actors try to control policy by using a dual strategy. On the one hand, they seek to 'control the prevailing image of the policy problem through the use of rhetoric, symbols, and policy analysis' (Baumgartner and Jones 1991: 1045). On the other hand, they try to 'alter the roster of participants who are involved in the issue by seeking out the most favourable venue for the consideration of these issues' (1991: 1045). Thus, in Baumgartner and Jones' model, it is actors' strategies that will provoke venue changes. There are no immutable rules, indeed, that determine which institutions in society will be granted jurisdiction over particular issues. Thus, in their view conflict expansion to new venues can occur in three ways:

1 'the loser's appeal strategy': those uncomfortable in the current venue or with the current image have incentives to seek out more favourable ones;
2 action by concerned outsiders, possibly allied with losers in a policy;
3 policy-makers from another venue can attack an existing policy arrangement trying to expand their own policy jurisdictions.

Furthermore, the interactions of image and venue may produce a self-reinforcing mechanism characterised by 'positive feedback mechanisms' (Baumgartner and Jones 1991: 1048). Indeed, each change in the venue of decision-making can lead to increased attention to a certain image of the policy problem, leading to further change of venue.

Thus, several hypotheses can be drawn from Baumgartner and Jones' framework:

• Images and venues are related because participants and decision-routines differ from one venue to another, thus favouring a particular image of a given policy problem. This means, attending to our case, that depending on the governance level ('venue') where policy-making takes place, the types of policy options that are chosen by policy-makers will differ in a predictable manner.

- When a policy/institutional actor succeeds in controlling the way a policy problem is portrayed, it also succeeds in controlling the policy. Thus, if EU institutions are successful in changing the policy image of the policy problem, we would expect governance to take place at the EU level, and individual member states to lose control over that policy. Reciprocally, if opposing actors succeed in keeping – or regaining control over – the image of a policy problem, we would also expect these actors to be able to control policy itself.
- In contrast, when a policy problem is dealt with in a given venue, a certain policy image is expected to prevail. Thus, when actors succeed in changing the venue of a policy, they also succeed in changing the image of the policy problem at stake and gain control over policy formulation. We would therefore expect, in the EU context, to see the stakeholders in a given policy issue practising 'venue-shopping', i.e. seeking the most favourable venue for the defence of their favoured way of tackling a policy problem.
- Certain policy actors (losers in a policy, outsiders and policy-makers from another venue wishing to expand their own policy jurisdictions) play a key role in provoking venue changes and therefore policy change.
- In a dynamic multi-level mode, it is this interplay between venues and images that has provoked the Europeanisation and the Communitarisation of the policies considered. The use by a given jurisdiction of images as a way of controlling policy (or the search for different venues by policy actors as a way of changing the images of policy problems) *induced* other jurisdictions to react and enter the rhetoric contest as a way of preserving or regaining control over policy. These dynamics provoked the 'locus of governance shift' from the national towards the European level.

Yet in the context of the EU, the model needs to be specified. It does not tell us which images are expected to prevail, and *why*, when the venue of decision-making moves towards the EU level.[9] It does mention that images are expected to change because decision routines and participants differ from one venue to another. However, we need to specify these propositions in the EU context. To complement their approach, the following hypotheses can therefore be proposed:

- Liberal images of given policy problems are more likely to prevail at the EU level, for three different motives:
  1 As argued by Scharpf (1996), EU decision rules ('decision routines') favour liberal policy solutions. Whereas negative integration can be implemented by the Commission and the ECJ, who make use of their

judicial and regulatory powers, positive integration requires the consensual agreement of fifteen – and now twenty-five – member states within the Council of Ministers. A distinction must be made between the unanimity rule, which tends to systematically provoke 'lowest common denominator' outcomes, and the qualified majority voting (QMV) rule, which can make high-level harmonisation more likely. Yet even with the QMV rule, the need for a nearly consensual agreement limits the room for manoeuvre of individual states. Whereas market liberalisation strategies can be implemented hierarchically by the ECJ and the Commission, market-correcting mechanisms require consensual agreement among member states (Scharpf 1996). Thus, the impact of decision rules must be examined in conjunction with a second explanatory variable: the multi-actorness of the policy-making process.

2 In a context characterised by the 'multi-actorness' of the decision-making process, it is highly unlikely that all participants in the EU-level decision-making process will share similar policy preferences. As argued by Baumgartner and Jones, images are likely to change from one institutional venue to another because *participants* change. At the EU level, policies are formulated by multiple policy actors: supranational institutions, member states and subnational interest groups. As already examined, an institutional bias incites EU institutions to apply the economic principles of the Treaty. Thus, market-correcting mechanisms can only be adopted if a majority of member states supports the principle. Yet, in view of member states' divergent policy traditions and conflicting interests in most policy sectors, we would also expect this to not often be the case.

3 Finally, the *nature of the status quo* has an impact on EU-level policy outcomes. If Europeanisation is the result of European institutions' *de facto* intervention in a given policy sector, then member governments might have a very restrained set of policy options available to them. Either they decide to preserve their policy sovereignty, in which case they will still be constrained by EU institutions' *de facto* use of their regulatory and judicial powers, or they opt for a common solution, in which case they will tend to be in a weak negotiating position if the 'veto' option is not desirable. This works in tandem with the predictions enunciated above. If the ECJ and the Commission have already been successful in shifting the locus of decision-making towards the supranational level (changing the 'venue' of policy-making), even only through their judicial and regulatory powers, then they will also control the 'image' of the policy problem at stake and member states will be in a reactive position

• Actors that will provoke 'locus of governance shifts' are actors that have an interest in applying a liberal image to a given policy problem.

As suggested by Baumgartner and Jones, 'losers in a policy' tend to look for more favourable venues for the pursuit of their preferences. Policy-makers from other venues can also attack existing policy arrangements in order to try expanding their own policy jurisdictions. Attending to the EU context, we would expect that the policy actors which feel disaffected in *dirigiste* countries would attempt to resort to the EU venue. As explained above, in the 'hierarchical' mode of governance (in which DG Competition within the Commission and the ECJ enact decisions and rulings without the participation of governments), EU decision rules indeed tend to favour the liberal image. We would also expect, since initial policy arrangements were organised at the national level, to see other jurisdictions that wish to expand their remit attacking them.

Case studies selection

Bearing in mind the number of variables that play a role in the explanation of integration and EU policy formation in any given policy sector, it would be too ambitious and possibly counterproductive to look at all EU-level activities in the cultural sector. Thus, the book focuses more specifically on EU legislative developments in the broadcasting, book pricing and copyright policy sectors.[10] Several motives justify the choice of these three policy sectors. First, the impact of support programmes and symbolic initiatives on national cultural policies has been marginal. EU support schemes' budget increased in the 1990s, but it is still insignificant in comparison to existing national aid mechanisms. The cultural programmes developed by the EU only complement national support programmes in these fields and do not impose any policy choices upon national governments as to which cultural sectors should be funded or promoted. There is simply no legislation at the EU level in the field of music, theatre or cultural heritage.[11] Since the objective is to understand why certain policies were Communitarised and how, it makes sense to look at the most far-reaching types of EU-level developments in terms of their impact on domestic policy choices rather than focusing on hardly controversial and essentially symbolic initiatives. In other words, the choices were determined by the need to look at sectors that had a Community dimension and were therefore caught up between culture and EU Single Market and competition policies. To look at sectors such as theatre, architectural heritage and museums would not really have involved this tension.

Among the various fields where EU Directives or Commission decisions and ECJ judgements had been initiated, it made sense to focus on three cases that would allow for a comprehensive account of policy processes in the cultural sector. Thus, it was necessary to concentrate on policy sectors in which the impact of EU-level developments on national policy choices was *substantial,* so that tensions between stakeholders[12] and their preferred policy options could be more easily observable. The rulings of the ECJ related to cultural matters provided a good indicator of the impact of EU developments on domestic cultural policies across various sectors related to the field of culture. The number of ECJ rulings on a given policy issue would indeed seem to be a clear indication of its salience in national or international arenas, and of the impact of EU-level policy developments on member states' policies. Indeed, the rulings of the ECJ often forced policy changes at the national level against the will of EU governments. The findings reveal that most culture-related ECJ rulings deal with audio-visual matters, fixed price systems in the book policy sector and intellectual property rights. More than 170 ECJ rulings have dealt with cultural policy issues.[13] Eighty-eight of these rulings were related to audio-visual matters, thirty-five to copyright issues and sixteen to the problem of fixed price systems for books.

In the audio-visual sector, the book looks more specifically at the Television Without Frontiers (TWF) Directive, in so far as it is the most comprehensive piece of EU-level legislation in this policy area.[14] It sparked wide and often heated debates involving member states, the European Commission, the European Parliament (EP) and interest groups. The impact of the TWF Directive on governments' legislative and policy choices is far-reaching (see Harcourt 2002). In the book policy sector, the issue of fixed price systems was the most debated one within EU negotiating arenas. No legislation has yet been implemented at the EU level but proposals have been made within the Council, and numerous ECJ rulings have been passed. It is possible to say that the policy area was 'Europeanised' in the sense that EU-level decisions have had an impact on the choices of member states in terms of policy-making. The Europeanisation of the regulation of book markets is therefore examined in the second case study. Finally, the copyright sector is, along with the audio-visual sector, the policy area where the most comprehensive EU policies have been implemented. It is also an area where there is a strong clash of preferences among member states. The latter are divided between the defenders of the 'Latin' tradition of the *droit d'auteur* and the advocates of the Anglo-Saxon tradition of copyright. Because most directives passed in the copyright sector were of a very technical nature and focused on narrow aspects of copyright law, it is necessary to examine *all* the directives that exist in this policy sector.[15]

Thus, the audio-visual and the copyright cases provide two examples where the Communitarisation of public policies took the form of EU legislation with member states and European institutions[16] both playing a role in the decision-making process. By contrast, the book sector offers an example where book-pricing policies were Europeanised as a result of ECJ judgements and Commission decisions, with these institutions exercising their competencies without the participation of member governments. In the first two cases, EU-level policies encompass elements of both negative and positive integration. In the book policy case, integration was essentially negative. Looking at policy areas where 'governance shifts' took a different shape will contribute to providing a more accurate and generalisable characterisation of the process of Communitarisation of public policies.

Outline of the book

Chapter 2 sheds light on the nature of the two different 'conceptions' of culture that were held by competing stakeholders in the decision-making process. Culture is the field 'par excellence' where policy preferences are not only determined by institutional, political and economic interests, but also by policy ideas. The chapter shows how policy ideas had an impact on the selection of policy models in the cultural sector at the national level, thus acting as the very shapers of policy actors' preferences, and the extent to which policy ideas were also acting as a weapon in actors' interest maximising strategies.

Chapter 3 sheds light on the tensions between distinct levels of governance in the course of the Communitarisation process of cultural policies. On the one hand, European institutions, and in particular the ECJ and the Commission, have played a role in the development of a new policy space at the EU level. In fact, EU-level intervention in the cultural sector began under the incentive of European institutions' agenda setting, judicial and regulatory powers as early as the 1970s. On the other hand, member states were careful to preserve their policy sovereignty in a policy sector considered as particularly sensitive. In the 1980s, the states whose legislative and policy traditions were at odds with the liberalisation policies developed by supranational structures attempted to develop their own initiatives that would take into account their favoured policy preferences. However, this chapter shows that despite states' intervention and following Treaty reforms, EU intervention remained dominated by the application of economic principles to the cultural sector.

Chapters 4, 5 and 6 present the case studies. The chapters differ in their structure because the narrative in each case is different. In the audio-visual and copyright cases, common solutions at the EU level were implemented, whereas this has not been the case in the book sector thus far. Therefore, the book policy chapter (Chapter 5) focuses more extensively on the effect of EU institutions' intervention on members states' policies. The chapters focusing on the audio-visual and copyright cases are divided between the analysis of this phenomenon, and that of the negotiations leading to the drafting of EU-level common solutions. Furthermore, the

Communitarisation of policies was initiated primarily by EU institutions in some sectors, and more predominantly by private commercial actors in others. Thus, the structure of the chapters reflects the narrative of the Communitarisation process in the different sectors.

Chapter 4 focuses on the TWF Directive, which establishes the principle of free flow for television programmes within the EU and harmonisation of EU states' broadcasting legislation. The chapter details the Communitarisation process of audio-visual policy as well as the negotiation phase at the EU level that led to the enacting of the TWF Directive in 1989 and its renewal in 1997. The very nature of broadcasting, as both a commercial activity and a cultural product, has created acute rivalries between policy actors. It is argued here that the TWF project was a supranational initiative developed by the European Commission as part of the drive to realise the European Single Market in the 1980s. France, whose interventionist tradition is evidenced in the audio-visual sector, along with other *dirigiste* states, felt strongly threatened by the mode of intervention developed at the EU level and attempted to wrest back control of policy by attempting to change the way the policy problem was framed at the EU level. If France's protests allowed for certain *dirigiste* concerns to be taken into account in European legislation, the unfavourable nature of the status quo meant that it was difficult for the *dirigistes* to pull their weight in the negotiations process by invoking their veto power.

Chapter 5 focuses on the developing of EU-level policies in the field of book pricing – where most EU states have implemented either legislative arrangements or contractual agreements between the stakeholders – from the 1980s until today. It details the impact of EU intervention on national policies, looking more specifically at France (one of the most 'interventionist' EU states in the cultural sector), Germany (where a cross-border agreement was in force), and the United Kingdom (one of the most liberal states in the EU). As in the audio-visual sector, economic principles were applied to the policy sector; yet no EU-level legislative solution was agreed in order to regulate book trade at the EU level. The chapter argues that although the ECJ and the powerful 'economic' DGs of the European Commission were successful – by making use of their judicial and regulatory powers – in imposing policy change in countries where *dirigiste* solutions were in place, most states did not feel that their own policy and legislative arrangements were under threat and thought that fixed price systems could best be preserved by respecting the subsidiarity principle.

Chapter 6 covers the Communitarisation process of policies in the field of copyright since the late 1970s – including in particular the first directives on copyright in the 1980s and the framework directive on copyright in the information society in 2001. Here, as in the audio-visual sector, European intervention initially started with the application of economic principles to the policy sector (ECJ judgements, Commission decisions) and common solutions were adopted when certain EU governments felt the need to develop positive policies. Yet two stages can be distinguished in the process of policy formation, with an evolution of policy priorities towards increased economic liberalisation. The chapter argues that the alteration of the constellation of actors involved in the policy-making process had an evident influence on the selection of policy options. In the 1990s, the constellation of actors' interests was much less favourable to the *dirigistes* than in the 1980s. New powerful economic actors had entered the 'game' and the constellation of actors was more likely to force the drafting of a 'political' compromise. This was reinforced by the fact that the interests of the new actors involved in the policy-making process were in line with the Commission's approach towards copyright issues.

The last chapter summarises the core observations of the book and their meaning in reference to the broader current theoretical debates on Europeanisation, Communitarisation and European integration processes. It compares the conclusions of the book to those of similar studies in other policy sectors (Parrish 2003), and concludes that the EU became an active regulator in the cultural sector as it did across a broad range of policy areas. European institutions' 'creeping competence' (Pollack 2000) extends to new policy areas through the application of economic principles to new issues where no Treaty competence otherwise exists.

Notes

1   The 'original Treaty' refers here to the Treaty of Rome and the 'Treaty' to its consolidated version.

2   As we shall see in the following chapter, whether it is accurate to use the term 'European cultural policy' is a controversial issue. There is no positive 'cultural policy' at the European level. Apart from a number of support programmes in the cultural field, most EU legislative developments aim at liberalising the cultural sector. Yet for the sake of convenience, we will use this term to designate the set of EU-level policy developments in the cultural field.

3   If the case studies discuss more extensively the role of the French government than those of other member states, it is because the French played a more active role than other EU states in the cultural policy sector. There is, however, no predetermined intention to focus specifically on the role of the French government in the construction process of EU cultural policy. Rather, the structure of the book results from the findings made when looking at the Communitarisation process of policies in the cultural field.

4   The term '*dirigiste*' will be used in this work to refer to regulatory and legislative developments that were of an interventionist nature, in contrast to legislative solutions that aim at liberalising markets.

5   The term 'Communitarisation' rather than 'integration' will be used in the book. If both terms name the same shift of governance level – from the

national towards the supranational level – the process of integration also involves the setting of new institutions as such (for instance the European Commission, the European Parliament). The process of Communitarisation is more strictly concerned with the developing of new EU level policies – rather than with the mechanisms that explain the creation of new institutions, literally speaking.

6   The '*dirigiste*' or 'cultural' coalition consistently encompassed France and certain Southern European States, representatives of the cultural community, DG Education and Culture within the Commission and most often the European Parliament (see also Collins 1994 for a detailed account of the conflicts between 'liberals' and '*dirigistes*' in the audio-visual field).

7   Yet see Checkel and Moravcsik (2001) for a recent attempt at drawing up hypotheses and methodological guidelines as to how to evaluate the independent causal effect of policy ideas in the policy-making process.

8   Chapter 2 will look, however, at how policy ideas have had an impact on which policy models were perceived as appropriate by policy actors.

9   I will not attempt, here, to draw hypotheses as to why certain images are expected to prevail in EU member states. This would require looking at the decision routines and participants in the decision-making process in fifteen different countries (if looking only at the pre-Eastern enlargement EU members). Testing such hypotheses, in addition to those already mentioned, would be unfeasible in a single research project.

10 Secondary literature was useful in order to 'map' these policy sectors. Yet a large part of the argument is based on primary sources. In this respect, the archives of the French Ministry of Culture were the most original and detailed source of information to which I had access. I have consulted the documents that were produced by the Ministry's services from the 1960s until the 1990s. In so far as the existing literature highlights the role of the French government in the construction process of EU cultural policy, having access to the archives of the Ministry of Culture was crucial in order to find out what the motivations and policy preferences of the French government were. However, the French archives were also a rich source of information on other states' policy preferences and EU negotiations more generally.

    Another central aspect of the research methodology consisted in carrying out an extended interview programme in Brussels, the UK and France (26 interviews in total). I interviewed EU officials from DG Education and Culture and DG Internal Market, as well as members of the European Parliament (MEPs) (Committee on Culture, Youth, Education, the Media and Sport). As it is widely accepted that France was the 'first mover' in the construction process of EU cultural policy (see Collins 1994; Pongy 1997; and also articles in the press, which presented France as the most active and influential state in the process), the initial national level research effort was concentrated on France. I interviewed several officials from the Ministry of Culture, and private stakeholders, such as interest group representatives (for example, cinema producers' representatives). As it is also widely suggested in the literature that Britain is the strongest opponent of French views, I also interviewed British officials from the Department of Culture, Media and Sport (DCMS). Interviewing British officials was crucial in terms of 'calibrating' French claims on the influence of the French during policy negotiations at the EU level.

11 There is no legislation on book prices either. However, there is a significant number of ECJ judgements in the field, which have an impact on domestic policies of EU states.

12 The term 'stakeholders' is used in this work to designate the actors that are part of the decision-making process and are interested in influencing the formulation of the policies discussed here.

13 The research was conducted in July 2003. I have used the Eurolaw database and the existing literature on the role of the ECJ in the field of culture in order to be able to reconstruct an exhaustive list of all the ECJ judgments in the field. I have based myself on the secondary literature concerning EU intervention in the field of culture and the role of the ECJ in the area as an indication of what 'ought to be included' in the 'cultural' sector. I did not include in the list the judgments related to education, the mobility of workers (even when the latter were working in the cultural sector), or industrial property (in contrast to intellectual property). However, I have included the rulings dealing with media concentration, for the latter have clear consequences in terms of cultural policy.

14 The European Commission had also laid down proposals for a media ownership Directive in the early 1990s (see Harcourt 2005 for a detailed account of EU-level negotiations over media ownership). Yet, the Directive proved to be politically infeasible.

15 The book does not, however, look at the 1986 Directive on the legal protection of topographies of semi-conductor products (87/54/EEC), the 1991 Directive on the legal protection of computer programs (91/250/EEC) or the 1996 Directive on the legal protection of databases (96/9/EC). These legislative elements essentially fulfil industrial policy objectives and do not affect the cultural sector as such.

16 The term 'European institutions' will be used in this book in its literal sense: it will be used to name the European Commission, the European Parliament and the ECJ.

2

Cultural policy at the heart of tensions between conflicting models of policy intervention

Culture is the field 'par excellence' where policy preferences are not only determined by institutional, political and economic interests, but also by policy ideas. Depending on how policy actors perceive a given policy problem, their views will also differ as to how the sector should be regulated. Thus, the Communitarisation process of the cultural sector was characterised by a competition between conflicting views of the problems at stake – which were expressed through the defence of conflicting models of public intervention. In the event, a coalition of actors conceiving culture as a mercantile activity opposed a competing coalition of stakeholders which pointed to the *specificity* of culture. 'Policy ideas' were both a tool for the control of policy and the furthering of actors' interests, and a shaper of these very interests.

The Council of Ministers was the typical *locus* of confrontation between conflicting policy models. Member states' positions during EU-level negotiations were dependent upon their own model of public intervention in the cultural sector, which they were trying to replicate at the supranational level. Tensions among and within European institutions added to the complexity of the policy-making process. The EP and the DG Education and Culture within the European Commission acted as the advocates of the 'cultural' view, while the most powerful Commission units sponsored an economic approach to cultural matters. If institutional dynamics – the desire of EU institutions and sub-units within them to maximise their competencies – were often a key motive of conflict between and within supranational institutions, the latter were also permeable to the influence of policy ideas – which found a favourable ground in certain institutional venues and not in others. Thus, this chapter sheds light on the nature of the two existing 'conceptions' of culture and cultural policy, the existing policy models in the cultural field and the role played by different venues as privileged *loci* of reception for certain views of the problems at stake.

Defining policy problems

Policy ideas can define the political discourse and eventually limit the number of policy solutions perceived as desirable. In the cultural policy sector, two conflicting sets of beliefs were supported by the stakeholders involved in the policy-making process. Opposed to those who conceived the cultural sector as an economic market to be submitted to EU competition law were those who argued that a so-called 'cultural specificity' justifies the exemption of the cultural sector from market mechanisms (see Collins 1994 for an account of this debate in the audio-visual sector). The latter view is based on the recognition that the main interest of cultural industries lies in the symbolic, aesthetic and the artistic nature of their output, because these outputs can potentially have such a strong influence on the very way we understand society – including of course cultural production itself. It is the boundaries between such symbolic, cultural production and other 'non-cultural' kinds of production that has been the object of heated debates. It is also possible to look at these boundaries in terms of the relationship between the utilitarian functions and non-utilitarian (artistic/aesthetic/entertainment) functions of symbolic goods (see Hesmondhalgh 2002). While many industries produce objects and services where both utilitarian and non-utilitarian elements are present, when it comes to books, television programmes, plays and fine art prints, at issue was whether the non-utilitarian elements outweighed other dimensions (or not).

In the audio-visual field, the debate lies around the issue of whether films are commodities like any others – in which case creating and bringing them to the market is a business to be governed by market forces alone – or the vehicles for transmitting intangibles that are the essence of a society, such as ideas, values, identity and a sense of shared experience and community. In the first event, cultural policies and programmes are seen as barriers to trade that must come down like any others as part of the trade liberalisation process. In the alternative, films have a value and significance that transcend the utility of commodities, requiring that they be treated differently in the context of the international trade rules. In his speech at the Symposium for a Europe of Culture in May 2005, Jacques Chirac clearly expressed the rationale upon which the *'dirigiste'* or 'cultural' view is based:

> Over the last decade, France and Europe together have fought unremittingly for the cultural exception, borne by their firm belief that the World Trade Organization [WTO] and the trade discussions that take place there are not the right forum for dealing with issues related to cultural exchange. Those working in culture, particularly filmmakers, have rallied to our cause and France, with others, has ceaselessly fought to defend this principle. It is a rough battle, waged without letup because so much is at stake economically.

But what is also at stake is our vision of what it means to be human. The cultural exception is based on a political and moral affirmation of the utmost importance: that there are human activities that cannot be reduced to their status as merchandise.[1]

Proponents of the 'cultural' view also oppose the idea that cinema is an entertainment industry, seeing it instead as an art and a heritage. The proponents of the 'economic' view, on the contrary, consider that cinema is entertainment, at heart an industry in the same way as any other; and thus reject any idea of protecting the industry.

In the field of copyright, the same tensions between different perceptions of the problems at stake can be observed. Intellectual property conceptualised as a universal human right differs in fundamental ways from its treatment as an economic interest under intellectual property law. A human rights approach is predicated on the centrality of protecting and nurturing human dignity and the common good. If intellectual property is conceptualised as an economic interest, intellectual property issues will be governed by economic goals such as improved competitiveness or profitability.

These different images of the policy problems at stake implied different conclusions as to how cultural industries, and the cultural sphere more generally, should be regulated or deregulated by governments.

Policy models

The Council of Ministers is the typical venue for confrontation between different domestic models of policy intervention – themselves based on different conceptions of the policy problems at stake. The systems of policy-making, as well as the allocation of responsibilities in the cultural sector, are very diverse in EU states. First, the management of the cultural sector can take place at different levels of government. In France, Luxembourg, Greece and Portugal, cultural affairs are dealt with by the state at the central level. Other states, such as Spain and Italy, have decentralised part of the responsibilities for the management of the cultural sector to local levels of government. In federal states, culture is formally within the remit of the regions/Länder. Another difference lies in the extent to which the state (either at a central or local level) involves itself in the promotion of culture and the arts.[2] It is therefore possible to distinguish essential traits that characterise policy models of different EU states in the field of culture. During EU negotiations related to cultural matters, what has determined the position of member governments was their acceptance of (or opposition to) the principle of substantial state intervention in the cultural field. This was conditioned, essentially, by the degree of state involvement (more *'dirigiste'* or more 'liberal') and the structure of public responsibilities (centralised/decentralised/federal) at the domestic level. Thus, cultural policy models are divided here along the following lines: 'liberal', *dirigiste* and federal models.

Liberal policy models
The liberal model is characterised by low levels of state involvement in cultural affairs. Other ways of promoting the arts (such as private sponsorship) have been implemented in liberal states but the principle of a public cultural policy is not widely endorsed. The UK as well as 'Northern' European states fit into this model.

The present UK arts funding system has its origins in the 1940s. The first national body to support the arts, the Council for the Encouragement of Music and the Arts (which evolved in 1946 into the Arts Council) sprang from the recognition that there was a role for government in funding the arts as an expression of a democratic society. Along these lines, Williams (1989) argues that the creation of the Arts Council took place at a time when the need for public intervention in the market was acknowledged. Until 1965, when responsibility was passed on to the Department for Education and Science, the UK government department responsible for allocating grants to the Arts Council was the Treasury.[3] However, after an expansion of arts expenditure in the 1970s, political and economic pressures in the 1980s led to a fundamental reappraisal of the funding and management of the arts. A market-driven approach was adopted and the emphasis was laid on measures to increase business sponsorship and achieving 'value for money' (Caust 2003).

In fact, a coordinated ministry to deal with arts, museums, heritage, media, sport and tourism was established only in 1992 – renamed in 1997 the Department of Culture, Media and Sport (DCMS). In return for increased investment in culture to end years of low funding, the government reduced the number of 'arm's length' cultural agencies. These agencies are public bodies, such as the Arts Council, the British Film Institute or the British Library, which administer the disbursement of government funds for culture and determine who the beneficiaries will be. However, the UK system of support for culture is still regarded as the archetypal 'arms-length' model.[4] The DCMS also has responsibility for regulating the running of the National Lottery, which was launched in 1994. Finally, the UK is characterised by the collaboration between the public and the private sectors in the promotion of culture. The DCMS has created the Creative Industries Task Force to bring together private and public sector players to work in partnership. The private sector is also involved in promoting creativity through sponsorship, donations and corporate membership schemes.[5]

If British cultural policy cannot be portrayed as being simply driven by market forces – the government does intervene, even if only in an 'arm's length' manner – the principle of a strong state-led public policy in the field of culture has never been on top of the British political agenda. More crucially, the UK has never been interested in developing a *dirigiste* policy in the field of culture at the EU level. The British government can be characterised, among EU member sates, as the defender of 'liberal' policy solutions at the EU level. It has, for instance, consistently opposed the reinforcement of EU cultural programmes.[6] The Netherlands, Finland, Sweden, Denmark and Ireland, who were often on the British side during EU negotiations on cultural issues, have policy models that present similar features to the UK's.

In the Netherlands during the 1970s, cultural policy was essentially part of the government's welfare policy. The social role of culture was perceived on the levels of both social class and geographical spread. However, with the economic stagnation of the 1980s, the government reconsidered its role in the cultural sector. In the 1990s, cultural organisations were encouraged to become more self-sufficient and to look at their market (their audiences). These policy goals appeared in the 1988 Arts Plan, which stated that the ministry's system of grants and subsidies should be tightened up. According to the 1993 Law on Cultural Policy, the government is now obliged to present a policy plan every four years, which reviews all foreseen and completed cultural activities.[7] In a manner, the expansion of public funding in the cultural sector was limited in Denmark in recent years.[8] The Danish government was one of the main opponents to the creation of a cultural policy at the EU level.

In the same way, the Finnish, Swedish and Irish policy models in the cultural sector have been subject to pressures for policy change.[9] In Finland, the reliance on public budgets and especially on legislation is undermined by the current process focusing on minimising state intervention, which includes the simplification of budgets and the multiplication of performance contracts. The idea that market forces should become the new promoter of culture is spreading among policy-makers (Kangas 2001). Likewise, the repercussions of the Swedish economic crisis on public finances led to the allocation of public functions within the culture sector to private entrepreneurs at the municipal level. Larsson and Svenson (2001) point to the fact that during the last twenty-five years, private cultural expenditure has constituted about 70 per cent of all total cultural expenditure – while public funds have provided about 30 per cent.

In Ireland, the cultural sector increasingly relies on private funding and cultural activities are increasingly subject to free market considerations. At the end of the 1980s there was still no coherent or explicit cultural policy in Ireland. More often the cultural issues were subsumed under the economic and cultural industry framework. Thus, the commercialisation of culture, as a dominant trend in Ireland's mass-media industry, means that cultural activities are increasingly subject to economic and free market considerations.[10] The consequence is that many state bodies which traditionally fund the arts have had to cope with drastic financial cutbacks, forcing them to seek industrial patronage. Others, such as the Film Board set up in order to support the development of the Irish film industry, have been abolished. Museums, art galleries and public libraries have been forced to introduce charges to the public for their services. Moreover, the cultural dimension of emigration has resulted in strong cultural links with the US and Australia. This dimension is clearly visible in the field of media policy, where no restrictions exist on Ireland's right to purchase television programmes from these two countries. Perhaps this explains why the Irish government has always opposed the French plan for a binding 60 per cent quota of made-in-Europe non-news programmes during the TWF Directive negotiations.[11]

The 'arm's length model', coupled with low levels of state financial involvement, is a distinctive feature of liberal policy models. In the Netherlands, the government established a number of independent foundations, such as the Press Industry Fund and the Dutch Film Fund, that are funded by the government. Each foundation allocates money to cultural institutions or individual artists according to its specific aims. The same tendency can be observed in Denmark, where all decisions on financial support for films or living arts are made by special committees of experts (Sticht 2000: 79).

The Finish cultural policy model is also one of horizontal and vertical decentralisation and 'arm's length' implementation. At central government level, a number of expert bodies advise the Ministry of Education and Culture and also implement agreed-upon policies. Horizontal decentralisation is also often of a corporatist type, with associations of professional artists playing an important role in the formulation and implementation of cultural policies. On the other hand, vertical decentralisation has implied the transfer of policy competence to municipalities (Kangas 2001).

The UK, the Netherlands and Denmark were the most fervent opponents to the development of EU *dirigiste* initiatives in the cultural sector. Ireland, Finland and Sweden usually provided them with their support. With the uncertainties of the financial climate of the 1980s and early 1990s, public intervention in the cultural sector was further limited and the principle of a strong public intervention in the cultural field increasingly contested.

Dirigiste *policy models*
France, Spain, Italy and Greece all share a tradition of state interventionism, which extends to the cultural sector. Thus, 'Southern' European countries are characterised by the existence of a strong public sector, which extends its influence beyond decisions about public resources and

is expected to take an active part in the general artistic and intellectual debates. Public policies in the cultural field are not equally developed in all Southern European states. Yet what distinguishes them is their acceptance of the principle of strong public intervention in the cultural domain.

In France, political actors support the view that a so-called 'cultural specificity' justifies the exemption of the cultural sector from market mechanisms. The then French Minister of Culture Catherine Trautmann, interviewed by *Le Monde* in 1999, explained that 'the liberalization of the audiovisual and cultural sectors will not bring about any benefits. Ever since Ricardo, we know that the logic of free-exchange implies that France and Europe renounce supporting their cultural and audio-visual industries, since foreign "products" can be imported at lower cost' (*Le Monde*, 11 October 1999). The history of French cultural policies is indeed marked by the central role the state has played in promoting and organising the arts and culture. A separate Ministry of Culture was established as early as 1959, headed by André Malraux. The essential activities undertaken were heritage protection, contemporary artistic creation and the regulation of cultural industry markets. By contrast with the Anglo-Saxon 'arm's length' model, the French system is highly centralised (Looseley 2001). During the two Jack Lang ministries in the 1980s the ministry's budget increased from 2.6 billion francs in 1981 to 13.8 billion in 1993 and its scope of activities was extended to new forms of arts and the development of new forms of communication (Looseley 1995). Major construction projects known as the *Grands Travaux* were initiated, such as the Bastille Opera House and the Grand Louvre. Furthermore, the ministry began to place more emphasis on cultural industries, such as books, cinema and the audio-visual, with a view to regulating the market.

Thus, the French model is characterised by substantial public intervention. The Ministry of Culture undertakes action in two ways: regulatory action and direct action. Regulations can involve, for instance, the institution of taxes and fees for certain cultural activity sectors and obligatory production and diffusion quotas (broadcasting quotas). Direct action involves the direct management of public cultural institutions, the development of national artistic heritage, artistic constructions and the delegation of grants to institutions, cultural actors and regional or local authorities.[12]

Another unique characteristic of French cultural policies is their conception of cultural diversity, which is considered with regard to globalisation. As mentioned above, the view of the Ministry of Culture is that the special nature of cultural goods and services must be recognised and that they are not simply tradable commodities like other products. The French government believes that cultural diversity must be fostered by promoting European cultural industries. In the audio-visual sector for instance, 60 per cent of broadcasting by television networks must be

European cinematographic and televisual productions with at least 40 per cent original French language content. Private radio station programming must also include a minimum 40 per cent content of French language songs.

France was noticeably the only state who consistently opposed the liberalisation policies developed by EU institutions in the cultural sector. During EU negotiations, France usually seeks to obtain the support of Southern European countries, such as Greece, Spain and Italy. The latter are the main beneficiaries of EU cultural programmes. Moreover, their political traditions present some similarities with French ones, making them more likely to support *dirigiste* positions (Pongy 1996).

Like France, Italy favoured the development of EU support programmes in the cultural field, and advocated a high level of harmonisation for cultural legislation. In recent years, public authorities recognised that some sectors of the cultural industry, like the cinema and press, were experiencing difficulties and were in need of subsidies.[13] The development of state intervention in the cultural sector has taken place rather recently in Spain, Portugal and Greece generally because of the fear of interfering in a policy sector that had been the channel for propaganda from authoritarian regimes. However, these states support the principle of public intervention in the cultural field. Spain, in particular, has experienced an accelerated development of cultural policies compared to other EU countries, and the cultural sector is now strongly regulated.[14]

Perceiving the implementation of the Single Market as a threat, *dirigiste* states asked for more intervention, subsidy and political control of the markets. Thus, two coalitions of actors trying to transpose divergent policy models at the EU level can be distinguished: 'Southern European' states, which tried to impose *dirigiste* measures to the cultural sector, and 'Northern European' states which supported liberal solutions. When looking at the domestic policies of 'Northern' and 'Southern' European states, characterising their policy model may not be as much of a straightforward endeavour – with the UK also having been making use of audio-visual quotas at home while France allowed, through a domestic liberalisation of its audio-visual market, the development of audio-visual 'champions' (Fraser 1996). Yet, in EU-level negotiations, these positions were quite clear-cut. Essentially, member states had fundamentally different views about the necessity to setting up market-correcting mechanisms in the cultural field at the supranational level.

Federal policy models
The principle of subsidiarity governs the organisation of competencies in federal states. The lowest level of government is in charge of cultural affairs, unless solutions to the policy problem are better dealt with by the federal government. In EU negotiations, federal states must under the

constitution refer to the regions/ Länder before delegating any competencies to the supranational level.

In Germany, the right to control cultural affairs is widely considered as an integral part of the autonomy of the Länder. Essentially, the latter are responsible for making decisions on all matters of cultural policy (Burns and Van der Will 2003). However, they are by no means the only public-sector actors in the area of cultural policy. The municipalities are responsible for the promotion of culture at the local level. As for the Federation, it is responsible for cultural policy in relation to third countries and federal legislation pertaining to cultural affairs. Following the 1998 parliamentary elections and the advent of an SPD–Green coalition in government, a Federal Commissioner for Cultural Affairs and the Media was appointed and a Commission for Culture and the Media was created in the Federal Parliament. This development was interpreted as the creation of a German National Ministry of Culture by international experts. The new Minister of State, however, has not really been given any new competencies for culture, but has rather taken over the culture-related tasks of the Ministries of the Interior and for Economic Affairs. A new virtual platform was created and helps to provide a 'public presence' for the Minister's activities.[15] Yet, the information supplied should not be mistaken for a coherent framework which, in fact, does not exist in Germany: cultural policy is shaped via funding and not through legislation. According to the Cultural Policy Yearbook (2000), municipalities fund 43 per cent, the Länder 47 per cent and the Federation 8 per cent of public cultural expenditure. The Länder have been extremely reluctant to cede any of their authority in cultural matters 'upwards to the level of the national government' (Burns and Van der Will 2003: 136).

Another distinctive feature of the cultural policy of the Federal Republic of Germany is the principle of government non-interference coupled with a strong sense of public sector responsibility for ensuring the existence and funding of cultural institutions and programmes. The constitution guarantees freedom for the arts which not only constitutes the basis of artistic autonomy and self-governing rights of cultural institutions, but also their protection from state directives and regulation of content. In the broadcasting sector, regional public service broadcasters are independent from the state and 'self-governing' (Humpreys 1994). However, it is also understood that the state is responsible for actively encouraging and supporting this artistic freedom, meaning that the bulk of the cultural infrastructure is under the public-law sponsorship of the cities and the Länder.

'Partly as a prophylactic response of the Allied occupying forces and the post-war German political class to the centralised "total" cultural policy of the Nazis, and partly as a return to the historically constituted distinct political identity of the regional states', Germany's federalism is particularly anchored in the cultural sector (Ahearne 2003: 1) As far as European integration is concerned, this means that the federal government often opposes the delegation of policy competence to the supranational level – although more flexibility can be observed in recent years. Since the first meetings of the culture ministers in the early 1980s, the German government has been very cautious in giving its approval to any strengthening of EU-level cooperation in the cultural field (Brossat 1999). However, it has sometimes been in favour of EU-level interventionist policies in the cultural field. In the book policy sector, the German government did not form its policy position on the basis of its institutional preferences (i.e. which level of government should have competence for cultural affairs) but of the *type* of policies (liberal or *dirigiste*) that it favoured.[16]

Like Germany, Austria and Belgium are also federal states. In Austria, most cultural assignments are devolved to the provinces (*Bundesländer*), while the federal government is expressly awarded competence for sovereign matters such as scientific and technical archives and libraries, artistic and scientific collections and federal museums. Since 1997 however, the Federal Chancellery administers cultural affairs, which have been assigned to the State Secretary responsible for culture, the arts, EU affairs and sport. Furthermore, about 60 per cent of total public expenditure on culture is spent by the federal government, the remainder being divided among the *Bundesländer* and Vienna.

In Belgium, the cultural autonomy of the three linguistic communities was gradually incorporated into the political structures in the late 1960s (Jaumain 1997). The *Loi du Pacte Culturel* of 16 July 1973 guarantees the representation of the autonomous communities and protects ideological and political minorities. The linguistic communities enjoy devolved legislative powers, and are responsible for the arts, audio-visual activities, education, sport and youth.[17] Very limited powers are reserved for the central government, such as the enactment of measures to guarantee the right to work and the right to social security, legislation on general taxation and copyright and the administration of certain major national institutions such as the Opera House. The subsidiarity principle was adopted in Belgium not only out a reaction to the experience of centralisation under fascism during the Second World War, but also to set itself apart from the communist countries' statist approach to culture and the US market-dominated approach.

Germany, Austria and Belgium, either for historical or linguistic motives, have therefore granted competence for cultural affairs to regional levels of government. During EU negotiations, the federal nature of domestic structures has either been a constitutional impediment to the construction of a new policy space at the supranational level, or, in certain instances, an excuse for federal governments that were not willing to further cultural schemes at the EU level (Pongy 1996). Thus, the position of federalist states is more difficult to predict.

Member states' positions during EU negotiations reflect their own model of public intervention in the cultural sector. As will be observed in the following chapters, member states either attempt to replicate their own policy model at the EU level or – when they do not feel challenged by EU institutions' intervention – they endeavour to preserve their domestic policies without delegating any competencies to the supranational level. Along with the trend in the 1980s and 1990s towards budget cuts in the cultural sector, the equilibrium among member states shifted even more clearly in favour of liberal countries. This tendency was confirmed after the entrance of three new states – Austria, Sweden and Finland – to the EU in 1995.

In a context where preferences strongly diverge, voting rules within the Council are also a contentious issue. Current debates within the Council focus on the efficiency of the decision-making process. France, in particular, supports the extension of the QMV rule to the cultural field, hoping that it could allow for the enactment of more substantial initiatives. In the Cannes Declaration of 15 May 2003, European Ministers of Culture stated clearly that European support actions should be decided with qualified majority voting (Cannes Declaration of European Culture Ministers 2003). The change of voting procedure was included in the Constitutional Treaty. Article 280 – which would have replaced Article 151 on culture, had the Constitutional Treaty been ratified – was indeed strengthened by the qualified majority voting principle. Jacques Chirac welcomed the change as a great step forward, since 'a single country will no longer be able to prevent initiatives from being taken' (Chirac 2005). Yet, the story is not so simple (for an account of the French position concerning voting mechanisms within the Council, see *Le Monde*, 8 December 2000). Most negotiations concerning cultural policy issues take place within the Single Market Council, where the QMV rule already applies. The only decisions taken within the Culture Council concern European support programmes – and even the Media Programme in the audio-visual sector is adopted under industrial policy objectives. This means that *dirigistes* are more concerned to ensure that legislative solutions concerning cultural industries, usually agreed upon with the QMV rule within the Single Market or General Affairs Councils, take into account cultural considerations. Furthermore, the French defended a completely different stance concerning the EU external trade policy in audio-visual and cultural matters. On that matter, the French government strongly advocated for the right to preserve its veto on changes in the common commercial policy.[18]

Policy models competition at the EU level

Each institutional venue carries with it a decisional bias, because both participants and decision-making routines differ from one venue to another. Thus, policy ideas can find a more favourable reception in some institutional venues than in others. The EU venue was a privileged interlocutor for the holders of liberal economic views and developed itself as a favourable ground for the defence of certain values and beliefs. In contrast, institutional venues use rhetoric or 'policy ideas' as a tool designed to extend their policy jurisdiction. Clashes *among* and *within* European institutions add to the complexity of the decision-making process.

The European Commission as a pluralistic unit
The European Commission has favoured an 'economic' approach to the cultural area. However, conflicts between the various Directorates (DGs) with responsibilities in the cultural sector have prevented the formulation of policy guidelines from being a straightforward process. The different DGs involved in the formulation of EU cultural policy defend diverging positions.

- DG Education and Culture is formally in charge of the formulation of policy orientations in the cultural sector. It is a small and non-influential administrative unit, which has sectoral competencies. DG Education and Culture is in charge of the Culture 2000 programme and the management of the 'European City of Culture' event. It is also the privileged interlocutor of professionals in the cultural field. If the DG's budget is very limited, it is the venue where the logic of a specific cultural action within the Commission is enunciated (Pongy 1997). Issues such as national cultural independence, the promotion of diversity and pluralism, and protection of ethical and moral standards – enshrined in the concept of public sector broadcasting – have shaped the sector wherein the DG's remit lies.
- DG Information Society and Media is, since 2004, in charge of EU audio-visual policy. Media Plus, which used to be under the aegis of DG Education and Culture, is now under the control of DG Information Society and Media. The eEurope 2005 Action Plan, a sort of high-level 'policy accelerator' that focuses attention on and pushes forward progress concerning broadband, eBusiness, eGovernment, eHealth and eLearning is also under the remit of the DG.
- DG Internal Market is one of the most powerful DGs within the Commission, invested with horizontal competencies. It defends liberal views and examines policy issues from the 'Single Market' perspective. Several policy areas, such as the audio-visual and the copyright sectors for instance, are under the remit of DG Internal Market.

- DG Competition is also very powerful within the Commission. Its liberal orientations are very strong and it can be characterised as the main opponent to *dirigiste* policies in the cultural sector. It has consistently made use of its regulatory powers in order to challenge national legislative arrangements that were not compatible with EU competition law. The application of exemptions to the general prohibition of State aid rests indeed exclusively with the European Commission, which possesses strong investigative and decision-making powers.
- DG Regional Policy is in charge of the administration of structural funds and regional programmes. It grants substantial funding to regions or rural areas in order to enhance the preservation of their cultural heritage. The Community Initiative Interreg III promotes the development of such projects across borders. One of the chapters of the Innovative Actions provides incentives for regions to build cooperation with each other on the theme of regional identity.

Different views of the policy problems at stake were rooted in the organisations (or institutions) that promoted them. The personal beliefs of EU civil servants, who are in their large majority lawyers or economists, might have played a role in the dominance of certain frames within the European Commission. Yet the portrayal of policy problems was also a tool for the different DGs, which aimed to maximise their influence and the remit of their competence within the Commission.[19] As influence is greatest where agents possess transnational constituencies or interest groups within member states which can bypass member governments (Pollack 1997), the DGs involved in the support or regulation of the cultural sector have been trying to institutionalise their connections with certain groups of private actors. The 'liberal DGs' have been particularly successful in gathering support from transnational constituencies. The advertising lobby is one of the strongest supporters of the liberalisation of the audio-visual sector. It has been a crucial partner for the Commission services and has played a decisive role in the elaboration of EU-level audio-visual legislation in particular (see Fraser 1996). Several advertising lobbies have united themselves under the name of the 'European Advertising Tripartite' (EAT) in 1980. The liberalisation of the audio-visual sector has also been supported by private television channels and private television producers. Among the major commercial channels involved in the policy debate were the Compagnie Luxembourgeoise de Télédiffusion (CLT) in Luxembourg, Télévision Française 1 (TF1) in France and Berlusconi's own television channels in Italy. Commercial channels have opposed the idea of EU-level quotas for European television programmes as well as any attempt to tighten advertising ceilings. Television producers – in contrast to cinema producers – have also supported the liberalisation of the audio-visual sector. Most of them rely upon private television channels for the broadcasting of television programmes, and the latter use advertising as their main source of revenue. In the book policy sector, private corporate actors such as supermarkets, large bookshops and on-line bookshops are in favour of the liberalisation of book trade. National legislative arrangements on book prices have consistently been targeted by private actors. DG Competition within the Commission has consistently supported the views of on-line bookshops in recent years (Littoz-Monnet 2005). In the copyright policy sector, private actors have also favoured the easing up of copyright regimes in most EU states. In the analogue environment, discotheque owners and record companies were the most fervent advocates of lenient legislative regimes in the field. Consumer organisations and libraries, for different motives, have also been part of the coalition which endeavoured to impose a more liberal regime on the regulation of intellectual property. With the development of digital technologies, new policy actors came to support the liberalisation of on-line services. The Information Technology (IT) sector and telecommunications operators perceive regulations as existing or potential barriers to the delivery of information and content. In this context, the question of whether new media services should be regulated along the lines of the broadcasting or telecommunication sectors has come to the fore. The most powerful DGs of the Commission, along with the IT sector and telecommunication companies, have favoured a light touch regulatory regime for on-line services, along the lines of the telecommunication sector regulatory system.

In contrast, DG Education and Culture relies on the support of the European creative community, and especially of the French cultural lobby, which played a particularly active role in EU-level cultural negotiations.[20] The artistic community has orchestrated EU-level lobbying campaigns in order to defend its interests, during which DG Education and Culture and the European Parliament acted as their favoured interlocutors. The Fédération Européenne des Réalisateurs Audiovisuels (FERA), which represents European film directors, and the Comité des Industries Cinématographiques Européennes (CICCE), the European cinema lobby, were among the most active interest groups in the campaigns for the creation of interventionist mechanisms at the EU level.

Thus, the Commission cannot be characterised as a unitary actor. DG Education and Culture, despite its lack of influence, ensures that 'cultural' interest groups find an interlocutor at the EU level. However, given the prevailing influence of DG Competition and DG Single Market within the Commission – itself a result of the European project being essentially an economic one – their views have dominated the policy debate on the regulation of cultural industries within the Commission.

The European Parliament: national and political dividing lines
Since the entry into force of the Maastricht Treaty, the co-decision procedure[21] allows the EP to play an increasingly important role in the formulation of EU legislative developments in the cultural sector. The EP has distinguished itself by its pro-integration positions and its positive stance towards *dirigiste* policy measures. It has produced numerous reports on cultural matters and the Culture Committee plays an active role within the EP (Pongy 1997). During legislative procedures, the EP has consistently used its 'amendment powers' in order to strengthen the proposals drawn up by the Commission and the Council. This has occurred for instance with legislation on television broadcasting, intellectual property law and the design of EU support programmes in the cultural sector. Concerning the sensitive issue of media ownership regulation, the EP has distinguished itself by its concern for ensuring pluralism and diversity of the media (Harcourt 2005: 70). Brossat (1999) points to the terminology used by the EP; whilst the Commission tended to use phrases such as 'cooperation in the cultural sector' when discussing EU intervention in this field in the 1960s and 1970s, the EP was already employing the term 'European cultural policy'.

Yet in the same way as conflicts occur within the Commission, debates within the EP often reveal intense divisions among MEPs (Pongy 1997). Political cleavages tend to shape divisions within the EP with the European People's Party (EPP) and Liberal parties on one side, and the Socialist Party and the Green Party on the other. Left-wing MEPs have consistently supported the reinforcement of cultural programmes and the design of *dirigiste* policy solutions in the cultural sector. However, political dissension is sometimes transcended by national cleavages. Thus, during the vote on the TWF Directive in 1989 (89/552/EEC), right-wing French political parties voted with the Socialist party in favour of strengthening the *dirigiste* aspects of the TWF Directive.

Tensions among MEPs and between the different DGs of the European Commission reflect the complexity of the decision-making process in the cultural sector. Yet it is possible to distinguish essential traits of the policy-making process in the cultural sector. Different institutional venues have given a more or less favourable reception to given 'images' of the policy problems at stake. The European Commission represented a favourable venue for the proponents of the 'liberal' view, while the EP gave more credit to arguments referring to the specificity of culture and the need for special laws that ensued from it.

Conclusion

The way policy problems were perceived by policy actors had a direct impact on which policy options were seen as relevant or appropriate. The policy-making process in the cultural sector has therefore been characterised by the permanent adjustment between two competing 'policy images' of the policy problems that are being considered. This phenomenon is true at the intergovernmental level, where member states try to impose their own views of the problem at stake in order to replicate their own policy model at the EU level, and at the supranational level, where European institutions and sub-units within them uphold conflicting frames.

Yet the extent to which policy actors' beliefs played an independent role is subject to debate. Actors' ways of portraying a policy problem also ensued from underlying institutional or commercial interests to focus on one aspect of a policy problem. For instance, French policy-makers have been presenting policy issues from a 'cultural' perspective, which also suited less obviously trumpeted commercial motives. France indeed has a strong audio-visual production to defend and groups of creators are extremely powerful economic actors. Britain, on the other hand, felt like it could benefit from the liberalisation of the broadcasting sector. As argued by Stone (1989), politics constantly involves strategic efforts to manipulate the understanding of reality. Because agenda 'redefinition' strategies can help provoke policy change – and at the same time allow certain actors, formerly disadvantaged under a given regulatory regime, to take control over policy – 'policy images' have been used strategically by institutional actors as weapons to provoke changes in the venue of decision-making and control policy. Member states have been trying to replicate their own model of policy intervention at the EU level, while EU institutions have endeavoured to extend their policy jurisdiction by applying a 'liberal' image on to cultural policy issues. It is these strategies, depicted in the following chapter on governance level competition, that have allowed for the 'locus of governance shift' from the national towards the European level to occur.

Notes

1   Speech by Jacques Chirac on the occasion of the symposium for a Europe of Culture, Elysée Palace, 2 May 2005.
2   It is not possible to compare the figures for cultural policy funding in EU states, for various reasons. First, the data available often does not cover the same year or the same periods of time. Second, cultural funding is not always allocated by central governments. In Germany, for instance, Länders will be responsible for a large share of public spending in the cultural field. Third, cultural funding will take into consideration only direct state aid, neglecting indirect aid such as tax incentives (see Schuster 2002 for a comprehensive presentation of the obstacles towards the creation of reliable statistics on cultural funding).
3   See country profile of the UK. Council of Europe (2006). Compendium, Cultural Policies and Trends in Europe, 7th edition, www.culturalpolicies.net.

4 See website of the Department of Culture, Media and Sport, UK: www.culture.gov.uk/arts/policy_for_arts/arms_length_principle.htm.

5 See country profile of the UK, footnote 3.

6 For instance, the UK opposed the Ariane Programme which promotes the translation of European works (Pongy 1997).

7 See country profile of the Netherlands. Council of Europe (2006). Compendium, Cultural Policies and Trends in Europe, 7th edition, www.culturalpolicies.net.

8 See country profile of Denmark. Culture Link Network, www.culturelink .org/culpol/dk.html.

9 See country profiles of Sweden, Finland and Ireland. Council of Europe (2006). Compendium, Cultural Policies and Trends in Europe, 7th edition, www.culturalpolicies.net.

10 See country profile of Ireland. Culture Link Network, www.culturelink .org/culpol/ie.html.

11 See Chapter 4 on the TWF negotiations.

12 See country profile of France. Council of Europe (2006). Compendium, Cultural Policies and Trends in Europe, 7th edition, www.culturalpolicies .net.

13 See country profile of Italy. Council of Europe (2006). Compendium, Cultural Policies and Trends in Europe, 7th edition, www.culturalpolicies .net.

14 See country profile of Spain. Council of Europe (2006). Compendium, Cultural Policies and Trends in Europe, 7th edition, www.culturalpolicies .net.

15 See country profile of Germany. Council of Europe (2006). Compendium, Cultural Policies and Trends in Europe, 7th edition, www.culturalpolicies .net.

16 See Chapter 5 on the regulation of the book trade for a detailed account on German preference formation in EU-level negotiations.

17 See country profile of Belgium. Council of Europe (2006). Compendium, Cultural policies and Trends in Europe, 7th edition, www.culturalpolicies .net.

18 See section on the external strategy of the EU in the cultural sector in Chapter 3 of this book.

19 See Cram 1997 for a detailed analysis on the competence maximising strategies of both the Commission as a whole and its individual directorates.

20 The representatives of creators, producers and of the artistic community more generally will be referred to as 'cultural' interest groups in the book.

21 In the co-decision procedure, the Parliament shares legislative power equally with the Council. If Council and Parliament cannot agree on a piece of proposed legislation, it is put before a conciliation committee, composed of equal numbers of Council and Parliament representatives. Once the Conciliation Committee has reached an agreement, the text is sent once again to Parliament and the Council so that they can finally adopt it as law. Both Parliament and Council have the power to reject a proposal either at second reading or following conciliation, causing the proposal to fall.

3

Cultural policy at the heart of tensions between governance levels

In 1957, when European states signed the Rome Treaty,[1] no mention was made of the cultural sector. By 1992, Article 128 of the Maastricht Treaty (now Article 151)[2] created a formal competence for EU intervention in the cultural field. How can this evolution be accounted for? Was it a linear process, which had already begun prior to the reform of the Maastricht Treaty? Or have Treaty reforms been the harbingers for major policy developments? Moreover, which policy actors can be considered to have played a substantial role in the development of a policy space that was not evoked in the original treaties? This chapter aims to provide an overview of the construction process of EU cultural policies. A broad synopsis of the historical evolution of EU intervention in the cultural sector is crucial for contextualising the developments examined in detailed cases later. It is in this broad overview that we gain our initial glimpse of the different phases in the creation process of a new policy space at the EU level, along with the core stakeholders that have come to be involved in the process.

When looking at EU-level policy developments in the cultural field, it appears clearly that already much ahead of Treaty reform, numerous resolutions, decisions and legislative instruments related to cultural policy issues had been adopted at the Community level. Accounting for the Communitarisation process of cultural policies is therefore not a straightforward story. Rather, the process that led to a shift from the national towards the EU level of governance was characterised by constant tensions between subnational, national and EU-level policy actors that were all competing to control policy. If various initiatives in the cultural sector had been taken in the 1960s by some member governments worried about the 'purely' economic nature of the European project, these were essentially symbolic endeavours, often implemented outside the Community framework. Communitarisation of the cultural policy sector began when a *negative* type of integration, which resulted essentially from judgements of the ECJ and decisions from the European Commission, was initiated. The process of negative integration, which did not involve the creation of a distinct EU policy in the cultural sector (in the sense that EU intervention mainly consisted of the application of economic principles to cultural matters), had however a strong impact on domestic policies. The European dimension penetrated national arenas of politics, and member governments had to adapt their legislative and policy traditions to EU-level developments. Thus, the initial phase of the Communitarisation process of the cultural sector resulted from an extensive application of the Treaty rules to new areas on the part of DG Competition and the ECJ. However, in a second stage, aspects of intergovernmental negotiations and supranational centralisation were combined. Member states whose legislative and policy traditions were at odds with the liberalisation strategies developed by supranational structures attempted to develop their own initiatives. In this 'joint decision' mode (Scharpf 2000: 18), the setting of EU-level common solutions resulted from initiatives that were laid down by the Commission and adopted by the Council of Ministers.

This chapter sheds light on the connection between the two successive stages of the Communitarisation process of cultural policies. In reaction to the wave of negative integration promoted by European institutions from the 1970s onwards, certain states decided to promote the development of a positive type of integration, which they hoped would favour their policy preferences. The second stage of the Communitarisation process of cultural policies, which was (essentially) a consequence of the wave of negative integration that had already taken place, entailed the creation of a new positive policy at the EU level. The role played by policy ideas in the competition between governance levels also comes to light. The liberal and the *dirigiste* views have been used by conflicting 'advocacy coalitions' of actors (Sabatier 1998) as weapons to control policy and the formulation of policy choices. Both groups, in an endeavour of 'issue definition' (Baumgartner and Jones 1993) have focused on a given aspect of the subject to further their goals. Thus, two competing views of the problems at stake were used strategically by institutional actors as weapons to provoke changes in the venue of decision-making and further their policy preferences. The interaction between issue definition and venue produced a self-reinforcing mechanism characterised by 'positive feedback mechanisms' (Baumgartner and Jones 1991: 1048). Change in the venue of decision-making led to increased attention for a certain 'image' of the policy problem, leading to further change of venue.

The chapter starts by focusing on the earliest aspects of Community intervention in the cultural sector, highlighting the role of EU institutions in extending the remit of EU law to the cultural sector. If EU states had discussed the need to promote European cultural cooperation during Heads of State summits in the 1960s, their declarations were bereft of practical effect. The chapter then explains why, in the 1980s, member states entered the 'game' at the European level and initiated the deepening of EU-level cooperation. It will however be highlighted that despite the desire of several EU states to develop more positive forms of intervention, EU intervention remained subjugated to the application of purely economic principles to the cultural sector. This remained true after the institutionalisation of EU-level policy initiatives in the field of culture and the insertion of a legal basis for EU cultural policy in the Maastricht Treaty – with the notable exception of international trade negotiations, in which the EU has so far defended a more protectionist stance.

The confines of political cooperation: member states' symbolic declarations

European governments began to envisage initiatives for greater cultural cooperation as early as the late 1960s and 1970s. While there was no reference to an EC competence in the cultural sector in the Rome Treaty, the latter placed the emphasis on the need to 'lay the foundations of an ever closer union among the peoples of Europe'.[3] Thus, developing European cultural policies was conceived as a means of promoting a sense of 'European awareness' among European citizens – thought of as a necessary prerequisite to any furthering of European political integration.

When culture was meant to serve Europe …
The call for a renewed awareness of the centuries-old unity of European civilisation had already begun among a restricted group of intellectuals during the First World War (Lipgens 1982). Historians and writers were captivated with cultural elements which, they perceived, were common to the whole European continent, and argued that European history consisted of fruitful exchanges between ideas and realities that were shared throughout Europe. The French writer Paul Valéry, in *La Crise de l'Esprit* (1919), pointed to what he interpreted as a renewal of European self-awareness in reaction to the First World War. In the wake of the Second World War, these ideas were further developed by resistance movements. To them, promoting European unity was the sole means of ensuring peace for the future. In the Declaration of the French Committee for a European Federation,[4] the leaders of the French resistance stated that 'the European federation … can only be the result of a free decision by the peoples, who in this way express their will to save their common democratic civilisation' (cited in Lipgens 1982: 129).

After the war, the idea that European unity could be used as an underpinning for peace was endorsed by intellectuals and political parties. Federalist groups, mainly issuing from former resistance movements, became active when tensions arose between the US and the Soviet Union. The European Union of Federalists (UEF), created in December 1946, engaged in an endeavour to define what differentiated Europe from the superpowers, strongly arguing that the concept of a distinctive European culture still made sense (Obaton 1997). Their ultimate objective consisted of constructing a political Europe served by federalist institutions. Along with the rediscovery of Europe's common heritage, federalists attempted to grasp the essential values that characterised European civilisation. To the European Movement,[5] Europe could be characterised by some 'essential' characteristics, such as the 'love of freedom, hostility to totalitarianism of every kind, the humble and conscientious search for truth, and, above all, respect for the human personality and for the individual as an individual' (cited in Lipgens 1982: 24).

However, divisions between 'unionists' and 'federalists' hampered these ambitions. 'Unionists' were in favour of an intergovernmental type of cooperation, which would leave national sovereignties unperturbed. Along these lines, Winston Churchill proposed, in a speech in September 1946, to build a union based on the reconciliation of France and Germany and include 'the European family or as much of it as we can' (cited in Lipgens 1982: 320). Yet, if these views did not give leeway to all the federalist ambitions, the inclination of a key European politician to foster the promotion of European unity was crucial to European movements' success.

After the Second World War, the conscious rediscovery of European heritage and European values was perceived as a prerequisite to any sort of political unification. Culture was meant to serve Europe, before Europe could subsequently serve culture. Such were the thoughts that animated the first projects of European cooperation along cultural lines.

... before Europe could serve culture?

In 1969, the French government initiated the Hague Summit (European Council 1969),[6] during which European Heads of State acknowledged that the construction of an ever tighter European peoples' union was 'indispensable for preserving an exceptional seat of development, of progress and culture, for world equilibrium and for peace' (European Council 1969: 12). Only a few years later, French President Georges Pompidou initiated the 1972 Summit of Paris (European Council 1972). The Summit Declaration states that 'Europe must be capable of making her voice heard in world affairs and making a creative contribution in proportion to her human, intellectual, and material resources and affirming her own concepts in international relations in line with her role in initiating progress, peace and cooperation' (European Council 1972: 15). Although Summit declarations were bereft of any legally binding power, they expressed the shared concern among European governments not to limit the construction of Europe to a purely economic project. At the Copenhagen Summit of October 1973 (European Council 1973a), Heads of State adopted the *Declaration on European Identity* (European Council

1973b), in which they concluded that special attention had to be given to intangible values, underlining the position of Europe as an ideal place for the development of culture, and the role of culture as one of the fundamental elements of European identity (European Council 1973b: 118–122). Again, the summit was called on the initiative of French President Georges Pompidou, displaying France's long-standing interest in the development of European cultural integration.

In the late 1970s, some member states seemed ready to suggest more tangible policy developments. In the Tindemans Report, the Prime Minister of Belgium argued that Europe should not be confined to being a purely technocratic project (Tindemans Report 1976). He added that Europe 'must make itself felt in education and culture, news and communications, it must be manifest in the youth of our countries, and in leisure time activities [and] protect the rights of the individual and strengthen democracy through a set of institutions which have legitimacy conferred upon them by the will of our people' (Tindemans Report 1976: 12).

In the 1980s, the 1981 Genscher-Colombo Plan (Genscher and Colombo 1981), initiated by the Italian and German Ministers of Culture, proposed the creation of a Council of Ministers for cultural cooperation. The plan proposed that the Council would meet on a regular basis in order to harmonise member states' views on cultural matters. The French and the Belgian governments firmly endorsed the initiative (Massart-Piérard 1986). From the Genscher-Colombo plan arose the *Solemn Declaration on the European Union*, signed in June 1983 (European Council 1983) by member states. The Declaration contains proposals related to the strengthening of European cooperation in the field of higher education, the safeguarding of cultural heritage, and, interestingly, the promoting of joint activities in the dissemination of culture, in particular with regard to audio-visual methods (European Council 1983: 28). However, few of these proposals entailed the unfolding of common actions or policies and the Declaration failed to take into account the breadth of the suggestions laid out in the Genscher-Colombo Plan.

Repeatedly, member states' declarations signified their concern not to confine European integration to the sphere of economics. The French, Belgian, Greek and Italian governments showed their inclination to promote 'political' and 'cultural' forms of cooperation. Political cooperation was the only way for European states to develop their partnership in the cultural field. However, the declarations drafted by European governments remained symbolic initiatives. If member states signified their desire to foster cultural cooperation within Europe as early as the 1960s, they continued to conceive intervention in the cultural field as a means of furthering broader political objectives. Cultural cooperation was perceived as an instrument designed to pursue the reinforcement of European political integration. A more concrete and extended form of intervention in the cultural sector was in fact initiated by European institutions, which have skilfully circumvented the absence of legal basis in the Rome Treaty. Yet, the latter tackled cultural problems from an economic perspective and did not consider culture as a policy interest *as such*.

European institutions 'get into culture' too: legitimising EU intervention in the absence of Treaty basis

In the late 1970s, the European Parliament and the Commission issued the first policy documents on Community intervention in the field of culture. The ECJ and the Commission accordingly made use of their judicial and regulatory powers in order to tackle cultural matters. Yet, EU intervention focused solely on the economic aspects of cultural products, thereby trying to project a liberal 'image' on cultural policy issues. As predicted by Baumgartner and Jones (1993), policy-makers from another venue attacked existing policy arrangements in member states in an attempt to expand their own policy jurisdictions. EU-level discourse was therefore showing a one-sided preoccupation for the commercial aspects of cultural products, as a way of *changing the venue* of policy action, and thereby extending the remit of EU institutions' powers. (For further analysis of the application of the treaty principles to the cultural sector, see Delcourt and Papini 1987; Dumont 1992; Frediani 1992; Granturco 1999.)

The first policy documents: preparing the ground for future policy intervention

The first interventions in the cultural sector were made in the form of EP resolutions. In May 1974, the EP adopted a resolution on cultural heritage (OJ C 62, 30.5.1974), which in fact focused on a far broader range of issues. The resolution was the first formal step towards the formulation of a 'would-be EU cultural policy'. The EP proposed 'to eliminate the administrative obstacles which still hamper the exchange of cultural work, to eliminate the legal, administrative, and social obstacles to the providing of services by cultural workers … to approximate the national law on the protection of cultural heritage, royalties and other related intellectual property-rights' (OJ C 62, 30.5.1974). The resolution also engaged the Commission in proposing concrete policy initiatives in the cultural sector in application of the provisions of the EC Treaty. Thus, these proposals heralded the *economic* focus of EU intervention in the cultural sector. Two years later, the EP reiterated its support of the strengthening of European cultural cooperation, reasserting that the Rome Treaty was applicable to cultural matters (OJ C 79, 5.4.1976).

After its first direct elections in 1979, the EP decided to establish a Cultural Committee, which produced, between 1980 and 1981, six reports on themes as diverse as the European Music Year, the European

University Institute, the Museum on European Unification, the social situation of cultural workers, minority languages and the opening to the public of Community archives. Resolutions on literary translation in the European Community (OJ C 39, 12.2.1979 and OJ C 342, 19.12.1983), the International Youth Year (OJ C 229, 9.9.1985) and the European Foundation[7] (OJ C 352, 31.12.1985), were adopted by the EP in the following years. Thus, despite the initial economic hue of its proposals, the EP progressively distinguished itself by its propensity to promote a policy agenda that conceived culture as more than just an economic market.

The European Commission first intervened in the cultural sector in 1977, with the *Communication on Community Action in the Cultural Sector,* which defined the cultural sector as 'the persons and undertakings involved in the production and distribution of cultural goods and services' (European Commission 1977: 5). The main objectives as set out in the Communication consisted, essentially, of ensuring free trade in the cultural sector, combating the theft of cultural goods, ensuring the freedom of movement and establishment of cultural workers, creating training periods for young cultural workers, harmonising fiscal systems and implementing legislation on copyright and related rights. The Commission justified the issuing of the 1977 Communication by referring itself to 'the factual material gathered by its departments concerning the economic and social difficulties of the cultural sector' (European Commission 1977: 5). Thus, the Communication essentially confined itself to considering the economic aspects of the cultural sector and set out to promote the liberalisation of cultural markets.

The 1982 *Communication on Stronger Community Action in the Cultural Sector* (European Commission 1982) was once again marked by caution and did not aim to create a new policy space at the EU level in the cultural field. The Commission suggested that Community action be organised along the following lines: promoting freedom of trade in cultural goods, improving the living and working conditions of cultural workers, widening the audience for cultural events and promoting the conservation of architectural heritage. The Commission approach was still, in essence, limited to the application of the Rome Treaty to the cultural sector. Only a limited number of suggestions concerning the setting of European schemes for the preservation of cultural heritage, support programmes for the European cinematographic industry and the promotion of cultural relations with third countries, could be characterised as genuine attempts to set up EU cultural policies (European Commission 1982). The Parliament welcomed the 1982 Communication in a 1983 resolution on Community action in the cultural sector (C 342, 19.12.1983).

Thus the Commission, in a successful agenda-setting exercise, succeeded in extending the reach of its competence to the cultural sector when its formal powers were limited to the economic sphere. Its strategy consisted of focusing on the economic value of cultural goods so that their treatment could fall under the scope of the Rome Treaty. However, if the Commission set out its policy orientations in the communications discussed above, it was by making use of their judicial and regulatory powers that EU institutions could impose their policy objectives (i.e. the liberalisation of cultural markets) on national level cultural policies far more effectively. In this respect, the ECJ was crucial: EU rulings provided EU intervention in the cultural field with the legitimacy it needed.

The role of the ECJ in legitimising the 'competence creep'
From the 1960s onwards, the ECJ issued judgements on cultural policy issues. The role of the ECJ as a political actor in the EU policy process has been widely discussed by political scientists. Academic lawyers have argued that the ECJ also succeeded in transforming the founding Treaties into a constitution (Weiler 1993; Wincott 1996; Dehousse 1998). The ECJ's assertive role can also be evidenced in the cultural policy sector. Although cultural policy motives were not accepted by the ECJ as a motivation for restricting the free movement of goods, the rulings of the Court – which defined cultural products in economic terms – contributed to legitimising Community intervention in the cultural sector.[8]

The rulings from the ECJ confirmed that Community action in the area of culture involved no more than the application of the Rome Treaty to this sector of activity (see Lane 1993). Repeatedly, the Court demonstrated its inclination to treat cultural issues from a purely economic perspective. To begin with, it was disinclined to rule on the scope of Article 36 (now Article 30) of the Rome Treaty on national treasures – the only Treaty basis which could have allowed cultural considerations to be taken into account.[9] The possibility of doing so arose in the 1968 case *Commission* v. *Italy* (ECJ 1968a), which focused on the legality of a duty imposed by Italian authorities on the export of art treasures. The Italian government argued that the products subject to the measures could not be defined as goods within the meaning of the Treaty and, in the alternative, that the exception of Article 36 covered the particular measure. The Court dismissed the first argument on the ground that anything capable of monetary evaluation constitutes a good. As for the second argument, the Court claimed that Article 36 could not be relied on to justify a tax.

In other events, the Court made it clear that it was reluctant to apply the developments of the jurisprudence to the cultural sector. In the 1979 *Cassis de Dijon* case, the Court had concluded that:

> Obstacles to movement within the Community resulting from disparities between the national laws relating to the marketing of the products in question must be accepted in so far as those provisions may be recognised as

being necessary in order to satisfy the mandatory requirements relating in particular to the effectiveness of fiscal supervision, the protection of public health, the fairness of commercial transactions, and the defence of the consumer. (ECJ 1979)

The *Cassis de Dijon* case raised the question of whether or not the protection of culture could be classified as a mandatory requirement and as such be invoked in order to restrict the free movement of goods within the European Community. In the 1984 *Cinéthèque* case (ECJ 1985a), concerning French audio-visual legislation, the Court recognised cultural protection to be a mandatory requirement which could justify restrictions otherwise incompatible with Community competition law. However, the conclusions of *Cinéthèque* were the result of lengthy lobbying campaigns from the French government and representatives of the cultural community.[10] In most of its rulings, the Court was disinclined to place the interests of cultural protection over those of the Internal Market. This was evident again in the 1990s *Tourist Guide* cases,[11] where limitations to the provision of services that were aimed at the protection of historical, artistic and cultural heritage were permitted only narrowly.

More generally, the Court has indicated that, wherever activities in a given field have economic consequences, they may for that reason be affected by the rules of the Treaty. Good examples of the ECJ's propensity to extensively interpret EU law can be found in the domain of intellectual property and the audio-visual sector.[12] In *Parke Davis* v. *Centrafarm* (ECJ 1968b), the Court ruled that national intellectual property rights were capable of creating obstacles both to the free movement of goods and competition within the Common Market. In the 1971 case *Grammophon* v. *Metro* (ECJ 1971), the Court drew a distinction between the existence of intellectual property rights, which remained unaffected by the Treaty, and the exercise of such rights, which was subject to the rules of the Treaty. The so-called 'doctrine of exhaustion of rights'[13] was applied to other cases, such as *Music Vetreib* v. *GEMA* in 1981 (ECJ 1981a), in which the Court expressly ruled that copyright fell within the scope of the free movement of goods provisions of the Treaty. In the same way, audio-visual media was recognised as falling within Treaty rules in the 1974 case *Sacchi* (ECJ 1974). In the early 1980s, the ECJ was called upon to adjudicate a series of disputes arising from the new commercial tensions attendant upon structural changes in European broadcasting. The Court effectively confirmed the *Sacchi* ruling and broadcasting was defined as a tradable activity.

The ECJ has benefited from the institutional support of the Commission. For the latter, initiating proceedings before the ECJ proved to be an efficient way of furthering its policy objectives. In the book policy sector, the Commission initiated the 'Net Book Agreement' (ECJ 1992 and ECJ 1995) and the 'VBVB/VBBB' cases (ECJ 1984), which dealt with fixed price systems in cross-border common linguistic areas. In the field of intellectual property, the Commission expressed its concerns about the compatibility of national legislation with the Treaty rules in the case *Commission* v. *France* (ECJ 1981b), arguing that a levy introduced by a 1976 French law on the sale of reprographic machines was contrary to EU law. In the audio-visual sector, the Commission opened infringement proceedings against several member states in order to halt various forms of discrimination which prevented the free movement of audio-visual works between member states. In cases where the Commission was not directly involved, it often expressed its views by submitting written observations to the Court. For instance, in the *Sacchi* case (ECJ 1974) the Commission argued that radio and television institutions should be defined as *undertakings* within the meaning of Article 85 (now Article 81) of the Rome Treaty. Thus, acting as a 'catalyst in the integration process' (Dehousse 1998: 71), the ECJ – benefiting from the support of the Commission – extended the remit of the EC's competence to the cultural sector even when the overall question of harmonising legislation in the audio-visual, book or copyright policy sectors was not discussed by member states.

The European Commission: technical or policy law?
The Commission's rule-making powers are, at first sight, confined to routine decisions and the implementation of Council legislation. Yet the Commission has proved that it could use its regulatory powers in an extensive fashion in the field of competition policy. By defining what constitutes 'discrimination practices' and 'unfair competitive practices', the Commission can find opportunities for enacting 'policy' law (Nugent 1999).

In the cultural sector, the Commission made extensive use of its regulatory powers. It developed a proactive strategy, which consisted of enacting decisions against national legislative arrangements regarded as incompatible with Treaty principles. To do so, the Commission defined policy issues in a way that would allow for the application of EU economic rules. In the decision *RAI/UNITEL* (78/516/EEC), the Commission indicated that the term 'undertaking' could cover an individual artist, to the extent that the exploitation of his/her skills could be considered to be an economic activity. This approach was adopted likewise in other decisions. In 1981, the Commission ruled against a German collecting society (81/1030/EEC), declaring that the collecting society's failure to conclude management agreements with foreign artists constituted an abuse of dominant position within the meaning of Article 86 of the Rome Treaty (now Article 82). In a decision (89/441/EEC) on aid granted by the Greek government to the national film industry, the Commission ruled that Greek law was incompatible with the common market within the meaning of Article 92 of the Treaty (now Article 87) – on the grounds that the award of aid was subject to conditions of nationality that were incompatible with EU law. Giving an economic definition to 'artists' or 'cultural products' allowed the Commission to intervene in new policy areas in the absence of Treaty basis, as also happened in other spheres, such as education and sport (see Dumont 1992).

Thus, neither the Commission nor the Court seemed ready to recognise any general exception to free market principles in favour of the cultural sector. It is nevertheless worth mentioning that several cases, in which French legislative arrangements were often at stake (such as the *Cinéthèque* case mentioned above), demonstrated that the ECJ could be permeable to states' policy preferences when the latter were particularly salient.[14] Yet if the ECJ did not apply EC competition law to the cultural sector in a systematic and technical manner, it certainly contributed, by applying an economic definition to cultural works, to extending Community competence to the sector. The rulings of the Court and the decisions from the Commission triggered the liberalisation of the cultural sector, thereby challenging interventionist policies that had been developed in certain member states. The Commission and the ECJ benefited from the complicity of a number of private commercial actors which used the legal sphere in order to challenge national policies that were not favourable to them. Private actors' 'Eurolitigation' strategies have been successful in provoking policy change at the domestic level in each of the sectors examined in greater detail in the case studies which follow. The role of 'losers' appeal strategies' in stimulating the application of EU competition law to national policies via resort to the Commission and the Court was crucial in securing policy change at the national level. The latter were using the European venue in order to change the way cultural policy issues were defined, and therefore provoke the Europeanisation of the policy debate and the liberalisation of cultural markets that they were hoping for. Private television channels and advertisers' associations were particularly active in the audio-visual sector, while discotheques protested against the alleged excessive royalties charged by authors' societies in the copyright sector.

Thus, the first stage of EU intervention in the cultural sector was essentially characterised by the application of the Rome Treaty to cultural markets and its pith and substance was economic. Member states recognised the need to further cultural integration in Europe, but their initiatives (which were mainly of a 'symbolic' nature) were carried out on a purely intergovernmental basis within Heads of State summits. The period ranging from the late 1960s to the early 1980s could be summarised as follows. During the first phase of EU cultural cooperation, cultural matters were tackled by European governments, but the latter did not take any concrete action in this field. During the second phase, the

ECJ and the European Commission actively intervened in the cultural sector, but they did not tackle cultural matters *as such*. They intervened through the 'economic back door', thereby setting out a liberalisation strategy in the cultural field. Because EU institutions had no legal competence to intervene in the cultural sector, the only way they could do so was through the use of their economic treaty-based powers.[15] EU-level policy discourse has therefore showed a one-sided preoccupation for the commercial aspects of cultural products. Using the liberal image has been a way of changing the venue of policy action, and thereby extending the remit of EU institutions' powers. Up to this stage, none of these initiatives (intergovernmental and supranational) taken could, even loosely, be understood as constituting the bases of a Community cultural policy.

Member states 'back' into the policy process: the institutionalisation of EU-level cooperation in the cultural sector

After a hesitant awakening, the gradual unfolding of EU intervention in the cultural sector in the 1980s proved that a new policy space could be gradually constructed and institutionalised in the absence of formal Treaty basis (see McMahon 1995 for an exhaustive overview of EU cultural initiatives in the 1980s). Abandoning their rather disinterested attitude towards supranational cooperation in the cultural field, those member states that were frustrated with the economic approach of European institutions succeeded in initiating policy initiatives that went beyond the mere application of the economic principles of the Rome Treaty to the cultural sector.

The first Council meetings: intergovernmental or supranational cooperation?

With the development of greater levels of intergovernmental cooperation in the early 1980s, EU-level cultural initiatives were extended beyond the scope of socio-economic matters. National Ministers of Culture initiated regular Council of Ministers meetings within a newly created 'Culture Council' and furthered the development of a new policy space dealing specifically with cultural issues.

The first meeting of the Culture Council took place on an informal basis, following an invitation from the French and Italian Ministers of Culture[16] in September 1982 (Culture Council 1982). EU Ministers of Culture were concerned with the preservation of European cultural heritage and the need to support the European film industry (Culture Council 1982, EC Bulletin 9–1982: 40). The French Minister of Culture proposed the creation of a support scheme for European audio-visual productions. However, clashes of interests among European states rapidly surfaced, preventing the implementation of far-reaching initiatives.

Invoking either institutional or budgetary motives, Britain, Germany, the Netherlands and Denmark expressed their hostility to the French proposal.[17] In November 1983, Melina Mercouri, then Minister of Culture in Greece, called for another informal meeting of European Ministers of Culture. However, the Danish Minister (for judicial motives) and the British Minister (for financial motives) expressed anew their suspicions concerning the development of EU-level cooperation in the cultural sector.[18] Greece, Italy and France have therefore played a central role in initiating the first steps towards EU-level cooperation in the cultural field. The role of personalities has been fundamental; Jack Lang in France, Melina Mercouri in Greece and Vincenzo Scotti in Italy provided the European Community with the necessary vision for the development of cultural cooperation.[19]

The first formal meeting of European Ministers of Culture took place in Luxembourg in June 1984 (Culture Council 1984). The Ministers of Culture agreed on the necessity to foster the teaching of languages within the Community, improve European citizens' knowledge of other European countries' cultures and histories and promote cultural cooperation with non-member countries. The Italian and French governments fashioned themselves into active agenda-setters. The Italian government proposed the creation of a European information centre on stolen works of art. The theft of works of art was indeed an essential concern for the Italians. During the same meeting, the French government suggested the introduction of uniform pricing arrangements for books within the European Community. Here as well, it is evident that domestic concerns were crucial; book-pricing policies are a key element of state intervention in the cultural field in France. Thus, a handful of European countries favoured the strengthening of EU-level initiatives in the cultural sector. Proposals in favour of EU-level policy solutions were, however, motivated by states' desires to 'export' their own policy traditions at the supranational level.

Throughout the 1980s, the activities of the Culture Council were still tentative. The intensification of European cultural cooperation was hampered at the Culture Council of November 1984 (Culture Council 1984). The UK opposed any kind of public intervention in the cultural field, while the Netherlands and Denmark favoured other forms of cooperation. Two resolutions, concerning measures to combat audio-visual pirating and the rational distribution of films throughout the audio-visual communication media (OJ C 204, 24.7.1984, OJ C 204, 3.8.1984), were adopted in July 1984. Yet, the resolutions were passed by the representatives of the governments of member states – and not by the Council of the European Communities. Symbolically at least, the distinction mattered. In fact, states that were interested in furthering supranational initiatives in the cultural sector decided to promote an intergovernmental mode of cooperation, which allowed them to circumvent the limits of the Community framework.

The French government as a 'first mover'
The presence of strong-minded politicians, such as Minister of Culture Jack Lang in France and Commission President Jacques Delors, partly explains the shift towards greater EU-level cultural cooperation. However, member states' attempts at initiating different type of policies at the EU level were also a reaction against developments that were orchestrated by European institutions. (For an interesting analysis of how cultural policies were also a reaction against the consequences of world-wide liberalisation trends, see Esmein 1999.) Member states initially defended their sovereignty in the sensitive area of culture. However, their room for manoeuvre in formulating domestic policies was reduced as a result of the *de facto* application of the EU Treaty on cultural matters by the ECJ and the Commission. Technological developments also increased the perceived need for supranational-level rules. In France, Jacques Thibau, then Director of the Cultural Affairs Department within the External Affairs Ministry, was asked to lead European negotiations on telecommunications.[20] His mission consisted of thinking of a minimal set of rules that could be applied to a 'European audio-visual space'. Thus, states where domestic policies were being questioned by technological developments and the EU-led liberalisation strategy of the cultural sector had to adapt their strategies. Two ECJ cases were particularly challenging for French policies in the cultural field.[21] In the book policy sector, the ECJ issued several rulings concerning the 1981 French law on book prices – the so-called 'Loi Lang'. The Loi Lang enforces a system of fixed prices for books, the aim of which is to ensure that there is no decline in the number of separate titles published and that cultural diversity is maintained. The cases brought before the ECJ triggered a two-year long struggle between French authorities and independent book shops, on the one hand; and the ECJ, the Commission and commercial actors, on the other (see ECJ 1985b). The two coalitions held conflicting views as to the compatibility of a fixed price system for books and EU competition law. The *dirigiste* coalition was eventually successful in securing French legislation; the core principles and values that were at the origin of the "fixed price system were not challenged. Yet, if the law was eventually maintained, at least in essence,[22] the ECJ's propensity to question domestic legislation clearly meant that the French government would be bound to take into account the requisites of EU law. In the audio-visual policy sector, French legislation was seriously endangered in the *Cinéthèque* case, which dealt with the rational distribution of films throughout the audio-visual communication media (ECJ 1985a). The French government developed arguments that were of a *political* nature in order to defend the

legislation before the ECJ.[23] The ECJ eventually concluded that a regulation ensuring the priority use in cinemas of cinematographic works of any origin in relation to other methods of broadcasting was compatible with Article 30 of the Treaty (ex Article 28). However, the French had to orchestrate fierce lobbying campaigns in order to protect the measure, and subsequently became aware of the confines of their room for manoeuvre in the field of culture.

Thus, the states that wished to preserve domestic *dirigiste* policies in the cultural sector sought to impose the setting of *EU-level* policies that would lock in their own policy preferences at the supranational level.[24] In order to protect its own model of policy intervention (and in so doing trying to replicate it at the EU level), the French government therefore developed a policy discourse that focused on the special characteristics of the cultural sector. In other words, France, along with other *dirigiste* states and the artistic community, attempted to impose a *dirigiste* or interventionist image onto those cultural policy issues that were being considered at the European level. It was however evident that certain states, such as the UK, the Netherlands, or Denmark, were hostile to developing supranational policies that were at odds with their own policy traditions. Thus, the most 'proactive' governments bypassed EC structures in order to promote projects that would allow them to further their policy objectives.

The first European support schemes in the audio-visual sector have indeed resulted from a successful attempt from the French to 'export' their policy model at the Community level. In 1985, impatience with the persisting lack of progress on the cultural front led the French to launch their own action plan (Wiesand 1995). In the *Blue Book*, a policy document produced by the French government and submitted to other member governments and EU officials, the French set out to develop voluntary cultural cooperation *à la carte* between as many EU states as would be interested. In the introduction of the *Blue Book,* the French government explains rather straightforwardly that 'rather than exhausting ourselves [i.e. the representatives of the French government] trying to reach an agreement between twelve states on the principles and means of an EC measure, we will try to take swift action together with those member states who wish to be involved' (French Government 1987: 5).[25]

The French government's pet project consisted of creating a European support scheme in the audio-visual sector. Already during a meeting of European Ministers of Culture in 1982, Jack Lang had pointed to the necessity of supporting the European audio-visual industry in order to prevent the disappearance of national cultural identities (*Le Matin*, 21 September 1982). In fact, setting up a Community level support mechanism in the audio-visual field was perfectly in line with French policy objectives.

However, during the Culture Council of June 1984 the French were confronted by opposition from Britain and Denmark (*Le Monde*, 25 June 1984). Thus, in order to circumvent the rigidity of the voting procedure within the Council, they initiated the creation of a project based on inter-governmental cooperation (*Le Monde*, 24 November 1984). Rather than setting Community level cultural policies, what mattered to the French was the possibility of furthering French policy objectives through supra-national mechanisms, whatever the latter would be. The project was further discussed during a meeting organised by the *Centre National de la Cinématographie* (CNC),[26] finally taking shape under the name of Eurimages in 1988. Eurimages is now implemented under the aegis of the Council of Europe and aims at promoting co-productions and the circulation of audio-visual works within Europe. The majority (almost 90 per cent) of the fund's resources – which originate from member states' contributions – goes to supporting co-production. Eurimages has so far supported the co-production of more than 900 feature films and documentaries. The sum committed to assistance for distribution amounts to some 762,245 euros a year, while that committed to assistance to cinemas amounts to 616,000 euros each year.[27] France has been, since the creation of Eurimages, a net beneficiary of Eurimages funding.[28]

Another audio-visual support scheme was initiated by French President François Mitterrand. The success of 'Technological Eureka', a support scheme in the field of research and development, led the French authorities to initiate a similar project in the audio-visual sector. The idea emerged on the French political agenda in the late 1980s (Collins 1994). In October 1988, François Mitterrand wrote to Jacques Delors, the President of the European Commission, emphasising the major importance of supporting the audio-visual industry in Europe.[29] In October 1989, 26 countries eventually signed up for the creation of Audiovisual Eureka. It was created under the shape of a pan-European inter-governmental association with thirty-five member countries and the European Commission and the Council of Europe as associate members. The main objective of Audiovisual Eureka consisted of contributing to the development of a wide-ranging European field for cooperation and exchanges in the audio-visual sector.[30] Thus, France succeeded in initiating the first European support mechanisms in the audio-visual sector – but the only way to do so was by bypassing EU decision-making mechanisms.

The proactive role of states that had strongly embedded policy traditions to defend had an effect upon Commission thinking. In the 1987 Communication *A Fresh Boost for Culture in the European Community*, the Commission states that it 'shares the concern expressed by the French government' on business sponsorship (European Commission 1987: 11). Furthermore, the Commission 'agrees with the French government that the quality of the initial and continuous training given to those working in the audio-visual industry is essential to the development of European cinema and television' (European Commission 1987: 21–22). The only literary reference quoted in the Commission Communication is a publication from the *Documentation Française*, published under the aegis of the French Ministry of Culture and the Council of Europe.[31] No reference is made to other states' views. Thus, the proactive role of the French, combined with the openness of the agenda-setting stage of EU decision-making processes, meant that they could influence the formulation of policy guidelines under the Delors Commission. The French government distinguished itself by playing the role of 'first mover' in the creation of supranational level mechanisms in the cultural sector. Yet not only were these initiatives based on an *intergovernmental* type of cooperation, but French international strategies have also been inhibited by EU institutions' liberalisation plans.

Institutionalisation of EU-level cooperation
In the second half of the 1980s, cultural cooperation was characterised by a greater 'supranationalisation' of its mechanisms. In the Culture Council meeting of May 1985, member states reaffirmed their intention to develop activities at the Community level. A number of resolutions were adopted on 'symbolically' significant actions, such as the 'European City of Culture' event (OJ C 153, 22.6.1985) and the European sculpture competition (OJ C 153, 22.6.1985). Further evidence of cooperation emerged in the form of resolutions concerning collaboration between libraries in the field of data processing (OJ C 271, 23.10.1985), the access of young people to museums and cultural events (OJ C 348, 31.12.1985) and transnational cultural itineraries (OJ C 044, 26.2.1986).

In the late 1980s, Community action in the cultural sector became increasingly structured, with regular meetings of the Culture Council and the establishment of a Committee for Cultural Affairs in 1988 (OJ C 197, 27.7.1988). Substantial initiatives were undertaken (EC Bulletin 12–1987: 10). Resolutions on the promotion of the translation of important works of European culture (OJ C 309, 19.11.1987) and the promotion of books and reading (OJ C 183, 20.7.1989) were adopted. In the following years, further resolutions on issues related to copyright and the export of cultural goods were to be adopted.

Jacques Delors had then become President of the European Commission and proposals for cultural cooperation within the Community framework were given greater credit.[32] An entire section of Jacques Delors' introduction to the 1985 Programme of the Commission was dedicated to 'the cultural and human dimension' of the European Community. He argued that culture had to become 'a driving force towards achievement of the European ideal, enabling the Community to assert its identity while respecting its diversity' (Delors 1985). In the 1987

Communication *A Fresh Boost for Culture in the European Community*, the Commission argued that 'the time ha[d] come – without departing from the principle of subsidiarity – to give cultural activities in the Community a higher profile' (European Commission 1987: 7). The Commission proposed a considerably wider range of actions than in its two former communications concerning cultural matters.[33] Among the fields of activity envisaged were the promotion of the audio-visual industry, ensuring access to cultural resources, improving training in the cultural sector and fostering cultural dialogue with the rest of the world. Japanese and US audio-visual products were indeed perceived as a threat, and the emphasis was laid on the necessity to protect European audio-visual works. The Communication was welcomed during an informal meeting of the Ministers of Culture in Copenhagen in December 1987 (Culture Council 1987).

Throughout the 1980s, supranational developments were paralleled with a growing concern for EU cultural cooperation at the intergovernmental level and regular meetings of the Council of Ministers responsible for Cultural Affairs. EU-level cultural cooperation was progressively institutionalised. A handful of 'cultural' projects were initiated by the governments that had a specific interest in furthering EU-level cooperation – and also in reaction to the liberalisation strategies set out by EU institutions. The role of France, in that respect, was evidenced. Simultaneously, European institutions initiated a policy discourse which was quite different from the all-economic approach they had so far applied to culture. The European Commission and the European Parliament started focusing on the need to further cultural cooperation in order to promote a sense of 'European identity' among European citizens.

The late 1980s: new 'European identity' rationale for EU-level intervention?

In the 1980s, EU official justifications for the deepening of cultural action were two-fold: on the one hand, European institutions focused on the role of culture as a facilitator of European integration; on the other, they argued that harmonising member states' legislation was a pressing need in order to meet the requirements of the Single Market. The rationale developed by European institutions was captured in the 1987 Communication, which reads that 'the Commission is convinced that increased cultural activity is now a political as well as a social and economic necessity, given the twin goals of completing the internal market by 1992 and progressing from a People's Europe to European Union' (European Commission 1987: 6).

Presenting Community level cultural policies as a political imperative was a new element in the European policy discourse. The rationale for EU intervention was simply put: if the European Union was to succeed as an entity, the feeling of belonging to a common culture had to be fostered. The two 1985 *Adonnino Reports on a People's Europe*[34] contained specific sections devoted to culture and communication, which suggested the creation of support schemes in the audio-visual sector, the establishment of a European Academy of Science, Technology and Art and measures meant to ensure young people's access to museums and cultural events (Adonnino 1985). The Adonnino Committee, chaired by the Italian MEP Pietro Adonnino concentrated on the theme of the image and identity of the Community, and suggested the introduction of concrete 'European' symbols to which citizens could relate. More specifically, the report proposed adopting a European Flag and a European anthem. The Committee also called for more active communication policies concerning the activities of the EU and a 'European dimension' in the field of education. In June 1985, when approving the proposals made by the Adonnino Committee, the European Council meeting in Milan adopted the flag, the anthem – Beethoven's 'Ode to Joy' – and Europe Day as the official symbols of the European Community. The resolution on the European Cinema and Television Year (OJ C 320, 13.12.1986) was also inspired by the reports' conclusions. The 1986 resolution on the protection of Europe's architectural heritage (OJ C 320, 13.12.1986) referred to the *1983 Solemn Declaration on the European Union* and its primary objectives. 'Symbolic' initiatives, such as the 'European City of Culture' (OJ C 153, 22.6.1985) and the 'European Cultural Month' (OJ C 162, 3.7.1990), were aimed at reinforcing the sense of European identity among European citizens.

The notion of a People's Europe was a fairly well-established one within the European Community of the late 1980s (Shore 2000). The term People's Europe related to the idea that the integration project should not be primarily concerned with market-making, but also with a more 'fundamental' project of community building as captured by the new European symbols. Thus, developments in the 1980s reasserted that the promoting of cultural policies at the EC level was part of a broader project, the objective of which was to foster a sense of European identity among Community citizens.

The 'European identity' rationale also underpinned the development of European audio-visual policy. Policy-makers believed that changes in the content of broadcasting would reshape the identities of European viewers. These powerful and long-standing sentiments – based on the assumption that television creates an informed and involved public (Harrison and Woods 2000) – prevailed among EU officials and the political class of the Community. With these presuppositions in mind, EU policy-makers formulated policies aimed at creating a unified European audio-visual market and establishing pan-European services (Collins 1994). In the

1982 'Hahn Resolution', the EP places emphasis on the role of the media in creating a sense of European awareness, arguing that:

> European unification will only be achieved if Europeans want it. Europeans will want it if there is such thing as a European identity. A European identity will only develop if Europeans are adequately informed. At present, information via the mass media is controlled at national level. The vast majority of journalists do not 'think European' because their reporting role is defined in national or regional terms. Hence the predominance of negative reporting. Therefore, if European unification is to be encouraged, Europe must penetrate the media. (OJ C 87, 5.4.1982)

The Report suggested the creation of a joint European channel under the auspices of the European Broadcasting Union (EBU). The project took concrete shape with the creation of Eurosport and Euronews by the EBU's first satellite ventures, Europa and Eurikon. The EP resolution inspired the 1983 Commission's Interim Report *Realities and Tendencies* (European Commission 1983), which also underlined the role of television as a vehicle for European culture.

Invoking the 'identity' rationale was, however, always a delicate enterprise, given the absence of treaty basis in the cultural policy sector before 1992. In any case, policies issued from the 'identity' line of thinking involved the creation of 'European' symbols, symbolic events, and the restructuring of European education programmes. Culture, in a more anthropological meaning, was at stake. The rationale did not serve as a ground for developing new market-correcting mechanisms in the art sector as such.

EU Legislative developments: back to the 'competence' issue

The 'economic' nature of the rationale for EU intervention in the cultural sector is evident when one looks at EU legislative developments in the cultural field (Dumont 1992). Throughout the 1980s and 1990s, EU legislation was based on economic arguments and essentially aimed at liberalising new policy sectors in the perspective of the Single Market.

The TWF Directive adopted in 1989 (89/552/EEC) and amended in 1997 (97/36/EC) established the legal frame of reference for the movement of television broadcasting services in the European Union.[35] It provided for coordination at the EU level of national legislation applicable to television broadcasts, such as access of the public to major sporting events, television advertising and sponsorship, the protection of minors and the right of reply. The Directive is based on the assertion that films are economic products to be dealt with by the Internal Market Directorate – a liberal image was clearly applied to the broadcasting sector. Quotas aimed at encouraging the production and distribution of European works were implemented, but only 'where practicable'. Essentially, the TWF

Directive, by allowing states to pick up and retransmit programmes from those EU states that meet the requirements of the Directive, establishes the free movement of television programmes within the EU.

In the copyright sector, the Council and the Commission did not initiate a genuine harmonisation of copyright law in the EU.[36] The 1980s copyright directives were limited to technical matters. In 1996, the Commission presented a legislative proposal concerning the harmonisation of artists' resale rights throughout the EU. After several years of bitter negotiations, the Directive on resale right (2001/84/EC) was formally adopted in September 2001. However the text of the final Directive does not implement a high level of harmonisation in the EU. The 2001 Directive on copyright and neighbouring rights in the information society (2001/29/CE) had a broader remit; it aimed to extend copyright protection to new forms of technology in the digital area, such as the Internet, CD-ROMs, CDs and DVDs. However, the 2001 Directive does not commit EU states to a high level of harmonisation and was received with angst by copyright holders.

Further EU legislative developments were linked to the necessity of harmonising EU law in the perspective of meeting the requirements of the Single Market. In view of the implications of abolishing frontier controls within the EU, trade of cultural goods with third countries had to be protected. A Council regulation on the export of cultural goods was therefore adopted in 1992 (3911/92). According to the regulation, the export of cultural goods is subject to the presentation of an export licence, which is valid throughout the EU. A licence may be refused if the goods in question fall into the category of national treasures covered by national legislation. In 1993, the Directive (93/7/EEC) on the return of cultural objects unlawfully removed from the territory of a member state was also adopted. The Directive ensures the return of cultural objects that are classified, before or after their unlawful removal from the territory of a member state, as national treasures possessing artistic, historic or archaeological value by national law or regulation in accordance with EU law. Thus, Single Market requirements and technological developments have provided the EU with solid motives, upon which EU-level legislative developments could be based far in advance of Treaty reforms. By contrast, the 'European identity' rationale did not provide a sufficiently firm legitimisation for EU-level intervention.

Throughout the 1980s, the EU extended the remit of its competence to the field of cultural policy. However, despite the emergence of a discourse concerned with the (non)emergence of a sense of European identity among European citizens, legislative developments were not based upon this rationale. The common concern of all EU legislative initiatives consisted of ensuring regulatory consistency among the member states with a view to deregulation of the sectors at stake. It will now be considered whether, with the insertion of a specific clause on cultural policy in the Maastricht Treaty, a 'positive' cultural policy was allowed to develop.

Treaty reform as *a posteriori* legitimisation of EU-level intervention in the cultural sector

The insertion of Article 128 in the Maastricht Treaty provided a legal basis for EU intervention in the cultural sector and legitimised actions that were already under way. However, as will be highlighted below, if Article 128 allowed for the strengthening of *dirigiste* measures, post-Maastricht EU intervention in the cultural sector can hardly be characterised as an attempt to develop a positive EU cultural policy.

The insertion of Article 128 in the Maastricht Treaty
The construction of EU cultural policy seems to have followed a familiar pattern in that Treaty reform eventually caught up with actions already under way. Approximately thirty decisions, resolutions or conclusions from the Council of Ministers were adopted before 1992 (Granturco 1999). Major legislative initiatives bearing clear cultural considerations had already been initiated. Thus, Article 128 of the Maastricht Treaty, which established a legal basis for EU cultural policy, was the logical outcome of developments that were already in hand. The Treaty states that action by the Community should be aimed at encouraging coopera-tion between member states and supporting and supplementing their action in the following areas:

> – 'improvement of the knowledge and dissemination of the culture and history of the European peoples,
> – conservation and safeguarding of cultural heritage of European signifi-cance,
> – non-commercial cultural exchanges,
> – artistic and literary creation, including in the audio-visual sector.[37]

Article 128 also states that cooperation with third countries should be fostered, and sets out that the Community must take cultural aspects into account in its action under the provisions of the Treaty. The Council can adopt incentive measures and recommendations. Unlike in the education sector, where the QMV rule applies, the cultural sector is still governed by the unanimity rule.[38]

The Maastricht approach aims to provide safeguards for national autonomy, which is ensured, essentially, with the principle of subsidiarity. The harmonisation of member states' legal and regulatory provisions is excluded from the scope of Article 128. Several states, worried that the Maastricht Treaty and the Single Market contained in themselves the potential for unleashing cultural homogenisation within the EU, were worried about the effects of additional EU intervention (Lane 1993). Craufurd Smith (2004) also explains that Article 128 was answering member states' concerns about the Community's capacity to disturb long-standing cultural practices. The UK was opposed to recognising EU competence in the cultural sector, as culture is not considered to be a major field of public action in Great Britain (*Le Monde*, 18 September 1992). These various sources of opposition resulted in a narrow definition of EU competence and in the upholding of the unanimity voting rule within the Council.

The reinforcement of dirigiste *initiatives at the Community level*

Since the reform of the Treaty, the EU has initiated (or developed) three support programmes – Kaleidoscope, Ariane and Raphael – which aim to develop cooperation between EU states and disseminate European peoples' culture.[39] Taken together these support mechanisms constitute the embryo of what could be characterised as a cultural policy *as such*. The Kaleidoscope Programme, set up in 1996, aimed to encourage artistic creation and the promotion of cultural exchanges, particularly in the fields of the arts, the performing arts and the applied arts. It replaced the project 'Europe Cultural Scene' that had been created by the Commission in 1990 (Granturco 1999). However, its budget was expanded considerably after the Treaty reform. Similar objectives are emphasised in the Ariane Programme, which deals with translation in the area of books and reading, and in the Raphael Programme devoted to European heritage. The Ariane Programme, created in 1997, aims to promote a wider knowledge of literary works within Europe by means of translation and improvement of skills of professionals. (Already in 1987, member states had decided to organise a pilot scheme called Aristeon in order to support the translation of European works (OJ C 309, 19.11.1987).) Under the Raphael Programme, which was adopted in 1997, the Community initiated the preservation and safeguard of cultural sites such as the Parthenon, Lisbon, the site of Sarlat, historic gardens and opera houses.

In response to demands from the EP, the Commission proposed to establish the first European Community Framework Programme in Support of Culture for the period 2000–2004 (508/2000/EC). The aim of the so-called Culture 2000 Programme consists of simplifying EU action by using a single instrument for financing and programming – grouping together Ariane, Kaleidoscope and Raphael. The Programme sets out to promote mutual knowledge of the culture and history of the European peoples; foster the creativity and the transnational dissemination of culture and the movement of artists; highlight cultural diversity and the development of new forms of cultural expression; and improve access to and participation in culture in the European Union for as many citizens as possible.[40]

The Culture 2000 programme, with a total budget of 167 million euros, has improved the financing and programming of EU cultural activities. Most significantly, it treats cultural action as a separate policy in its own right for the first time, by grouping together all the former aspects of Community intervention in the field.

In the audio-visual sector, the Media Programme was created in order to respond to *dirigiste* policy actors' demands for more substantial intervention at the EU level. The Programme, set up in 1988 for a probationary period, was renewed until 1995 after having been endorsed by the Council in December 1990.[41] The Media Programme was then replaced by Media Plus, with a total budget of 350 million euros for the 2001–2005 period. Media Plus was extended until December 2006, and new proposals have now been laid down by the European Commission for a 2007 Media Programme.[42] Its basic objective consists of making the European audio-visual industry more competitive and creating an environment that encourages businesses in the sector – essentially by providing loans and technical assistance. It also encourages the programming of European films and improves the conditions of promotion and access for independent producers and distributors to the European market. In recent years, award-winning films such as *Le Fabuleux Destin d'Amélie Poulain*, *La Pianiste* and *No Man's Land* benefited from the support of the Media Programme.[43]

Thus, instruments supporting EU cultural initiatives were either created or consolidated in the 1990s. Support mechanisms constitute the embryo of what could be characterised as a *dirigiste* cultural policy at the EU level. Yet, when one examines EU legislative developments, the impact of the 1992 Treaty reform is far less obvious.

Television transmission standards: success of a dirigiste *initiative?*
The other key *dirigiste* element of EU audio-visual policy (aside from the Media Programme) consisted of setting common technical standards for satellite broadcasting. The harmonisation of TV transmission standards bears clear techno-industrial policy objectives, but it also has, especially in the digital context, implications for audio-visual policy. Since most digital broadcasts are encrypted, viewers require a conditional access decoder to receive those broadcasts. These conditional access systems 'operate as electronic turnstiles in the home, controlling which broadcasts and other services viewers can receive, and which viewers and customers broadcasters and other service providers can reach' (Levy 1999: 63). Without adequate regulation, conditional access operators and broadcasters can be tempted to develop vertical integration strategies, thus preventing viewers from accessing a full range of television channels. Adequate regulation can therefore play a role in terms of preserving media pluralism.

In the analogue context, attempts to harmonise transmission standards essentially aimed at reviving the European consumers electronics industry (Goldberg, Prosser and Verhuslt 1998). EU officials believed that the plurality of transmission standards which existed in the EU (PAL and SECAM[44]) was hindering the possibility of making economies of scale and was thus disadvantageous for the industry (Collins 1994). The Commission also argued that the establishment of a European standard (D2 MAC, of the 'MAC' family[45]) would make an incremental approach to an EU standard for High Definition Television (HDTV) possible – HDTV, which allows for cinema-quality broadcasting, is a major innovation in electronics (Moussis 2001). The Commission thought that the HDTV definition standard would provide a bulwark against Japanese and US competition and thus boost the European audio-visual industry. Thus, the 1992 Directive on satellite television transmission standards (92/38/EEC) was aimed at finding policy solutions to the problems which resulted from the existence of two incompatible transmission standards.

However, the successive revisions of the Directive that resulted from dissension among EU states weakened the requirement to use MAC standards (Collins 1994, Caudron 1992). The 1992 Directive opened the door to a non-MAC digital route to HDTV. It allowed for the use of PAL standards and stated that only those services that would be established after 1995 would have to use the MAC standard. In fact, the Directive favoured UK interests (as well as those of Denmark, Spain and Ireland) and did not give way to French, German and Dutch efforts aiming at re-establishing the mandatory use of MAC standards. In June 1993, the Council of Ministers agreed to an action plan (93/424/EEC) for the development of HDTV including incentives for programme production in MAC. Yet, the plan was again a compromise devised to satisfy UK demands for less interventionist policies (see Collins 1994). Production subsidies were limited and producers had to provide 50 per cent of the additional costs of HDTV production from commercial sources.

The 1995 Directive on the use of standards for transmission of television signals (95/47/EC) requires that digital television services use standardised transmission systems. However, the Directive does not specify which standards are to be used. In fact, by then the introduction of HDTV services was no longer the immediate objective. Instead, market players thought that the introduction of the HDTV screen format (16:9 widescreen) was more strategically important and achievable. The advantage of 16:9 as a policy is that it bypasses the debate on technologies; 16:9 can be delivered using analogue or digital technologies. There is no longer a single objective – HDTV – with a particular approach mandated. The *dirigiste* strategy failed, largely because conflicting interests could not be brought up together.

Thus, EU legislative developments were still dominated by liberal concerns even after the Treaty reform. This is all the more true in that legislative and regulatory initiatives – as well as ECJ cases – have a much greater practical impact on national cultural policies – at least in terms of policy choices and policy-making – than EU support programmes in the cultural sector. Article 128 was not used as a legal basis for Community action to redress any of the negative consequences of market liberalisation. Legislative developments did not initiate market-correcting mechanisms, but rather ecouraged the liberalisation of cultural industries' markets. Furthermore, if interventionist policy measures were further developed after the reform of the Maastricht Treaty, their impact is still rather marginal (*Le Monde Diplomatique*, September 1999). Only 0.9 per cent of the EU budget has been dedicated to cultural expenses in recent years.[46] In the mid-1990s, the budget of the Centre National de la Cinématographie (CNC) in France equalled that of Media II (the programme which was the predecessor of Media Plus).[47]

An external *dirigiste* strategy?

The formulation of the EC's commercial policy: culture as a special case?
Dirigiste states have actively defended their ability to control the position of the EC concerning cultural and audio-visual issues in international trade negotiations. Article 133 of the Nice Treaty rules that the Council of Ministers has to 'act unanimously when negotiating and concluding an agreement ... where that agreement includes provisions for which unanimity is required for the adoption of internal rules or where it relates to a field in which the Community has not yet exercised the powers conferred upon it by this Treaty by adopting internal rules'.[48] This ensures that every member state can preserve its 'right of veto' within the Council when the latter negotiates external agreements on cultural matters. Furthermore, Article 133 includes a specific clause on audio-visual services, stating that 'trade in cultural and audio-visual services, educational services, and social and human health services, shall fall within the shared competence of the Community and its Member States'. During the Nice Treaty negotiations, France was the most vocal opponent of exclusive competence for the Community in the audio-visual sector, since 'it did not trust the Commission to defend Europe's Maginot line against Hollywood' (Ludlow 2001: 1). It benefited from the support of the Spanish government, and to some extent Portugal. Non-governmental organisations, such as Attac, which launched its 'Red Alert on the 133' campaign, also pulled their weight on final outcomes, allowing the *dirigistes* to secure the principle of a shared competence between the European Community and Member States.

During the negotiations on the future Constitutional Treaty, *dirigiste* states and the cultural lobby succeeded in preserving special rules for EU commercial policy in the cultural and audio-visual sectors. Article III 315–4 of the Constitutional Treaty gives member states a veto on changes in the common commercial policy in 'the conclusion of agreements in the field of trade in cultural and audio-visual services, where these agreements risk prejudicing the Union's cultural and linguistic diversity'. However, how such risk is defined is open to interpretation. It might become difficult to protect, for example, cross-border agreements on book prices on the sole ground that they are indispensable to preserve linguistic and cultural diversity. Given, however, that the Constitutional Treaty has not been ratified, such speculations have at this stage no substantial *raison d'être*. What the Constitutional Treaty negotiations highlight was the ability of *dirigiste* actors to maintain member states' right of veto in international negotiations on audio-visual and cultural services. The representatives of the cultural community had set up a Vigilance Committee for the Defence of Cultural Diversity, which strongly lobbied for the maintenance of the Nice Treaty rules in international audio-visual negotiations (Comité de Vigilance pour la Diversité Culturelle 2003). Within the EU, France and the cultural lobby have, to some extent, succeeded in reigning in the Community's 'competence creep' (Pollack 2000) in the sphere of commercial policy.

The EC's external strategy: cultural exception or cultural specificity?
The European Community is often presented as the defender of the so-called 'cultural exception' principle – which ensures that trade liberalisation does not apply to the audio-visual sector – within WTO negotiating arenas. Paradoxically, while the Community was promoting the liberalisation of cultural industries within the European Union, it adopted a protectionist stance in international trade negotiations.

Initially, the remit of the 1947 General Agreement on Tariffs and Trade (GATT) was limited to goods. The doctrine of the 'cultural exception' was first reflected in the decision to include Article IV of Part II of the GATT agreement, which concerns 'Cinematograph Films' and allows the parties to the agreement to make use of screen quotas requiring the exhibition of domestically made films for a specified minimum proportion of total screen time.[49] The 1947 GATT also maintains a general exception for measures designed 'to protect national treasures of artistic, historic or archaeological value' (Article XX.f). All other cultural goods – except for developed films and home-recorded videos – are subject to the GATT disciplines.

Yet the United States quickly made it clear that they would be seeking a liberalisation of the audio-visual sector. As early as the 1960s, they asserted that European limitations on the import of television programmes contravened the GATT provisions. They argued that television programmes were different from cinema films, and that any special treatment was therefore not justified for them. Yet Europeans were not ready to make any concessions on that matter. Perhaps the European plea that culture is not a product like any other was also more acceptable then, as discussions were held exclusively on liberalising trade in industrial and agricultural goods (Pauwels and Loisen 2003).

Twenty years later, the contours of the policy debate were quite different. It had been decided, further to a proposal from the United States, to extend the GATT framework to services at the launch of the Uruguay Round in 1986. The European Community agreed with the principle of liberalising the services sector, although with different sector-based interests than the United States (Kennet 1996). Agricultural subsidies were at the centre of most of the Uruguay Round talks, and little progress was made concerning services. Yet, in autumn 1993, the audio-visual dossier came to dominate the negotiations. The European Commission favoured the notion of a 'cultural specificity', under which all services would be included in the agreement, but the separate status of audio-visual services would nevertheless be stipulated in the agreement. Yet Jack Lang, then Minister of Culture in France, played a prominent role in imposing the principle of the 'cultural exception'. Arguing that the specificity of the film industry justified its protection from foreign products through a series of subsidies and quotas, he strongly opposed any liberalisation of the audio-visual sector. The French initiated a lobbying campaign towards EU institutions in the hope that the European delegation would uphold French demands in international trade negotiations. In September 1993, French Minister of Communication Alain Carignon, accompanied by numerous cinema personalities, pleaded before the European Parliament in favour of the defence of the 'cultural exception' (*Le Monde*, 17 September 1993). As a result of French lobbying campaigns, the Commission eventually acknowledged that the principle of a cultural specificity would not offer sufficient guarantees for the achievement of European objectives (De Witte 2001).

Yet the principle of a 'cultural exception' was unacceptable to the United States and the outcome of the Uruguay Round negotiations was a compromise between the conflicting objectives of the parties. There is indeed no genuine 'cultural exception' in the current General Agreement on Trade in Services (GATS) context. When signing the Uruguay GATS Agreement in 1994, the European Union agreed to be subjected to the 'general' obligations and disciplines of the GATS. However, the annex to Article II allowed WTO members to exempt some services from these basic 'general' disciplines for a period of ten years. The European Community has invoked this clause not only for the audio-visual sector but also for some other services, such as water, road and air transport, press agencies, non-life insurance and financial services. In practice, this means that services in the audio-visual field were not liberalised and a series of most-favoured nation (MFN) exceptions to the agreement were included.[50] Exemptions to the MFN (i.e., non-discrimination between foreign trading partners) concern, among other things, co-production agreements and privileged treatment for audio-visual works originating in the EU and other European countries. They have allowed the European Union to develop public policies to support the audio-visual sector, such as broadcasting quotas, financial aid (for production and distribution programmes like MEDIA) and regional co-production agreements (like Eurimages).

In January 1995, the WTO started to administer the sectoral agreements drawn from the 1986–94 Uruguay Round of the GATT. With the transition towards the so-called 'Information Society', the advocates of the liberalisation of the audio-visual sector tried to dismantle the audio-visual protective measures via the points of contact between various types of service. The increasing convergence between traditional media and telecommunications services is leading to a situation where formerly isolated concepts such as 'audio-visual services' and 'electronic commerce' are becoming blurred (Wheeler 2000). Furthermore, the MFN exemptions in the audio-visual sector were due to run out in 2005 (Freedman 2003). Thus, when a new round of negotiations over trade in services started in January 2000, the situation of the audio-visual dossier was expected to change. In the first background note produced by the WTO services ahead of GATS 2000 (WTO 1998), audio-visual services were indeed categorised as a sub-sector of communication services. It was agreed at the Doha ministerial meeting in November 2001 that initial requests for commitments on market access would have to be made by June 2002 and initial offers in March 2003. Divisions on various issues prevented the negotiating parties from submitting their requests and offers on time. In June 2005 the United States, together with Hong Kong, Japan, Mexico and Taiwan, made a joint statement on the negotiations on audio-visual services, requesting commitments from other member states to open up audio-visual markets. US service providers were pressuring the European Community to ease up trade restrictions. Yet the Community proposal, which was submitted to the WTO on 2 June 2005, proposed a careful opening of the EU market. It would allow lawyers, accountants, book-keepers, architects and engineers to open offices in the EU or to offer their services from abroad. Other areas regarded by the Commission as being more sensitive, such as the education and health sectors and the audio-visual sector, would remain off limits (*Euractiv*, 3 June 2005). After arduous negotiations, WTO members agreed on a compromise declaration in December 2005, but many issues remain unresolved (*Euractiv*, 19 December 2005). Thus, the EC has defended a more *dirigiste* position externally than internally so far. Such a stance is however likely to be increasingly challenged in the current context of convergence between telecommunications and audio-visual services.

Conclusion

We have observed that two parallel processes were at the origin of the Communitarisation process of public policies in the cultural sector. On the one hand, the ECJ and the Commission proved capable of developing autonomous agendas and engaged in a strategy aimed at liberalising the cultural sector. Already in the very first Commission communications on cultural issues, the economic hue of EU intervention was clear. Even after 1992, EU policies remained dominated by liberal concerns. As examined in the first section of this chapter, ECJ judgements and Commission decisions could reveal themselves as extremely challenging for national legislative and policy traditions in the EU. In their attempts to question existing policy arrangements in order to expand their own policy jurisdictions, the European Commission and the ECJ benefited from the support of policy actors that felt disaffected in states where *dirigiste* policy traditions were in place.

On the other hand, the developments examined here shed light on the role of member states in the generation of EU-level cultural cooperation. The first meetings of European Ministers of Culture were initiated by Melina Mercouri, the Greek Minister of Culture. The first supranational aid systems in the audio-visual sector were initiated by the French government in the 1980s, and so were the first proposals for a European-wide fixed price system for books. Thus, it is evident that states' policy preferences were based on their own model of public intervention. States that had developed interventionist cultural policies at the national level were seeking to replicate their policy model at the EU level. Yet it seems that member states' determination to further EU-level policies was also a reaction to European institutions' intervention. When member governments felt that their policy traditions were challenged by European intervention, they attempted to impose alternative policy solutions at the EU level. Indeed, the type of cooperation that was initiated by certain states *before* recognising that their own policy traditions were being threatened was essentially intergovernmental. Furthermore, states' initiatives essentially aimed at setting supranational aid mechanisms. It was only *after* the 1980s wave of ECJ judgements and Commission decisions that certain states began to propose EU-level *legislative* solutions, which, they hoped, would lock in legislative arrangements that were more favourable to them. Not only does this show that it is essential to focus on the interaction between developments that take place at different governance levels, but also that competition for policy competencies can induce certain actors, which were initially 'out' of the policy-making process, to enter it in an attempt to reshape it from within. European institutions were in fact successful in altering the contours of the policy debate so as to make the nature of the 'default position' less desirable for member states.

Despite the introduction of a Treaty basis on cultural matters and the increasing involvement of member states in projects of EU cultural cooperation, there is still no comprehensive and positive 'European cultural policy'. Rather, EU intervention in the cultural sector is a mixture of *dirigiste* support schemes, symbolic initiatives and attempts to harmonise EU law in the perspective of the Single Market. The multifaceted nature of EU cultural intervention is the result of a complex process of interaction and negotiation between multiple actors with different policy objectives. The case studies which follow elucidate why certain actors could impose their preferences better than others in the EU decision-making process, resulting in *dirigiste* policy options not being adopted at the EU level.

Notes

1   I will use the term 'Rome Treaty' in this chapter when referring to policy developments that took place before entry into force of the Maastricht Treaty in November 1993.
2   For greater consistency, the 'culture' article will be referred to as in the Maastricht Treaty numbering (Article 128) in the book.
3   Treaty of Rome, as amended, Preamble.
4   The *Mouvement de Libération Nationale* was an umbrella organisation of eight non-communist resistance groups, which conceived a European federation as the goal of their future foreign policy. In June 1944, leading personalities of the movement, such as Albert Camus and André Ferrat, resolved to form a French Committee for a European Federation, especially designed to further this common purpose.
5   The European movement was created in 1948 at The Hague Congress by the UEF and other federalist groups.
6   The French government laid down a proposal on this matter in July 1969.
7   The European Cultural Foundation is independent and promotes cultural participation and cooperation in Europe and beyond. It was founded in 1954 in order to help add a cultural dimension to the European integration process.
8   The essential jurisprudential developments are presented here; the rulings related to the audio-visual, book and copyright policy issues will be examined in further detail in the case studies.
9   Article 36 of the Rome Treaty (now Article 30) states that: 'The provisions of articles 28 and 29 shall not preclude prohibitions or restrictions on imports, exports or goods in transit justified on grounds of public morality, public policy or public security; the protection of health and life of humans, animals or plants; *the protection of national treasures possessing artistic, historic or archeological value*; or the protection of industrial and commer-

cial property. Such prohibitions or restrictions shall not, however, constitute a means of arbitrary discrimination or a disguised restriction on trade between Member States.'

10   This point will be further discussed later in this chapter.

11   Case *Commission* v. *France* (ECJ 1991a); Case *Commission* v. *Italy* (ECJ 1991b); Case *Commission* v. *Greece* (ECJ 1991c).

12   ECJ judgments related to broadcasting and intellectual property will be examined in further detail in Chapters 4 and 6.

13   The doctrine states that, where goods are lawfully placed on the market in a member state, copyright cannot be relied upon to restrict the free circulation of those goods.

14   The flexibility of the Court in interpreting EU law will be depicted in greater detail in Chapter 5 on book pricing regulation.

15   For an explanation of the increasing support of the liberal project by the Commission's services, see also Hooghe and Marks (1997).

16   Jack Lang in France and Vincenzo Scotti in Italy.

17   Minutes of the SGCI meeting (Secrétariat Général du Comité Interministériel pour les questions économiques Européennes) on the informal Culture Council of 17–18 September 1982 in Naples, Archives of the French Ministry of Culture.

18   Minutes of the SGCI meeting on the informal Culture Council of 28 November 1983 in Athens, Archives of the French Ministry of Culture.

19   Interview with Jack Lang, former Minister of Culture in France, 16 January 1999, Paris.

20   Note from the SAI on the European Audiovisual Space, 10 May 1983 – Archives of the French Ministry of Culture.

21   Interview with Jack Lang, former Minister of Culture in France, 16 January 1999, Paris.

22   See Chapter 5 on book trade regulation for further detail.

23   Summary of the observations presented by the French Government to the ECJ on 1 June 1984, Archives of the French Ministry of Culture.

24   Notes from the Service des Affaires Internationales (SAI) between 1896 and 1989, Archives of the French Ministry of Culture.

25   Author's translation.

26   Minutes of the SGCI on the Culture Council of 13 November 1986 in Brussels – Archives of the French Ministry of Culture.

27   See website of the Council of Europe: www.coe.int/t/e/cultural_co-operation/ eurimages/about_eurimages/Missions_&_Objectives/objectives.asp# TopOfPage.

28   See Report for the CNC from Jacques Renard on Eurimages, October 2002: www.cnc.fr/b_actual/r5/ssrub4/eurimages/eurimages.htm.

29   Confidential document, Archives of the French Ministry of Culture.

30   The coordinators of Audiovisual Eureka terminated the existence of the scheme in June 2003.

31   *Le mécénat en Europe*, by Jacques de Chalendar.

32   Interviews with French officials, Paris, 2000.

33   A Belgian official working for DG Education and Culture within the European Commission highlights the propensity of the Commission and of

the ECJ to act in an 'expansionist' fashion throughout the 1980s. Interview in Brussels, 21 September 2001.

34   These reports were produced by the ad hoc Committee on a People's Europe.

35   The origins of the TWF Directive are explained in Chapter 4.

36   See Chapter 6 for a detailed analysis of intellectual property law harmonisation in the EU.

37   Article 151 paragraph 2 (ex Article 128 paragraph 2, which has not been modified).

38   See Appendix 1 for the full version of Article 128.

39   Decision of 29 March 1996 for Kaleidoscope (719/96/EC), of 6 October 1997 for Ariane (2085/97/EC), and of 13 October 1997 for Raphael (2228/97/EC).

40   See Appendix 2 for a detailed account of the objectives of the Culture 2000 Programme.

41   Europa website: http://europa.eu.int/scadplus/leg/en/lvb/l24109.htm.

42   The Media Plus Programme was created by a Council decision of 20 December 2000 (2000/821/EC).

43   Website of the Media Programme: (http://europa.eu.int/comm/avpolicy /media/index_en.html).

44   PAL (phase-alternating line), is a colour encoding suptem used in broadcast television systems in most parts of the world. SECAM (*Séquentiel couleur à mémoire*) is an analogue colour television system that was first used in France.

45   HD-MAC, a complex mix of analogue signal, multiplexed with digital sound, was first proposed by the Commission in 1986.

46   Website of DG Budget, Europa: http://europa.eu.int/comm/budget/pubfin /index_en.htm.

47   For the year 2002, the budget of the CNC reached 651.3 million euros (www.cnc.fr/cncinfo/286/tendances_1.htm), twice as much as the budget of Media Plus for five years and fifteen countries (350 million).

48   Treaty of Nice amending the Treaty on European Union, the Treaties establishing the European Communities and certain related acts, OJ C 80, 10.3.2001.

49   Article IV on 'Special Provisions relating to Cinematograph Films' states:
'If any contracting party establishes or maintains internal quantitative regulations relating to exposed cinematograph films, such regulations shall take the form of screen quotas which shall conform to the following requirements:
(*a*) Screen quotas may require the exhibition of cinematograph films of national origin during a specified minimum proportion of the total screen time actually utilized, over a specified period of not less than one year, in the commercial exhibition of all films of whatever origin, and shall be computed on the basis of screen time per theatre per year or the equivalent thereof;
(*b*) With the exception of screen time reserved for films of national origin under a screen quota, screen time including that released by administrative action from screen time reserved for films of national origin, shall not be allocated formally or in effect among sources of supply;
(*c*) Notwithstanding the provisions of subparagraph (*b*) of this Article, any contracting party may maintain screen quotas conforming to the require-

ments of subparagraph (*a*) of this Article which reserve a minimum proportion of screen time for films of a specified origin other than that of the contracting party imposing such screen quotas; *Provided* that no such minimum proportion of screen time shall be increased above the level in effect on April 10, 1947;

(*d*) Screen quotas shall be subject to negotiation for their limitation, liberalization or elimination' (GATT 1947).

50   The GATS is based on the application of market access and national treatment on a voluntary basis. The market access principle obliges the members to open their domestic markets to all service suppliers from other members. The national treatment principle obliges the members to grant all service suppliers, whatever their nationality, the same treatment accorded to domestic services suppliers. However, the second logic of the agreement lies in the applicability by default of the Most Favoured Nation (MFN) clause – which states that the most favourable treatment which is granted to the service suppliers from any foreign country must be offered to all foreign suppliers of this service. Members can indeed exempt services from the application of the MFN principle by listing these services in their list of exemptions.

4

The Communitarisation of broadcasting regulation: the 'Television Without Frontiers' Directive

The very nature of broadcasting, as both a commercial activity and a cultural product, created acute rivalries among policy actors desirous of imposing their own concerns on public political agendas. Broadcasting is also a policy sector closely associated with member states' 'sovereignty', thus resulting in unwavering tensions between EU institutions' propensity to intervene in the audio-visual field and member states' reluctance to delegate their policy competencies to the EU level. Yet, the TWF Directive adopted in 1989 (89/552/EEC) and renewed in 1997 (97/36/EC)[1] can be considered to be the most comprehensive piece of legislation related to cultural policy issues enacted at the EU level. Essentially, it establishes the principle of free flow for television programmes based on the liberal principles of 'country of origin regulation' and 'mutual recognition', in so far as television programmes observe a minimum of harmonised rules. Thus, this chapter deals with two questions. First, it explains how the shift of competence from the national to the EU level could occur. Second, it spells out policy outcomes at the EU level, once the Communitarisation of the policy sector had taken place. The Europeanisation process of broadcasting policy has already been examined in several detailed studies (see for instance Collins 1994; Venturelli 1998; Levy 1999; Krebber 2002; Harcourt 2005), which have discussed the major debates related to broadcasting regulation in the EU, highlighted the role played by different policy actors in the decision-making process and explained EU-level policy choices in the field. The research conducted here builds upon existing work in the field and agrees with Harcourt (2005) that 'although Member State governments have played a significant role in European policy-making, the EU is not just an arena where one can plot the interaction between different actors and find a result' (Harcourt 2005: 3). Yet the chapter adds to existing research by shedding light on the dynamic quality of multi-level governance in the policy sector as well as locating these findings within broader theoretical debates on European integration.

The argument goes thus. As early as the 1970s, the ECJ and DG Competition within the Commission exploited their Treaty-based powers in a 'hierarchical direction' mode (Scharpf 2000) in order to extend their remit to audio-visual activities in advance of Treaty reforms. By applying a liberal image to audio-visual policy issues, they could efficiently assert their competence in this sector. Simultaneously, private commercial actors were using the European venue in order to change the image of audio-visual policy issues at the national level, hoping to promote further market liberalisation. EU institutions' intervention challenged both national prerogatives and the interests of public broadcasters. In particular, France, whose interventionist tradition is indeed evidenced in the audio-visual sector, felt strongly threatened by the mode of intervention developed by EU institutions. Thus, *dirigiste* actors attempted to wrest back control of policy by changing the very image of the policy problem at the EU level. Two competing coalitions of actors – the *dirigiste* (or 'cultural') coalition led by France and the liberal coalition led by the Commission and Northern European states – aimed to formulate EU policy orientations in the audio-visual sector in directions that were favourable to their interests. The *dirigiste* coalition, in its attempts to change the prevailing image of the policy problem, aimed to direct the locus of policy-making towards the venue where member states were the most powerful – the Council of Ministers.

This chapter argues that France and other interventionist states were initially passive towards the development of an audio-visual policy at the EU level – the French government's initiatives were limited to the promotion of support schemes that had a limited impact and were often implemented outside the Community framework. However, in a context where EU institutions' *de facto* intervention was challenging domestic policies, France eventually had to *react* in the face of external developments and accept that the game had to be played at the EU level. But imposing *dirigiste* preferences via the European medium was particularly difficult. Were it not for the use of informal strategies – such as lobbying campaigns and coalition-building strategies – the wide diversity of actors' interests would have led all negotiations to a deadlock. Informal strategies allowed the cultural coalition led by France to impose some of its concerns – such as protectionist schemes for European audio-visual works – on the EU agenda. However, at the stage of policy negotiations, the *dirigiste* camp was constrained to accept a political compromise. Since most states favoured liberal policy solutions (in a context where consensual agreement was required), the French government's room for manoeuvre was constrained to securing national arrangements and a minimal set of rules at the EU level. The constellation of actors' interests within the Council of Ministers (with a majority of liberal states), the nature of the status quo (characterised by the *de facto* intervention of EU institutions) and decision rules (the need for consensual agreement) were the three factors that determined the choice of policy options at the EU level. EU institutions succeeded in altering the contours of the policy debate so as to make the nature of the status quo less desirable. In this context, the veto option was no longer available for *dirigiste* governments, making their room for manoeuvre very limited during EU negotiations.

After examining those aspects of member states' audio-visual policies that were relevant to understanding EU-level broadcasting negotiations, the chapter examines the role of supranational institutions in extending EU competence to broadcasting, and the impact of EU intervention on domestic policies. EU-level negotiations over the content of the 1989 TWF Directive are then analysed. The last section finally scrutinises the renewal process of the Directive.

EU states: 'broadcasters' versus 'producers'

Patterns of national broadcasting policies are characterised by a wide regulatory diversity,[2] which stems from the very different political and cultural agendas of EU states (Levy 1999).

An embedded tradition of public intervention in the audio-visual sector exists in France. Since 1946, support mechanisms that contributed to the development of the national cinematographic industry have been in place. Supporting the national audio-visual industry became a deliberate policy after 1981, and benefited from the doubling of the cultural budget in 1982.[3] Thus, the French system is heavily regulated, and sometimes even accused of sustaining productions never watched by the public.[4] Besides, all the broadcasting operators in France are subject to a large set of common regulations aimed at ensuring pluralism, protecting young audiences and limiting advertising on screen. One of these obligations, which distinguishes France from other European States, consists of imposing programming and investment quotas. Terrestrial television stations must ensure that 60 per cent of their programming is of European origin, and that this output includes a minimum of 40 per cent of French works. Programming quotas are completed by investment quotas: television channels can choose to invest either 15 per cent of their turnover in French audio-visual works productions and 20 per cent in European audio-visual works, or 15 per cent of their turnover in French audio-visual works and broadcast a minimum of 120 hours of European/French audio-visual works in prime time.[5] The attention devoted by legislators to the promotion of national programming reflects the significance granted to film as a way to promote French culture and language. But it also derives from the fact that the French have always perceived the commercial benefits of promoting the French audio-visual industry. The French cinematographic industry is stronger than that of other EU states (Kruse 1994; Pongy 1997), perhaps as a result of the strong public intervention in the sector, but French TV production is weaker than that of other EU countries. British TV broadcasting production, for instance, has been more successful at exporting TV products. Thus, arguably, France has felt the need to protect its TV industry – as well as cinema – because it has not been so strong. This means that France was more interested in the implementation of protectionist mechanisms at the EU level than were other EU countries. The personal beliefs of Jack Lang, then Minister of Culture in France, in the necessity to foster European culture and European identity also contributed to the development of a European strategy by the French government.[6]

However, France was isolated in its demands for *dirigiste* policy options at the EU level. The UK broadcasting landscape had been the object of a marketisation strategy in the 1980s under Margaret Thatcher. Thus, Britain was more favourable than France to the principle of transfrontier television.[7] An obvious explanation is that the UK possesses a competitive audio-visual sector and is more able to compete in international markets than most other EU states (Collins 1994). The long-standing presence of the factors required for audio-visual competition gives the UK the potential for being an important centre of audio-visual production; and the UK also has a comparative advantage over other EU states in that English is the world's most widely-used language. Another reason lies in the presence in the UK of a special system of 'on-demand' non-domestic satellite licences. During the Thatcher era, audio-visual companies 'could obtain a non-domestic licence from the Independent Television Commission (ITC) more or less on demand' (Levy 1999: 34). The licences permitted the benefiting channels to 'escape' constraining domestic legislative regimes that were in force in other EU states, making the UK an attractive location for TV channels. When the European Commission issued its first policy proposals in the field of broadcasting in the 1980s, the British government therefore thought that EU liberalisation measures would bring European broadcasters to Britain to beam their programmes abroad (Levy 1999). Yet the UK initially contested the European Commission's right to exercise jurisdiction over broadcasting. Broadcasting was perceived as a national matter. This position also resulted from more pragmatic motives: the UK trades more with the US and Australia than with European countries (Levy 1999). Thus, if the British eventually accepted the principle of EU-level regulation, they always opposed the *dirigiste* elements of the Directive (i.e. programme quotas). Furthermore, the UK also came to realise that its non-domestic licence system would in fact not benefit from the Communautarisation process of broadcasting regulation. In 1994, in response to complaints from other countries, the Commission brought a case against the UK to the ECJ, challenging the UK's interpretation of what the TWF Directive actually allowed. The Commission objected to the UK's claiming of control over non-domestic broadcasters, arguing that it amounted to a failure to embrace the principle of mutual recognition that underpinned the Single Market created by TWF (Harcourt 2005: 105). The ECJ accepted the Commission's case. Subsequently, the 1997 revision of the TWF Directive clarified that a member state only had jurisdiction over broadcasters when their headquarters were located within their territory and editorial decisions about the schedules of the channels were taken in that state. The UK duly abolished its category of 'non-domestic' licences, but maintained its light touch regulatory regime for all satellite broadcasters. Under EU law, the UK is so far not required to apply the TWF provision to satellite broadcasters, since they are considered to be new services with minority audience share (Harcourt 2005).

In Germany, broadcasting is the responsibility of the Länder, thus constraining the Federal government's ability to negotiate on broadcasting issues with other states. In any case, programme quotas have never been central to the domestic debate. Commercial broadcasting developed rapidly further to the liberalisation measures initiated by the Kohl government in the 1980s (Levy 1999). Essentially, by developing a massive state-led plan to equip Germany with a cable infrastructure – telecommunications fall under federal jurisdiction – the federal government introduced an incentive for the Länder governments to introduce legislation permitting commercial broadcasting. The CDU/CSU (Christian Democratic Union) was particularly keen on removing the monopoly of public service broadcasters, hoping that the political tone of commercial broadcasting would be more in tune with its political positions (Humphreys 1994). The German production sector has therefore benefited from the competition between broadcasters for attractive programme content. If smaller and medium-sized production companies have, on several occasions, complained that the market was dominated by a few large production groups, the issue of language, culture and identity, which has been a strong driving force in media policies in France, has never played a similar role in Germany. The aspect of European regulation most heavily debated in Germany has been the limitations on television advertising, because these run squarely against the interests of the big private broadcasters, which usually call for maximum freedom in advertising.

The Luxembourgian delegation also pulled its weight during EU negotiations. One distinctive feature of cultural policy in Luxembourg is the absence of public television broadcasters. In the audio-visual field, Luxembourg has always relied on private business initiatives. The country did not set up a public-service radio station but rented instead available frequencies to a private consortium. Since then, Radio Télévision

Luxembourg (RTL) has become an important tax generator for the country. With the creation of the satellite consortium SES/ASTRA in 1983, also organised along private lines, and the Mediaport, Luxembourg has pursued this policy. Astra has attracted both analogue and digital channels from other EU states, which broadcast to markets in EU states and an increasing number of non-EU states (Harcourt 2005: 134). Thus, Luxembourg's EU strategy was clear-cut: to promote market liberalisation and minimal standards. In the same way, most other countries were not interested in supporting European audio-visual products. Most small EU states thought that they would not be able to rely on their national production to comply with content quotas and would not be able to afford a large amount of expensive European programmes.

The role of European institutions

The Commission, the Court and, to a lesser extent, the European Parliament played a crucial role in the emergence of an EU-level legislative regime in the audio-visual sector. In the early 1980s, the gradual process of developing EU-level policies concerning retransmission, programming and advertising was initiated by European institutions, which acted as policy entrepreneurs. Simultaneously, several member states initiated further cooperation at the intergovernmental level in order to develop support schemes for the audio-visual industry. The French government acted as a 'first mover' in the development of interventionist schemes at the EU level. However, the *dirigiste* policy image defended by France and 'cultural' interest groups came into conflict with the intervention from the ECJ and the Commission, which was aimed at the liberalisation of market forces in the audio-visual sector.

ECJ cases: defining broadcasting as a 'service'
Having no legal competence in the audio-visual sector, the ECJ justified its intervention by invoking its responsibility for ensuring the free flow of television programmes within the EU (see Lange and Renaud 1989; Negrine and Papathanassopoulos 1990; Machet and Robillard 1998). With the expansion in trans-frontier broadcasting during the 1980s, tensions between European media systems were exacerbated. Member states were free to prevent the retransmission of foreign programmes within their territory if the latter infringed their domestic legislation (Humphreys 1996). Thus, the diversity of legislative regimes in the EU (concerning in particular advertising) often led states with stricter legislation to ban the broadcasting of foreign programmes, thereby 'infringing' upon (according to the interpretation of the ECJ) the principle of free circulation laid down by the Treaty.

For the first time, in the 1974 *Sacchi* case (ECJ 1974), the ECJ ruled that broadcasting was covered by the Treaty of Rome. In this judgement, a cable operator, Giuseppe Sacchi, claimed that Radio Audizioni Italiane (RAI), the Italian public service broadcaster, could not continue its monopoly over advertising revenue as it created obstacles to the trade of goods from other member states. The ECJ concluded in its preliminary ruling that RAI's monopoly did not restrict the trade of goods within the EC. Yet, the case established that a television signal was a *service*, thus legitimising EC intervention in the broadcasting sector. The *Sacchi* case was subsequently quoted in the 1984 Green Paper on broadcasting regulation and presented by the Commission as a legal basis for the TWF Directive (European Commission 1984). In the 1980s, the Court confirmed the *Sacchi* ruling and established a body of European case law treating broadcasting as a tradable activity; the rulings focused solely on the economic aspects of audio-visual products, thereby altering the way policy problems related to audio-visual regulation were tackled.

The 1980 *Debauve* case (ECJ 1980a), which focused on whether cable television and terrestrial television should be accorded similar treatment, reasserted that discrimination between signals on the basis of their national origin was unlawful.[8] However, the *Coditel* cases (ECJ 1980b and ECJ 1981c) established that holders of intellectual property rights in one member state were able to forbid distribution of such property. Thus, limited exceptions to free market principles were granted by the Court, but no general principle in favour of cultural policy concerns was established. In a 'hierarchical' decision mode, the Court applied the prohibitions of the Treaty against national policies constituting barriers to the free mobility of goods and services, or distortions of free competition. By portraying broadcasting as a service, the Court allowed for the extension of EU competence to the audio-visual field. Further ECJ cases confirmed the ECJ's propensity to intervene in national policy in the late 1980s and 1990s (see Harcourt 2005 for a detailed presentation of the role of the ECJ in the broadcasting sector).

In the cases that were brought before the ECJ, domestic commercial actors which were uncomfortable with the existing image of the policy problems at stake in domestic arenas invariably supported the application of EU competition law. In the *Cinéthèque* case (ECJ 1985a) for instance, French videotape distributors tried to challenge national legislative regimes they perceived as too constraining. At issue was a French law which regulated the distribution of cinematographic works by prohibiting their simultaneous exploitation in cinemas and in video-cassette form for a limited period. Videotape distributors argued before the ECJ that the French legislation had the effect of restricting intra-Community trade. In the case of *Bond van Adverteerders* v. *Netherlands* (ECJ 1988a), the Dutch association of advertisers brought an action before the ECJ claiming that the Dutch cable regulation infringed Treaty rules on the free circulation of services. Private actors had particularly strong incentives to use European structures in states where the audio-visual sector was strictly regulated. The European venue afforded them the chance to change the way policy problems were approached and thereby induce policy changes that could not have been provoked through national policy channels. For the ECJ, presenting the audio-visual sector as an economic market was an efficient way of shifting the venue of decision-making and thereby furthering its competencies. Thus, the ECJ and private actors had a common interest in focusing on the economic and commercial aspects of broadcasting.

The European Commission's agenda-setting exercise
In the 1980s, the introduction of satellite television and the anticipated media revolution raised new regulatory issues. Acting as a purposeful agenda setter, the European Commission pointed to the inadequacy, in the new technological environment, of the legislative arrangements that were then in force. In an attempt to encompass the rationale for EU action within a broader cultural project, EU discourse referred to the necessity of promoting a sense of European identity among European citizens – which could be fostered via the creation of a European media. Yet, without any legal competence to act in the cultural sector, EU institutions had no choice but to intervene through the 'economic back door'.

In 1982, the European Parliament issued a resolution on radio and television broadcasting (the 'Hahn' Resolution), which stated that 'if the Community and its institutions do not participate in this decision-making process [i.e. in the audio-visual field], developments might take place which would not be in the interests of the Community' (OJ C 87/110, 5.4.1982). The idea that rules should be drawn up on European radio and television broadcasting was clearly expressed. As explained in greater detail in Chapter 3, the Hahn resolution further stated that if European unification was to be encouraged, Europe had to penetrate the media. Thus, the EP was essentially concerned with the role of the media in fostering cultural integration within the European Union (see Goldberg, Prosser and Verhulst 1998). The Commission's Interim Report *Realities and Tendencies in European Television* (European Commission 1983) endorsed the EP's views. The Commission proposed the creation of a European broadcasting channel, meant to foster European consciousness (European Commission 1983: 1). More significantly, the Commission's Report laid the basis for the development of a general framework for the European broadcasting system constituted by satellite, cable, and traditional networks. The role of the Community was conceived as one of facilitating the transmission of national and international programmes within member states. In that respect however, the Commission justified the need for EU intervention by referring to the economic principles of the

Rome Treaty. The Commission clearly stated that 'the respect of the EEC Treaty rules on the free flow of services, in the television field, must be guaranteed and certain aspects of television and copyright law coordinated' (European Commission 1983: 24). Thus, the Commission invoked economic motives in order to legitimise its intervention – in contrast with the 'cultural' rationale developed by the Parliament. By stating that broadcasting is primarily an economic activity, which it is therefore competent to regulate, the Commission disavowed the cultural dimensions of broadcasting (Collins 1994).

The project for European broadcasting regulation took a concrete form with the 1984 *Green Paper on the Establishment of the Common Market for Broadcasting* (European Commission 1984).[9] The Green Paper proposed to set minimal EU standards concerning advertising, the right of reply, minors' protection and copyright. However, broadcasting was again defined exclusively as a commercial activity, and as such as being within the remit of Community intervention. The Commission made it clear that 'the EEC Treaty applies not only to economic activities carried out for remuneration but, as a rule, also to all activities carried out for remuneration, regardless of whether they take place in the economic, social, cultural, sporting or any other sphere' (European Commission 1984: 6).

Thus, the supranational project clearly favoured the liberalisation of the audio-visual sector. Because the Commission's rights in the cultural sector are stronger with respect to the liberalisation of markets than in their regulation, the Commission's action reflects this bias (see Scharpf 1996) – as will also be shown in the book and copyright cases. Like the Court, the Commission showed a one-sided preoccupation for the economic aspects of the policy problems at stake in order to extend the remit of its competence to a new policy sector.

However, in the audio-visual case, the predominance of liberal ideas was also accentuated by other factors. Between 1984 and 1988, DG Internal Market was directed by Lord Cockfield and DG Competition by Leon Brittan. According to Collins (1994), the presence of two British Commissioners encouraged the application of competition regulations and promoted the establishment of a single broadcasting market. The influence of the British Commissioners was all the more significant since DG Internal Market was in charge of producing the 1984 Green Paper, while DG Culture did not get involved with the preparatory work of the TWF Directive until 1986 (Fraser 1996). Moreover, when DG Culture eventually became implicated with the design of the Directive in 1986, Jean Dondelinger had been nominated as new Commissioner for Cultural Affairs. The Luxemburgian politician favoured more liberal positions than his predecessor Carlo Ripa di Maena (*Le Monde*, 18 January 1989). The *dirigistes* could therefore not mount a strong countervailing force within the Commission.

The Commission was also heavily influenced by the advertising lobby (*Broadcasting*, 23 June 1986). In the 1984 Green Paper, successive references to the position of the European Association of Advertising (EAA) reflect the influence of the advertising community on the formulation of the Commission proposals. Gaston Thorn, originally from Luxembourg, was then President of the European Commission. He was also about to become President of the CLT, the advertising ceiling of which was the most flexible among EU states. Personal interests might have propelled him to favour lenient legislative regimes for EU broadcasting.

The combination of commercial actors' influence, the prevalence of liberal views within the Commission and the EU institutional 'liberal bias' derived from the Treaty powers gave the liberal coalition a strong advantage in framing the policy debate.

Venue and image competition: films as commodities v. films as art

States where domestic policy traditions were of a more interventionist nature felt particularly threatened by the governance shift that was occurring as a result of EU institutions' *de facto* intervention. The wording of the 1984 Green Paper challenged both national prerogatives and the interests of public broadcasters. DG Culture, backed by the EP, the European Broadcasting Union (EBU) and a number of member governments protested against the idea of broadcasting as an economic activity (Collins 1994). The protest was particularly acute in France. *Dirigiste* states responded by attempting to reorient the policy debate within the Council of Ministers, in which they could best influence policy formation at the European level.

Imposing a dirigiste *policy image at the EU level*
While EU institutions were enacting a market liberalisation strategy of the audio-visual sector, some member states – France and Southern European states – endeavoured to further intergovernmental forms of cooperation outside the Community framework. In the early 1980s, most states were becoming aware of the limitations of national regulations with the development of cable and satellite technologies. The Cultural Affairs Department within the External Affairs Ministry was made responsible for formulating proposals aimed at setting a set of minimal rules within a 'European audio-visual space'.[10] The French wanted to construct a 'European audio-visual space' in which the European audio-visual industry would be promoted, but they did not attempt to use the Community framework.

However, developing intergovernmental forms of cooperation was not an efficient *modus operandi,* in terms of preventing the Court and the Commission from applying competition law to the audio-visual sector.[11]

Jack Lang, interviewed by *The Times*, attacked European officials for being the prime enemies of culture, saying that:

> They hate culture; they hate the artists. When we write the history of Europe it should be stated that the civil servants of the Community are the enemies of culture. [...] I would like to consider culture as a part of the economy, and economy as part of culture, but this is dangerous because culture must not be considered as a mass-production industry. Cultural assets are not like others; they need special laws. (*The Times*, 15 August 1985)

Thus, the French recognised that transposing *dirigiste* policy solutions *within the EU framework* was the best possible strategy in a context where the status quo was characterised by the *de facto* application of economic principles to the audio-visual field. They decided to enter the 'game' in order to change the way policy problems were tackled at the EU level and use the EU as a medium to further national policy objectives.[12] However, the Commission and the ECJ were not the most favourable structures for the French government to practise 'venue-shopping' (Baumgartner and Jones 1991). As examined above, the latter favoured economic actors with a strong stake in market liberalisation. Therefore, the member governments that felt challenged by their political agenda attempted to shift the decision-making process away from the hierarchical mode and back to a venue dominated by intergovernmental negotiations. Reaching a political agreement with other states within the Council of Ministers was the only way through which the *dirigistes* could try locking in their favoured policy solution at the European level and prevent the ECJ and the Court from exercising their judicial and regulatory powers in a hierarchical manner. The Council of Ministers subsequently became the main locus for France's attempts to shift the agenda.

During the Culture Council of June 1984, which took place during the French Council presidency, Jack Lang suggested various initiatives: the creation of a European development fund for films, a joint action to deal with pirate videotapes and an EU-level regulation aimed at preventing television broadcasts for films during a fixed period after their release in cinemas (*Irish Times*, 23 June 1984). Several resolutions dealing with measures to combat audio-visual pirating and the rational distribution of films through all the audio-visual communication media were adopted in July 1984 on the basis of the French proposals (OJ C 204, 24.1984, OJ C 204 3.8.1984). Jack Lang also suggested the incorporation, in the TWF Directive, of a clause imposing European-produced programme quotas as a defensive measure against US imports.

In an attempt to reorient the policy debate at the EU level, the French government also initiated events outside the Community framework. Relocating the agenda appeared particularly crucial to the French during the phase of transition towards the Single Market, and all the more given that policy objectives in the field of broadcasting were formulated solely as part of the Single Market project. When the French led the presidency of the Council during the second semester of 1989, they organised a multi-lateral meeting in Blois where several questions related to copyright, audio-visual and education policies were raised.[13] The Commission responded auspiciously to the demands of the French Ministry of Culture. In particular, the Commission expressed its support to Audiovisual Eureka, a scheme meant to foster the cooperation between European audio-visual enterprises that had been strongly supported by the French. It also agreed to adopt policy proposals concerning national treasures, another pet project of the French.[14] Thus, if the French did not succeed in initiating regulatory developments at the EU level, they successfully imposed a competing image of the policy problems at stake.

The cultural lobby as the sponsor of the dirigiste *image*
The cultural lobby, and especially the French artistic community, played a proactive role in the policy-making process both at the national and at the supranational level. The cultural community reacted vehemently against the liberal approach developed by the Commission. While the French lobby opposed the definition of broadcasting as an economic activity, British broadcasters feared that the Commission would dictate rules concerning the programming of the British Broadcasting Corporation (BBC) (Collins 1994). French interest groups, such as associations of independent producers and representatives of the cultural community, were particularly dismayed by the pro-market approach of the 1984 Green Paper, which failed to treat television programmes as cultural products (see Humphreys 1996; Fraser 1996). Because of the specificity of the French model of public intervention in the audio-visual sector, the French lobby was the most actively involved in the process of formulating European rules for broadcasting from the late 1980s onwards. For instance, the representatives of the French cinema industry are particularly well established under the aegis of the organisation Eurocinema, which, in fact, is essentially composed of French lobbyists.[15] Thus, located in Brussels, professionals' representatives have been trying to anticipate any policy change likely to affect them.

The French cultural community also benefited from strong governmental support at the domestic level. Traditionally, the cultural community has defended values and ideas associated with the left; thus it supported the socialist party during the 1981 presidential election. Once elected, François Mitterrand and his government were therefore more inclined to develop policies that would favour the artistic community.[16] This can be generalised to the whole left-wing political elite, which has a tradition of sharing common values with the cultural community. However, more utilitarian motives also led French authorities to support professionals in the audio-visual domain. Interest groups made use of their high profile in the media in order to put pressure on successive governments and protect vested interests. Thus, the 'cultural exception' was defended by both left- and right-wing governments. When still in opposition, the right vehemently attacked the government's cultural policy in the early 1990s. French television quotas were labelled as 'anti-freedom' measures and public aid systems were criticised as abuses.[17] However, when the 'cohabitation' period commenced in 1993, with the right's victory in legislative elections, right-wing politicians changed their position, and the new Prime Minister Edouard Balladur defended the 'cultural exception' during the GATT negotiations.[18] This could be explained by the fact that François Mitterrand was actively involved in the 'cultural exception' battle. A highly publicised battle ensued, during which the Prime Minister and the President tried to obtain the support of the cultural community in favour of their respective parties (*Le Monde Radio-Télévision*, 11 October 1993). As a result, the French have always defended, rather successfully, the cultural exception principle in international negotiations.

Thus, beliefs and interests both explain the attachment between public authorities and the cultural community in France. The unity of the cultural coalition – which benefited from the high profile of the artistic community in the media – has given significant weight to French preferences in international negotiating arenas and was undoubtedly a crucial aspect in French strategies aimed at imposing a new policy image on cultural policy issues at the supranational level. At the policy formulation stage, cultural lobbyists succeeded in altering the image of policy issues at the EU level.

The 1986 TWF draft directive: an attempt to satisfy French special interests
The 1986 TWF draft directive included cultural goals in response to the disquiet of those alarmed by the definition of broadcasting as an economic activity (see Papathanassopoulos 1990). Broadcasting was still defined as 'a service within the meaning of the relevant provisions of the EEC Treaty' (European Commission 1986: 6). Yet the Commission also stated that the objectives of European broadcasting policy form part of 'a wider set of goals of which cultural objectives are an important component' (European Commission 1986: 7). Also, the Commission dropped its proposals concerning the legal license (means by which the right to *copy* an audio-visual work is eased), which were designed to settle the matter of copyright for audio-visual works. Copyright matters were not harmonised in the final version of the TWF Directive because of the impossibility of reaching an agreement within the Council (Collins 1994).

For Fraser (1996) the TWF Directive became, under French influence, a '*Grand Projet*', including objectives on programmes, equipment and technical standards. The cultural lobby, supported by the French government, was successful in reorienting the agenda in the mid-1980s. With the arrival of Jacques Delors as Commission President in 1985, French cultural demands also benefited from the presence of a more sympathetic interlocutor in the Commission.[19] In his introduction to the 1985 Commission Programme, Jacques Delors stated that 'the cultural and human dimension of Community action must become a driving force towards achievement of the European ideal, enabling the Community to assert its identity while respecting its diversity' (Delors 1985). The *laissez-faire* approach in the broadcasting sector was clearly opposed by the Commission President, who stressed the need to 'stimulate television production on a European scale and boost the Community market' (Delors 1985). Thus, the prevalence of liberal policy ideas within the Commission was tempered by the presence – and charisma – of Delors as Commission President and the cultural community could more easily impose its views at the EU venue usually dominated by liberal concerns.

Thus, if the TWF Directive was essentially a supranational initiative aimed at eliminating trade barriers, then certain states, and France in particular, developed strong resistance against supranational entrepreneurship. France initially defended its sovereignty in the sensitive area of culture; the form of cooperation promoted by the French government was mainly intergovernmental. However, member states intervened in a context constrained by the contours of the policy debate – which the Commission successfully altered so as to make the status quo (situation without a common solution) less desirable. Thus, the *dirigiste* coalition reacted by entering the 'game' at the EU level, in an attempt to reorient the agenda and lock in its own policy level at the supranational level.

The 1989 TWF Directive: 'mandatory liberalisation, optional interventionism'

At the policy negotiations stage, institutional constraints, states' conflicting interests and the precedence of a diplomatic logic made it difficult for the *dirigistes* to impose their concerns. Furthermore, they were not able, in last resort, to invoke their right of veto. The Court and the economic DGs of the Commission had made it clear that in the absence of a European Directive, domestic legislative arrangements would be subject to the *de facto* application of EU competition law.

The common position of April 1989
A constellation of interests favourable to liberal concerns   In April 1989, under the Spanish Presidency, the Internal Market Council agreed on a common position, which was a compromise between the divergent

interests at stake; namely, the common position did not include any binding obligations concerning broadcasting quotas. The 'softening' of the dirigiste camp resulted from its incapacity to impose its concerns in the face of the dominance of the liberal coalition.[20] Not only were a majority of EU states still in favour of liberal policy options – despite the lobbying campaigns of the French – but the political context also gave weight to liberal concerns.

The UK was leading the liberal coalition which opposed the very existence of quotas for European works. Already during the Culture Council of June 1984, Lord Gowry, then British Minister for the Arts, told Jack Lang that the French should stop being protectionists, and instead try to become competitive (*Les Nouvelles*, 5 July 1984). In 1989, the British position had become even more radical under the pressure of the US, which feared that European markets would be made less accessible to American audio-visual products. Allegedly, Prime Minister Margaret Thatcher seems to have opposed the principle of legally binding quotas 'after a phone call from Reagan'.[21] More fundamentally, she considered audio-visual regulation to be a national matter, arguing that 'there must be certain standards the television channels don't go beyond. We don't want channels going pornographic. It is that standard we are anxious about. What they tend to be doing in addition is saying when advertising can be transmitted. That's really not a matter of standards. It's not their job' (*The Times*, 22 September 1988). Other states embraced the British position for distinct reasons. Italy argued that implementing content quotas would not be possible; Luxembourg was anxious not to hamper the development of the Coronet satellite; and Denmark was simply not keen on delegating any sovereignty in this policy sector.[22] As examined in the first section of this chapter, very few countries had an interest in the implementation of interventionist policies.

Furthermore, the negotiations on the Audio-visual Convention of the Council of Europe (Council of Europe 1989), which were simultaneously taking place, gave weight to liberal concerns. The Convention, which intended to impose a very flexible quota system for European works[23] gained the support of a majority of states. The French delegation accepted the so-called 'Stockholm compromise' in November 1988, which gave away the principle of compulsory European quotas. Not only did France believe that the Convention would have been voted on even without its consent, but it also feared the political cost of a veto vote. The re-election of Catherine Lalumière, then President of the Council of Europe, could indeed have been endangered.[24] The 'Stockholm compromise' heavily influenced the TWF negotiations. The final *communiqué* of the European Council of Rhodes of December 1988 invited the Commission and the Council of Ministers to align the Directive content on the dispositions contained in the draft Convention (Maggiore 1990). It seems that French

President François Mitterrand also agreed to line up the TWF Directive
with the Council of Europe Convention in return for the acceptance of his
pet project Audiovisual Eureka, the intergovernmental audio-visual
production support scheme sponsored by the French meant to stimulate
cooperation among European audio-visual enterprises (*Le Monde*, 5 April
1989).

Political costs of the compromise: reactions from the cultural lobby   The
cultural lobby, essentially composed of representatives of the French
cultural community, was disappointed by the content of the Council
common position. Famous artists and film professionals initiated a lobbying campaign directed both towards European institutions and the French
government. In particular, they organised high profile events designed to
publicise their concerns and pressurise policy-makers. For instance, the
'Train Named Culture' event was meant to mobilise the cultural community and lobby the EP (Fraser 1996). The EP, and in particular the
Parliamentary Committee for Cultural Affairs, was sympathetic to the
cultural lobby. Roberto Barzanti, an Italian MEP responsible for writing
a report on the TWF Directive, protested against the content of the political compromise reached in April. In particular, the report criticised the
flexible nature of the quotas, suggesting instead that 'member states shall
do everything in their power via legally effective and appropriate means
to ensure that every television broadcasting body reserves, based on its
present situation and in a progressive manner, a majority proportion of its
broadcasting time to European works within a period of four years starting at the adoption of the Directive' (European Parliament 1990: 22).
However, very few of the amendments suggested by the EP were eventually upheld by the Commission.

Professionals' lobbying campaigns were also directed towards the
French government, accused of having accepted a political compromise
that was against 'French cultural interests' (*Le Monde*, 5 April 1989).
Several personalities wrote an open letter addressed to President François
Mitterrand in which they denounced a policy 'resigned to decline and
neglect'[25] (*La Croix*, 5 April 1989). The Ministry of Culture was the most
amenable to special interests' pleas. Officials from this ministry thought
that 'softening' the French position in EU negotiations would provoke
strong protests against the government.[26] Foreseeing the electoral
campaign of the European elections, it was concerned that the artistic
community would refuse to support the electoral list of Laurent Fabius,
then leader of the Socialist list. Such arguments were used by the Ministry
of Culture in order to pressure the other ministries that were involved in
the negotiation process.[27]

In a state where the 'cultural exception' theme was, and still is, a highly
publicised one (see *Financial Times*, 19 January 2002) such fears had an

impact on the governmental position. In June 1989, the Council of Ministers met in Luxembourg for the Directive's formal adoption. The French delegation strengthened its position and opposed the compromise reached in April. Germany, Denmark, the Netherlands, Belgium and Greece (although for different reasons) were also part of the 'blocking' minority that refused the plan proposed during the Council. In its attempt to strengthen the *dirigiste* elements of the Directive, the French government succeeded in transferring the dossier from the Internal Market Council to the General Affairs Council dealing with trade policy (Krebber 2002: 117).

The approval of the Directive

On 3 October 1989, the Directive was eventually approved by the General Affairs Council in Luxembourg. If the *dirigiste* coalition strengthened its opposition after the 'April compromise', the final Directive eventually gave weight to liberal concerns. Why were the *dirigistes*, then, unsuccessful in imposing their favoured policy options, in the last resort?

A diplomatic logic at the origin of the compromise   At the last stage of the TWF negotiations, a diplomatic logic took priority over sectoral interests, resulting in the ease of the dirigiste position. Ministries for External Affairs and national delegations in Brussels behaved as 'policy-brokers', trying to achieve the design of a common solution, whatever the latter would be. Indeed, supporting strong policy preferences in one sector might have endangered the policy negotiations in other areas. In EU-level negotiations, national representatives must take into account all the policy issues that are on top of the agenda (Lequesne 1993).

In France, the Ministry for External Affairs pulled more weight in EU-level negotiations than the Ministry of Culture. Edith Cresson, then Minister for European Affairs, was in charge of the TWF dossier. Backed by Roland Dumas, then Minister for External Affairs, she seems to have pressured the Ministry of Culture to accept a political compromise.[28] President François Mitterrand himself urged Roland Dumas to find a solution in order to avoid any deadlock in the negotiation process. The position of the French President can most likely be explained by the close connections between Helmut Kohl and François Mitterrand. Because the Ministry for External Affairs participates directly in negotiations in Brussels, it ultimately benefited from a greater influence than other ministries.

The final negotiations also took place while the French held the presidency of the Council in autumn 1989. The Council presidency is, according to Hayes-Renshow and Wallace, 'under pressure to look for agreement and to manage business in such a way as to foster agreement' (1997: 146). Paradoxically, it can be the most difficult time for a government to openly defend its views if the latter are not shared by a majority of EU states. This was the case for content quotas, regarded by most states as a measure meant to satisfy vested interests in France. Unlike at the agenda-setting stage, therefore, it was difficult for the French government to support strong *dirigiste* views within the Council of Ministers.

'Avoiding the status quo'   As examined earlier, France was isolated in its demands for dirigiste policies, such as programme quotas. Therefore, dirigiste states were facing a double dilemma. On the one hand, they could not gather a sufficient majority in favour of a dirigiste policy solution within the Council of Ministers. On the other, vetoing the Directive would imply the upholding of the status quo, which appeared as the most undesirable policy option to most governments, and in particular to France. Indeed, at the most crucial stage of the policy negotiations, DG Competition sent a reasoned opinion to the French government.[29] The reasoned opinion questioned the legality of a French legislation concerning the definition of audio-visual works that were eligible to be counted as 'European programmes' for the purpose of the fulfilment of the content quotas imposed on television channels. The Commission strategically took action after the General Affairs Council of 17 July 1989, during which the French delegation had expressed its reticence towards the content of the common position. Similar notices were sent to the Netherlands and Belgium, which had also opposed the common position. This was interpreted by the Secrétariat Général du Comité Interministériel pour les questions économiques Européennes (SGCI) within the French government as a warning message for the French: their room for manoeuvre, even in the absence of EU-level legislation, was increasingly limited.

Thus, the best the *dirigistes* could do was to resort to the use of 'policy trade-offs'. The French Ministry of Culture thought that by adopting a more flexible stance on advertising issues and granting derogations for small EU states which were not able to cope with content obligations, France might obtain a qualified majority within the Council.[30] Also, the French Ministry of Culture had already started to develop informal bargaining strategies with the Spanish government, which was holding the Council presidency during the first semester of 1989. A typical strategy for policy entrepreneurs consists of developing informal contacts with preceding or following presidencies (the 'troika' mechanism). Jorge Semprun, then Spanish Minister of Culture, offered his support to the French delegation in exchange for greater flexibility on the advertising chapter.[31] In fact, acting as a 'policy broker', the Spanish government seems to have favoured the policy options that were the most likely to gain a consensus within the Council. Spanish officials hoped that the

Directive could be adopted under Spanish presidency, hence bestowing upon Spain a degree of diplomatic prestige.

Thus, the best *dirigiste* countries could do was obtain the 'best possible compromise' in a situation where the status quo was not a desirable option. If the very maintenance of the article on quotas for European works[32] shows that the *dirigiste* coalition succeeded in imposing some of its concerns,[33] the essence of the Directive was dominated by liberal concerns.

Securing national arrangements and obtaining policy pay-offs   If the French and their dirigiste allies failed to impose their own model of intervention at the EU level, they nevertheless succeeded in securing their national legislative arrangements and obtaining side-payments. Most significantly, the French government successfully secured the maintenance of French legislation on linguistic quotas, authors' rights and media chronology (which guarantees that cinema productions cannot be sold as videotapes during a fixed period after their release). In March 1989, the French Prime Minister Michel Rocard asked Edith Cresson not to give up two crucial requests during the negotiations: the possibility for France to preserve its legislation on the distribution of audio-visual works and the maintenance of national linguistic quotas.[34] He however recommended that the French delegation should not prevent the adoption of the Directive.

Concerning the regulation of the distribution of audio-visual works, France orchestrated a successful 'coalition-building' strategy and obtained the support of Belgium, Greece, Italy and Germany. The Commission had conditioned the acceptance of an amendment on this issue to the existence of a significant support from the member states.[35] France obtained this support in September 1988 and an amendment on the distribution of audio-visual works proposed by France was included in the Directive.

In the field of authors' rights, France staunchly opposed the principle of a compulsory copyright licence, which would have prevented authors from controlling the use of their work. In a letter sent by Jack Lang to Commission President Jacques Delors in August 1988, the French Minister of Culture suggested that the chapter on authors' rights be either removed or completely redrafted. The letter reads:

> Concerning the issue of authors' rights and neighbouring rights, France is, like most other member states, firmly attached to the principle of the exclusivity of authors and their rightful claimants. Therefore, any system of compulsory licence can only meet the opposition of the French government. [...] The chapter of the Directive which concerns authors' rights must be either removed, or rewritten in order to give its entire value to the principle of the voluntary licence.[36]

In fact, most member states felt that the legal licence would have threatened their legislative traditions, and opposed it in principle. The *dirigiste*
coalition could therefore easily block the measure. If the French were not
successful in transposing their own policy model at the European level,
they ensured that French legislative arrangements and public support
mechanisms were preserved.

Moreover, the French government obtained several 'side-payments' as
a counterpart for accepting the liberalisation of the audio-visual sector
(*Le Monde*, 15 November 1990). The 1989 *Assises de l'Audiovisuel*,
organised by the French External Affairs Ministry, were designed to lay
the foundations for future developments of European audio-visual policy.
In particular, France succeeded in imposing the creation of a multilateral
support mechanism for the European film industry suggested during the
Assises. Audiovisual Eureka, which aimed at fostering cooperation
between European audio-visual enterprises, was signed by 26 countries in
1989. Furthermore, the 1990 Commission Communication on audio-
visual policy (European Commission 1990) stated that the Commission
policy proposals were informed by the *Assises*. French initiatives outside
the Community framework seem to have been successful in pushing new
policy issues to the top of the EU agenda.

The French government acted as a policy entrepreneur during the TWF
Directive negotiations. Mainly, its proactive strategies allowed for French
schemes to be maintained. The principle of quotas for European works
was also transposed at the EU level despite the firm opposition of several
EU states. However, a lot was conceded to liberal concerns in the content
of the EU Directive. Fundamentally, France and other *dirigiste* states
opted for a political compromise, because the nature of the status quo,
characterised by the *de facto* intervention of EU institutions and the development of trans-frontier broadcasting, was less desirable than a
'middle-course' EU-level solution.

The 1997 TWF Directive: 'new actors, new rules, similar outcomes'

The renewal of the TWF Directive confirmed the dominance of the liberal
image at the EU level. Both within the Commission and within the
Council of Ministers, the constellation of actors' interests was favourable
to liberal demands. At the time of the Directive renewal, decision rules
had changed (the co-decision procedure gave more powers to the EP) and
new actors had entered the decision-making process (that is three new
member states and a new Commission President). Thus, coalition patterns
were likely to be altered by the new parameters of the decision-making
process.

*Designing new policy solutions: renewed conflicts between the liberal
and the* dirigiste *DGs*

The overall assessment of the TWF Directive was due by 3 October 1994. Lengthy conflicts between the Commission DGs delayed the formulation of new policy orientations. Joao de Deus Pinheiro, then Commissioner in charge of the audio-visual sector, was in charge of producing the 1994 *Green Paper on Strategy Options to Strengthen the European Programme Industry* (European Commission 1994a).[37] Jacques Delors presented the 1994 Green Paper as a logical following through of the *White Paper on Growth, Competitivity, and Employment* (European Commission 1993), which supported the development of a positive industrial policy in the audio-visual sector (*Le Monde*, 24 March 1994; *Libération*, 8 April 1994). Thus, *dirigiste* concerns were taken into account in the formulation of EU policy orientations (*Le Monde*, 9 April 1994). The Commission manifested a clear intention to *anticipate* the demands of the cultural lobby. The experience of the 1984 Green Paper, which provoked fierce opposition from interest groups, is likely to have informed the renewal process of the Directive.

Informal policy proposals were issued by DG Culture in November 1994. The proposals suggested that the words 'where practicable' be deleted from the text of the Directive in order to make quotas for European works legally binding (European Commission 1995a). DG Culture also proposed that stage programmes, such as variety and talk shows, would not be considered as 'European programmes' for the purpose of fulfilling quota obligations, thus implying a stricter application of content quotas for television channels. In order to satisfy liberal pressures, video on demand services were not regulated, television-shopping was not construed as advertising and member states could not oppose themselves to the broadcasting of a programme already broadcast in another country (*Le Monde*, 17 November 1994).

However, the Commission was unable to draw up formal policy proposals by the end of 1994. Dissent among competing DGs prevented the Commission from reaching an agreement on revised quota rules (De Witte 1995). Martin Bangemann, in charge of the Internal Market, and Sir Leon Brittan, then responsible for external economic affairs and trade policy, were vehemently opposed to the system of quotas. For Martin Bangemann, 'quotas were not a good way to promote an industry' (cited in *Les Echos*, 1 February 1995).

A formal proposal was finally adopted in March 1995 under the French presidency. Marcelino Oreja, who took over the audio-visual portfolio in early 1995, submitted a project built along the lines of the proposal drafted in November 1994: the words 'where practicable' did not appear, game shows and studio-based programmes could not be used to fulfil quota obligations and thematic channels had investment obligations in European production. However, new services were excluded from the scope of the revised Directive despite the opposition of the French Commissioners, Yves-Thibault de Silguy and Edith Cresson, of the Portuguese Joao de Deus Pinheiro and of the Belgian Karel van Miert (*Libération*, 18 March 1995).

Thus, conflicts between liberal and *dirigiste* policy actors reappeared at the agenda-setting stage. As argued by Cram (1997), concentrating on the Commission as a 'monolithic unit' fails to highlight institutional divisions within the Commission. In the TWF case, disparities of views between DGs were very salient and the drafting of the proposal was hampered.

The strengthening of the liberal coalition within the Council of Ministers
During the preparatory work for the Council of Ministers meeting of September 1995, differences between member states were already obvious (Cornil 1996). The promotion of European works (content quotas) and the scope of the revised Directive were the most controversial issues during the policy negotiations stage (*European Report*, 24 March 1995). In its original version, the Directive applied to all services that consisted of pre-determined programme schedules broadcast simultaneously to more than one receiver. With the renewal of the Directive, it was envisaged that the scope of the Directive would be extended to interactive services, such as video-on-demand for instance.

The UK, Germany, the Netherlands, Denmark, Sweden and Italy were acutely opposed to the renewal of the quotas (*European Report*, 18 October 1995). Therefore, the Ministers responsible for audio-visual and cultural matters rejected the Commission's proposal during the Council meeting of November 1995. They agreed, instead, to embrace a compromise prepared by the Spanish delegation that preserved the status quo concerning content quotas – meaning that their implementation was to remain discretionary. Furthermore, member states decided to phase out the quotas after ten years (Keller 1997). However, non-binding quotas were extended to thematic channels and the Council decided to set up a contact group in charge of monitoring the Directive implementation. Although this compromise was presented by the French press as a success mainly due to French determination (*Figaro-Economie*, 21 November 1995), European content requirements remained discretionary and the scope of the revised Directive was not extended to new media services.

As had already happened in 1989, the *dirigiste* coalition was facing a hostile majority of liberal member states within the Council and was forced to accept a political compromise. Only Belgium and Greece offered their support to the French delegation (*Les Echos*, 5 October 1995). Germany and the UK, in particular, were strongly against the inclusion of any kind of quotas. Furthermore, three new states with liberal policy traditions – Austria, Finland and Sweden – had become members of the

EU in January 1995, thereby modifying the potential coalition patterns during the negotiation process. Moreover, Jacques Santer, the new Commission President, was less favourable to quotas than his predecessor Jacques Delors. Thus, the French government eventually accepted the policy option proposed by the Spanish government. Perhaps France, anticipating a less favourable climate under the forthcoming EU presidency of Italy – with Silvio Berlusconi as Prime Minister – preferred to preserve the status quo as a minimal guarantee.[38]

The co-decision procedure as a new opportunity structure for the dirigiste *coalition*

Under the co-decision procedure, the text prepared by the Council had to be examined by the EP in first reading. The new decision rules were seen by the cultural coalition as an opportunity to give weight to their concerns. In the Information Report on the TWF Directive issued by the French Parliament in 1995, the *rapporteur* recommended that French MEPs be mobilised in order to defend the strengthening of the Directive. The Report states that 'when there is still enough time, it is required that the initiatives necessary to the mobilisation of our representatives in the European parliament, and, there from, of all its members, be taken' (Assemblée Nationale Française 1995a: 20).[39]

As expected, the EP proved to be a strong ally for the *dirigistes*. This might be explained by the fact that the EP attracts lobbyists who, historically, might not have enjoyed such easy access to the Commission and national governments (Mazey and Richardson 2001). MEPs disapproved of the position adopted within the Council. In January 1996, the Cultural Commission of the EP voted in favour of a report prepared by Karsten Hoppenstedt (EPP, Germany) and Gerardo Galeote Quecedo (EPP, Spain), which differed radically from the Council's position (*Europolitique*, 27 January 1996). In first reading, 292 deputies voted for the strengthening of the quota mechanism against 195 MEPs who opposed it. The ten-year termination provision for quotas was dropped and quota rules were extended to new services (*Libération*, 15 February 1996). All the French MEPs – apart from the members of the National Front Party – unanimously voted in favour of the suppression of the words 'where practicable' (*Figaro-Economie*, 6 February 1996). The text as amended by the EP included most of the demands upheld by the cultural coalition. Defending an autonomous agenda was also a way for the EP to assert its competence and maximise its influence on the selection of policy options at the EU level.

However, the Council and the EP reached a predictable impasse in June 1996, when the Council of Ministers refused to accept the modifications proposed by the EP and chose to maintain the November compromise. In fact, most of the EP's amendments had already been eliminated by the

Commission when the text was transmitted to the Council. The Commission's changes paid scarce heed to the EP's demands (*European Report*, 25 May 1996). The Council merely adopted the proposal as modified by the Commission (*Europolitique*, 15 June 1996) – only Sweden, Belgium and Greece voted against the text, and Ireland abstained. The only amendments that were accepted by the Council concerned:

- the clarification of the definition of 'television advertising', 'television sales' and 'European works';
- the acceptance of a minimum delay of 18 months between the first release of a film in cinemas and its broadcast on general access television – unless the right-holders of the film agree to a shorter delay;
- the setting up of a contact committee for consultation between the Commission and the member states concerning all matters related to the Directive's application.

During the second reading in November 1996, an absolute majority – 314 votes – was necessary in order to modify the Council decision; but only 291 votes were attained (*European Report*, 16 November 1996). All the amendments that would have tightened content quotas and forced the inclusion of new services in the scope of the Directive did not appear in the final text. The time limits for advertising and teleshopping were doubled and the 'teleshopping windows' and 'telepromotions' were excluded from the total ceiling of advertising time (Harcourt 2005: 81). The weight of the European People's Party (Christian Democrats), the Liberal Group and Forza Europa led by Berlusconi prevented the EP from attaining the necessary 314 votes to modify the Council decision. Obtaining an absolute majority is a constant problem faced by the EP in second readings.[40] Even with a large majority, it was unable to influence the decision of the Council. The French were disappointed by the outcome of the TWF vote; Jack Lang commented that 'the European Parliament ha[d] passed up another chance to justify its existence' (cited in *European Report*, 16 November 1996).

However, the EP proposed the introduction of a so-called 'v-chip'[41] in order to categorise violent or sexually explicit programmes (*International Herald Tribune*, 13 November 1996) and voted in favour of guaranteeing universal access to broadcasts of major sporting events. The conciliation procedure was set up in order to allow the Council and the EP to find a settlement. Concerning the compulsory fitting of v-chips, the EP's calls were abandoned in return for the promise of a Commission study into the subject (Levy 1999). Concerning the broadcasting of sporting events, the Commission and the Council favoured a mechanism that would allow states to draft their own list of major sporting events, but the principle of having a 'list' was retained in the final text, adopted on 20 June 1997 (89/552/EEC).

Thus, the revised Directive further anchored the path towards the liberalisation of the audio-visual sector – although the cultural coalition was successful in maintaining the existence of at least 'symbolically' powerful quotas.

Impact of international technological developments

Technological developments had already reduced member states' sovereignty in the audio-visual sector during the negotiations for the 1989 TWF Directive. Indeed, two periods of transition have affected the television landscape. In a first stage, television became transnational with the arrival of cable and satellite technologies. An important contribution to the development of satellite services was made by two international satellite organisations, Intelstat and Eutelstat, which provided satellite capacity for satellite-to-cable television transmission. The European Space Agency (ESA) also played a role by carrying the original Sky Channel before it transferred first to an Eutelstat satellite and then to the Astra satellite, based in Luxembourg. The World Administrative Radio Conference (WARC '77) finally allocated Direct Broadcasting Satellite (DBS) frequencies and orbital slots to each European country for 'high-powered' DBS satellites (Humphreys 1996). The development of satellite television allowed television channels to relocate themselves in states where more lenient legislative regimes were in place. This challenged the possibility for states to adopt stricter quotas than the ones required by the TWF Directive, as the French government had done with the 1991 Tasca decrees (Fraser 1996).

In a second stage, digital technologies allowed traditional and new communication services to be provided over the same networks. The traditional distinction between broadcasting (non-interactive point-to-multi-point services) and telecommunications (interactive point-to-point services) had been thrown into question. In this new context, many EU and national telecommunications policy-makers argue that sector-based broadcasting regulation should be replaced by much greater reliance on competition policy. Moreover, it could be said that legitimacy for government intervention based on spectrum-scarcity has disappeared (Keller 1997).

Thus, national level regulations were *de facto* challenged by international technological developments, making the nature of the 'default situation' increasingly undesirable to most governments. As a result, disagreements among member governments focused on the *content* of the broadcasting Directive ('the selection of policy options') but not on the *level* of public intervention. If at first sight, member states seem to have evaluated rationally whether a common solution would/would not suit their interests, governments did so in a context which was altered by supranational level policy developments. Along with the new technological challenges at the international level, the Commission had indeed initiated the liberalisation of the European audio-visual market far in advance of treaty reforms and showed its constant ability to attack national regulations even in the absence of legal competence to do so.[42] Thus, accepting a directive which was 'half-satisfactory' was a rational option for the French government and other *dirigiste* states. The French Minister of Culture argued, in front of the French Parliament:

> In the face of this situation, we have only two solutions. The first one is to be maximalists, and to favour, thereby, the strengthening of this coalition [i.e. the liberal coalition]. We will then be able to say that we supported firmly and vehemently the 'colours of European culture'. We will also be able to say that we have lost, and we will have to take responsibility for the consequences. The other solution consists of trying to secure the essential, i.e. a minimal set of rules already accepted at the Community level and the maintenance of our national support mechanisms. (Assemblée Nationale Française 1995b)[43]

The French government was forced to adopt an increasingly defensive strategy in the face of external developments that it could not control, a tendency that was exacerbated by international technological developments. The current revision process of the TWF Directive confirms this tendency in an even more obvious manner. According to the European Commission, the key issue that regulators – both national and European – need to address today is that rules devised for one-to-many broadcasting are being rendered obsolete by the shift to one-to-one, on-demand services. It further argues that 'enhanced end-user control means less need for regulation'.[44] Thus, the proposal laid down by the Commission in December 2005 sets up a substantial deregulation of audio-visual rules (European Commission 2005). The Commission proposal distinguishes between scheduled broadcasting via traditional TV, the internet, or mobile phones, which 'pushes' content to viewers, and non-scheduled broadcasting, such as video-on-demand and web-based news, which the viewer 'pulls' from a network. Current broadcasting rules would apply to scheduled broadcasting, albeit in a more flexible form, whereas non-scheduled broadcasting would be subject only to a basic set of minimum principles, such as protecting minors and preventing incitement to racial hatred.

Conclusion

Looking at the audio-visual sector confirms that two parallel processes originated the Europeanisation and the Communitarisation processes of public policies in the cultural field. With the support of a number of commercial actors, the ECJ and the Commission made use of their judicial and regulatory powers and asserted their sovereignty in the audio-visual sector by giving an 'economic' definition to audio-visual works. The ECJ defined films as a 'service', while the Commission highlighted the need to liberalise the audio-visual market in the EU in order to complete the Single Market. By promoting a liberal image of the policy problem, EU institutions asserted their policy competence in a new policy area. As predicted, policy change was provoked by institutional actors that wanted to extend their own policy jurisdiction and therefore attacked existing arrangements and, subsequently, change in the image of the policy problem allowed for change of venue. With the change in venue came an increased attention to the liberal image, leading to further change in venue as an increasing range of private actors became aware of the new venue as an opportunity structure for the defence of their preferences. Such dynamics originated the Europeanisation of the policy area, in the sense that national level policies were increasingly constrained by EU-level policy developments.

In the audio-visual case, EU institutions' intervention was harmful for states where legislative traditions were the most interventionist. France felt particularly challenged by the liberalisation process initiated at the EU level, which came into conflict with its own plans for a 'European audio-visual space' along *dirigiste* lines. Thus, instead of being passively subject to EU-level policy developments, the French decided to 'enter the game' and tried to lock in their preferred policy model at the EU level against potential attacks from the Commission and the ECJ. To do so, the French attempted to portray audio-visual policy issues from a cultural perspective and pulled the decision-making process back to an intergovernmental mode, hoping that the Council of Ministers would be a more favourable venue in which to defend *dirigiste* concerns. Thus, in a dynamic multi-level mode, developments at the supranational level induced the intervention of member governments; the latter attempted to promote the creation of a positive audio-visual policy in a 'joint-decision' mode which would allow them to participate to the EU policy-making process.

The role of France as a major policy actor in the Europeanisation process of cultural policies is particularly noticeable in the audio-visual sector – although the two other case studies will also highlight, to a lesser extent, the important role played by the French government in cultural negotiations. However, if France can be characterised as a 'policy entrepreneur' in the decision-making process, in the sense that it was successful in creating a *dirigiste* policy agenda at the EU level, the policy options that were selected were a political compromise between *dirigiste* and liberal views. Moreover, the move towards the liberalisation of the audio-visual sector was furthered during the phase of renewal of the Directive.

Fundamentally, disagreements focused mainly on the content of the broadcasting Directive ('policy options') but not on the level of public intervention ('integration'). For *dirigiste* governments, the default position was even more undesirable, in so far as it was characterised by the *de facto* intervention of EU institutions along liberal economic lines. At the EU level however, the constellation of actors' interests was in favour of liberal concerns; and thus the room for manoeuvre for the *dirigistes* was limited to obtaining the 'best possible compromise' within the Council of Ministers. Technological evolutions in recent years exacerbated the undesirable nature of the default position, as the regulation of audio-visual activities appeared to be escaping any individual state's control. Therefore, in the case of audio-visual regulation, vetoing the Directive would not have prevented national legislative and policy traditions from being challenged by the internationalisation of television broadcasting. Fundamentally, in so far as European institutions, using technological developments as a 'window of opportunity' had succeeded in changing the venue of policy, the image of policy issues was likely to change too. EU decision routines, the participants ('multi-actorness') and the undesirable nature of the status quo combined to make the selection of liberal policy options more likely.

Notes

1 Hereafter referred to as 'the TWF Directive' and 'the revised TWF Directive'.
2 Only those aspects of EU states' audio-visual policies that are relevant to understanding EU-level negotiations on the TWF Directive are presented here.
3 Interview with Patrick Olivier, French Ministry of Culture, Paris, 22 March 2001.
4 Interviews with French officials, Paris, 2000.
5 French Ministry of Culture website: www.culture.fr/culture/infos-pratiques /droit-culture/index.htm.
6 Interview with Jack Lang, former Minister of Culture in France, Paris, 16 January 1999.
7 The BBC was less favourable to the principle, arguing that in Britain the tradition is that the government keeps its distance from day-to-day running of broadcasting.
8 In the same manner, the ECJ ruled, in the case *Bond van Adverteerders* v. *Netherlands* (ECJ 1988a), that the prohibitions on advertising imposed on the broadcasting of television programmes from other member states were unlawful. The provisions of Dutch law were considered to be a direct discrimination against television programmes from other member states. The same stance was defended by the Court in the case *Commission* v. *Netherlands* (ECJ 1991d), in which the Court held that the obligation contained in Dutch legislation for national broadcasting organisations to make use of the facilities of a national television production company in producing their own programmes, was contrary to the freedom to provide services.

9   Hereafter referred to as 'the 1984 Green Paper'.

10 Note from the SAI on the European audio-visual space, 10 May 1983 – Archives of the French Ministry of Culture.

11 See also section 2 of Chapter 2, in which EU law interference with national regulations was discussed with reference to the *Cinéthèque* case (ECJ 1985a).

12 Anand Menon (1996) analyses French European policy as an attempt to achieve national objectives via the medium of European integration.

13 Note from the DAI (Département des Affaires Internationales) on the French Presidency, 23 May 1989 – Archives of the French Ministry of Culture.

14 Note from the DAI on the meeting of Blois of 2–8 November 1989 – Archives of the French Ministry of Culture.

15 Interview with Gaetanno Stucchi, Director of the Television Department of the EBU, Geneva, 27 March 2001.

16 Interviews with French officials, French Ministry of Culture, 2000.

17 Jacques Toubon, then Member of the French Parliament, was actively fighting against the 'Tasca' decrees which imposed on television channels the commitment to broadcast 60 per cent of French programmes. He however defended the cultural exception when he became Minister of Culture.

18 Interviews with French officials, French Ministry of Culture, 2000.

19 Interviews with French officials, French Ministry of Culture, 2000.

20 Interviews in France, French Ministry of Culture, and in the UK, DCMS, 2000.

21 Interview with Carole Tongue, former British MEP, London, 5 March 2001.

22 Minutes of SGCI meetings between 1986 and 1989 – Archives of the French Ministry of Culture.

23 Article 10 of the Convention states that broadcasters are under the obligation to reserve, 'where practicable and by appropriate means', a majority proportion of their transmission time for the broadcasting of European works.

24 Confidential document – Archives of the French Ministry of Culture.

25 Author's translation.

26 Note to the President of the Republic from Jack Lang and Catherine Tasca, 4 April 1989 – Archives of the French Ministry of Culture.

27 Note to the President, footnote 26.

28 Interview with Francis Beck, Head of Jack Lang's cabinet between 1988 and 1991, Paris, 8 January 2001.

29 Minutes of the SGCI meeting on the TWF negotiations, 23 July 1989 – Archives of the French Ministry of Culture.

30 Confidential document – Archives of the French Ministry of Culture.

31 Confidential document – Archives of the French Ministry of Culture.

32 Article 4 states: 'Member States shall ensure where practicable and by appropriate means, that broadcasters reserve for European works, within the meaning of Article 6, a majority proportion of their transmission time, excluding the time reserved to news, sport events, games, advertising and teletext services'. See Appendix 3 for the full version of the Directive provisions on the promotion and distribution of audio-visual works.

33 The introduction of a content quota in the Directive was the exact replication of the French system at the European level (Keller 1997). In the 1986 draft directive, the Commission had already stated that the article dealing

with European quotas was 'based on arrangements that already exist or are planned in certain member states' and further explained that: '[U]nder the specifications applicable to French television broadcasters, for instance, sixty per cent of the programming time consisting of non-documentary works produced for television or the cinema are reserved for works originating in the member states of the European Economic Community' (European Commission 1986: 14).

34 Note from the DAI on the Council of 13 March 1989 in Brussels – Archives of the French Ministry of Culture.
35 Confidential document – Archives of the French Ministry of Culture.
36 Author's translation. Letter from Jack Lang to Jacques Delors in 1989 (no exact date) – Archives of the French Ministry of Culture.
37 Hereafter referred to as 'the 1994 Green Paper'.
38 If Italy was often on the *dirigiste* side during cultural negotiations at the EU level, this was not the case during negotiations on broadcasting quotas.
39 Author's translation.
40 Earnshaw and Judge (1996) analyse the case of the directive on motor vehicle emissions, in which an absolute majority was denied by a combination of absenteeism and dissenting votes from certain political groups. The same phenomenon happened for the TWF Directive.
41 The amendment, sought with some passion by members of the EPP group, seeks to compel television manufacturers to fit electronic chips to all TV sets. This should enable parents to bar their children from gaining access to certain broadcasts deemed to be harmful.
42 As illustrated by the 1989 reasoned opinion sent to the French government by the Commission in the middle of the negotiations on the TWF Directive.
43 Author's translation.
44 See press fact sheet 'Why Europe needs to modernise its TV Without Frontiers Directive': http//europa.eu.int/information_society/services/doc _temp/tvwf-sht1_en.pdf.

5

The Europeanisation of the regulation of book markets: fixed price systems for books in the EU

Although no European legislation on book prices has been adopted so far, it is reasonable to argue that the ECJ and the European Commission have been successful in Europeanising the policy area by making use of their judicial and regulatory powers. The ECJ and DG Competition within the European Commission indeed began examining the compatibility of member states' legislation with competition rules as early as the 1980s. Acting far in advance of Treaty reforms, these institutions extended the remit of their competence to the area of book policy through the 'economic back door', as they did in the audio-visual sector. The ECJ and DG Competition within the European Commission issued decisions and judgements on fixed price systems for books throughout the 1980s, which clearly constrained domestic policy choices in member states. The Commission also made use of its agenda-setting powers and published two communications on the European dimension with regard to books in 1985. It was capable of developing an autonomous agenda – the liberalisation of the book sector – and playing a decisive role in the policy-making process. European institutions benefited from the complicity of subnational private actors, such as large bookshops and supermarkets, which hoped that European legislators would impose more lenient regimes than national ones on them. As early as the 1980s, private actors engaged in the frequent use of 'Eurolitigation' strategies as a means of altering the way book policy issues were tackled in states where national legislative arrangements were not favourable to them. If private actors played an important role in the audio-visual sector, their influence in the Europeanisation process of the book sector is particularly crucial; they triggered the application of EU law in several member states. During this phase, the European dimension penetrated into national arenas of politics and policy – forcing member governments to adapt their legislative and policy traditions to EU-level developments.

However, another process developed in parallel with the EU-led liberalisation strategy of the book policy sector. As in the audio-visual sector, member states that felt that their legislative and policy traditions were challenged by European institutions' economic approach attempted to reorient the focus of the EU policy debate. The Commission and the ECJ promoted a negative form of integration in a 'hierarchical direction' mode (Scharpf 2000), which allowed for the extension of EU competence in the absence of Treaty basis. In response to supranational entrepreneurship, national governments attempted to impose an alternative image of the policy problem at the EU level, portraying books as a special product, in order to lock in legislative solutions that were more favourable to their policy preferences.

How can we explain the fact that certain policy options were chosen over others, when two coalitions were competing in order to further their favoured model of policy intervention? It will be argued here that because the constellation of actors' interests at the European level was favourable to liberal policies, and because few states actually felt challenged by the intervention of EU institutions, the coalition potential for the *dirigistes* was not strong enough to enable the drafting of a common solution. In fact, in a situation where states' preferences were highly divergent and where the status quo appeared as the most desirable option to a majority of governments, the policy sector remained characterised by a negative form of integration.

The structure of this chapter follows the thread of the general argument. After presenting, for the sake of clarity, the legislative traditions of EU states in the book policy sector, the role of EU institutions as a favourable venue for the defence of liberal preferences will be discussed. It will then be explained, by focusing on France, Germany and Britain, that when EU liberalisation policies came into conflict with national legislative traditions ('venues competition'), governments attempted to lock in another model of policy intervention at the EU level. Finally, a section devoted to the strategies of the interventionist coalition will examine how the *dirigistes* attempted to impose their policy preferences ('images competition') at the EU level and why their strategies failed.

EU states' policy traditions: books as a 'special case'

The idea that books are not just a saleable commodity but constitute a key cultural heritage as well as a foundation for upholding freedom of opinion, freedom to teach and freedom to conduct research, was the main rationale behind public intervention in the book market. The main objective set up by policy-makers in most EU states was that publishers should be encouraged to publish not only commercially successful books, but also smaller runs of works with 'high cultural value'. Most member states therefore have a system of fixed book prices, as a result of their conviction that price fixing is the only means to ensure that there is no decline in the number of separate titles published and that cultural diversity is maintained. This rationale has also justified the existence of cross-border agreements between states when common linguistic areas involving several countries existed, as was the case in Germany and in Austria, for instance.

In member states, fixed price systems for books are either based on inter-professional agreements, as in Germany, Denmark, the Netherlands and Luxembourg, or established by law, as in France, Spain, Austria, Greece and Portugal (Conference on The Economics of the Book Industry in Europe, 29–30 September 2000). In France, the law on book prices came into effect in August 1981. It established that all retailers had to comply with a price fixed by publishers. Retailers can then offer a maximum discount of five per cent on the publisher-fixed price. Book sales in Spain come under a system of fixed prices as established by the law on books passed in 1975, and further developed by the Royal Decree of March 1990 on book prices. The laws in Greece and Portugal were adopted more recently. In fact, both Portugal and Greece adopted laws, in 1996 and 1997 respectively, based on the principles of French legislation. Austria adopted a law on fixed prices in June 2000, after the Commission ruled out the agreement between publishers and bookstore owners in the entire German-language area.

Germany, Luxembourg, the Netherlands and Denmark have had contractual agreements between professionals since the end of the nineteenth century. In Germany, retail price maintenance has existed since 1888. There is a contractual system between publishers (who can choose whether to comply with the system or not) and bookstores. The same system is in place in Luxembourg. The book trade in the Netherlands has been defined since 1923 by a booksellers' system involving a collective agreement between all the groups of professionals involved in book distribution. The agreement was exempted from the law of 1956 on free competition. In Denmark, since 1830 a retail maintenance system has been based on an agreement between the Association of Danish Publishers and the Association of Danish Bookstore Owners. The system is considerably more flexible today, however, with numerous restrictions to the application of the publisher-fixed price. Furthermore, the Danish body for fair trade is putting pressure upon the Association of Bookstore Owners to accept greater competition. In Sweden, Ireland, Finland and the UK, inter-professional agreements defining the retail price maintenance systems have been abolished during the last thirty years.

Thus, EU states do not all grant the same significance to the protection of books as a special commodity. In fact, traditional divisions between liberal and interventionist states – with Northern European countries increasingly oriented towards free competition, and Southern states as proponents of stricter interventionism – also appear in the debate on the regulation of book trade.

Book pricing practices in fifteen EU member states (new accession states not included)

Country	Book pricing system
Austria	Fixed price system established by law since 2000
Belgium	No legislation in force – current debate on a law project
Denmark	Fixed price system by contractual agreement (flexible system)
Finland	Contractual agreement suppressed in 1970
France	Fixed price system established by law since 1981
Germany	Fixed price system by contractual agreement since 1888
Greece	Fixed price system established by law since 1997
Ireland	Contractual agreement suppressed in 1989
Italy	Fixed price system by contractual agreement – law project pending
Luxembourg	Fixed price system by contractual agreement (does not apply to imports)
Netherlands	Fixed price system by contractual agreement since 1923
Portugal	Fixed price system established by law since 1996
Spain	Fixed price system established by law since 1975
Sweden	Contractual agreement suppressed in 1970
United Kingdom	Contractual agreement suppressed in 1995

Source: Littoz-Monnet, Annabelle (2003) D.Phil Thesis, Oxford University.

However, the debate on book trade regulation was made even more complex by the existence of divisions within states. Two sets of actors often contend with one another over the definition of a problematic policy situation and vie for control of the policy-making process. Thus, in countries where retail price maintenance systems have been abolished, legislative reforms were often implemented despite the protests of professional associations. In most Northern European states for instance, the abolition of retail price maintenance systems could not be prevented. In a context where the national government was favourable to the liberalisation of the sector, associations of independent bookshops and publishers did not benefit from any support. In states where fixed price systems are in force, various commercial actors attempted to dismantle them. This was the case in France and Germany, where large and on-line bookshops fought against national laws perceived as impediments to their commercial strategies. When embedded legislative and policy traditions appeared unchangeable, private actors who believed in greater market competition used EU structures as a channel to promote their interests.

The role of European institutions

The propensity of the ECJ and DG Competition within the Commission to behave as competence maximisers was also evident in the book policy sector. As in the audio-visual sector, their institutional interest in extending their remit to new policy areas in the absence of Treaty basis resulted in the projection of a liberal policy image on to cultural policy issues.

Thus, EU-level policies focused solely on the economic aspects of cultural products. In the 1985 *Communication on the Creation of a Community Framework System for Book Prices* (European Commission 1985a), the Commission made it clear that the various arrangements in member states with respect to pricing should be examined: if the arrangements should have effects on trade between member states, the provisions of the Treaty were to be relevant. In the Commission Communication, *Books and Reading: a Cultural Challenge for Europe* (European Commission 1989), the Commission stated that fixed book prices have never proved to be the best suited means for improving editorial production and promoting distribution. Finally, in the *Report on the Consideration of Cultural Aspects in European Community Action* (European Commission 1996), the Commission repeated that there was no need for European legislation on books. Thus, the Commission entered the symbolic contest, showing a one-sided preoccupation for the commercial aspects of book policy issues. Presenting policy solutions through a 'free-market' lens and promoting negative integration was probably the only way to extend EU competence to the book policy sector.

The Court and DG Competition started making use of their judicial and regulatory powers as early as the 1980s. DG Competition interfered mainly when cross-border agreements were regulating price fixing in common linguistic areas (see Riou 1996; Zandvliet 1998). First, the Commission ruled, in a 1981 Decision (82/123/EEC), that the agreement between the Dutch VBBB and Belgian VBVB (organisations for the promotion of book trade), relating to the trade in Dutch-language books between Belgium and the Netherlands, was contrary to EU competition rules. The Dutch Associations brought the Commission decision before the ECJ in an action for annulment (see ECJ 1984). However, in the case *VBBB and VBVB* v. *Commission*, the ECJ dismissed the action for annulment, stating that the infringement of EU competition rules by the associations was not justified and that the agreement did not contribute to an improvement of the production and distribution of books. In response to a question from the ECJ, the Commission stated that 'Article 85(3) does not permit the Commission to conduct a cultural policy' (cited in McMahon 1995) and the Court did not comment on the relationship between cultural policy and competition rules on competition in its ruling.[1]

The propensity of the Commission to act in an extensive fashion was also evident in the *Sammelsrevers* case, concerning Germany and Austria.[2] In 1998, DG Competition filed a suit against the parties to the agreement for violation of European regulations. On 30 June 2000, the agreement was condemned for being contrary to intra-Community trade rules and both publishers and bookstore owners abandoned their agreement. Finally, the trans-border aspects of the Net Book Agreement (NBA) in the UK were also prohibited by the Commission, since the NBA also applied to Ireland.[3] In applying EU competition rules to the book sector, the Commission and the ECJ favoured considerations relating to the integration of national book markets over cultural interests. Therefore, the EU was a critically important institutional structure for the advocates of the liberal image. The following section now turns to examining the connections between private actors and EU structures, and the impact of EU intervention on member states' legislative and policy traditions.

Competition between venues

Connections between private actors and EU institutions, and the liberalisation strategies of the book market which stemmed from it, challenged member governments' policies. This phenomenon will be examined in three EU countries: in France (one of the most 'interventionist' EU states in the cultural sector), Germany (where a cross-border agreement was in force), and in the UK (one of the most liberal states in the EU).

The French case: when interventionist and liberal images collide

The French Act of 10 August 1981, which states that retailers must charge an actual public selling price of between 95 per cent and 100 per cent of the price fixed by the publisher or importer, was challenged at various times by large bookshops and supermarkets. During the 1960s, bookshops began to merge into large groups that dominated the book market. In 1974, the Fédération Nationale d'Achat des Cadres (FNAC), now one of the largest booksellers in France, opened its book department and offered discounts of 20 per cent on the price recommended by the publisher (*Le Monde*, 19 March 1987). Large groups, such as Hachette and Presses de la Cité were also holding an increasingly large percentage of the market share in the book policy sector. After having been unsuccessful in their attempts to oppose the creation of a fixed price system for books in the late 1970s, large bookshops tried to dismantle the regulation by invoking European law during the 1980s (Surel 1997). In 1984, the FNAC initiated the 'European price' action, which consisted of bypassing French legislation by exporting books bought in France, before importing them back and fixing a lower price than the one fixed by the publisher.

Similar practices were initiated by the Association des Centres Distributeurs Edouard Leclerc, a group of retail shops which had extended its activities to books. The Centre Leclerc charged selling prices for books which were lower than those permitted by the 1981 legislation. Following the issuing of a writ from several bookshops and the Union Syndicale des Libraires de France, which represents French bookshops, a

French court prevented the Centre Leclerc from charging selling prices which were not in conformity with the 1981 Act. However, Leclerc recognised that the issue could be considered in an alternative institutional context, possibly more favourable to its own interests. In the case *Leclerc v. Au Blé Vert* (ECJ 1985b), the Court of Appeal of Poitiers referred a question to the EJC on the compatibility of the 1981 French law with various provisions of EU law. The European venue presented the possibility of changing the way the initial problem was framed.

A real struggle therefore developed between the French government and 'cultural' interest groups on one side, and the ECJ, DG Competition and private actors on the other. 'Cultural policy' advocates, defining books as cultural products, were facing the proponents of a strict application of competition rules to the book policy sector. The latter attempted to present a quite different image – namely, that books were not special and were like any other tradable commodity. Again in the following years (ECJ 1985c, ECJ 1986a and ECJ 1986b), the Centre Leclerc invoked EU law in order to challenge French legislation. Thus, at repeated intervals, attacks on French legislation were initiated by private actors, who benefited from the support of national courts in facilitating access to the European venue.

Far from remaining passive, the French government attempted to prevent EU institutions from interfering with French legislative arrangements and developed informal strategies aimed at imposing its policy preferences.[4] In particular, France sought the support of other member states in order to lobby the ECJ and DG Competition. Jack Lang, then Minister of Culture, entertained regular contacts with German officials and succeeded in mobilising German domestic interests. In fact, he convinced book publishers and booksellers that their own system could be dismantled if the principle of state interventionism in the book policy sector was not acknowledged at the EU level.[5] It is believed that the German judges who were members of the ECJ recognised the legitimacy of French legislation following pressure from the French government. Consumers' associations denounced the 'tacit agreement' of the Commission for maintaining the 'Lang regulation' (*Le Soir*, 3 November 1985). *The Economist* concluded that the ECJ argued 'against the spread of chain bookstores' in the 1985 *Leclerc* case (*The Economist*, 19 January 1995). The ECJ decision was confirmed in several other judgements,[6] thereby strengthening the legitimacy of the French law. Further to another 'Eurolitigation' strategy by Leclerc in 1987, the ECJ supported the arguments of the French government (ECJ 1988b). In fact, the law was attacked only in its technical aspects, but the core principles and values that were at the origin of the fixed price system were not challenged (Surel 1997).

The high political support granted to the 'Lang regulation' made its dismantling extremely difficult. Indeed, as no legislative measure could be contemplated at the European level, despite repeated proposals from the French delegation (see section on *dirigiste* governments' strategies below), the Commission committed itself to hold back the infraction procedure engaged against France before the ECJ.[7] Furthermore, the Commission welcomed several French proposals, such as the idea of a pilot project on translation – in effect a typical example of side payments. A resolution was adopted in 1987 (OJ C 309, 19.11.1987), in which EU governments agreed to undertake a suitable pilot scheme in order to provide support for translations of European works. French proposals for a European translation scheme suggested the adoption of mechanisms that were similar to the ones already implemented in France.

The French case sheds light on the propensity of private actors to use the European venue in order to challenge national-level policies that are not favourable to them. However, the developments examined here also show that when a government strongly opposes the policy developments induced by supranational and subnational common strategies, it is able to prevent the dismantling of its legislation at the national level – if not to impose its own model at the EU level. In the French case, the ECJ showed that it could bend its liberal stance when fundamental opposition existed at the national level (and as a result of active lobbying campaigns).

The German case: legitimacy for EU intervention and dominance of the liberal image

In a similar fashion, commercial actors played a proactive role in the process which led to the dismantling of the fixed price system that was in force in Germany and Austria. The book price system in Austria and Germany was based until 2000 on agreements between publishers and bookstore owners in the entire German-language area – the so-called *Sammelsrevers* agreements. The Commission was notified of the latter in 1993 (Soriano 1999), and DG Competition made it known in July 1994 that the agreements were compatible with the rules set down in the Treaty. In a letter addressed to the parties to the *Sammelsrevers*, the Commission had even stated that it had no objections related to the agreements (*Agence Europe*, 10 August 1994).

However, complaints from Libro, an Austrian bookseller which wanted to sell German best-sellers at a discounted price, resulted in the Commission's probing of the system (*Financial Times*, 12 June 1999). Thus, by 'Europeanising' the policy debate, private actors were hoping to impose an alternative image of book trade policy issues and thereby provoke national policy reforms. Proving again its propensity to extend the remit of its competences to new policy sectors, DG Competition eventually filed a suit against the parties to the agreement for violation of European regulations in 1998. For Eric Hardin, President of the Union

Syndicale des Libraires de France (Union of French Bookshops), this case is representative of the battle between 'the technocratic and ultraliberal power of DG IV [DG Competition], which does not accept the existence of derogations for books, and the position defended by politicians, attached to fixed book price systems' (interview cited in *Livres Hebdo*, 30 January 1998).[8] Indeed, Karel Van Miert, then EU Commissioner for Competition, repeatedly expressed the view that such pricing agreements for books violated EU competition law (*European Report*, 25 October 1997). He was utterly insensitive to the arguments put forward by German editors, who signed the Declaration of Leipzig on 26 March 1998. Mario Monti, who replaced Karel Van Miert as Competition Commissioner in 1999, also favoured banning the agreements (*Agence Europe*, 21 October 1999). At the other end of the spectrum, Michael Naumann, Minister of Culture in Germany since 1998, vehemently defended the existing agreements between Germany and Austria. Thus, allied to tensions between the European and the national levels of governance, were tensions between the liberal and the interventionist images and their associated coalitions. Domestic protests were however unsuccessful, and the agreement was condemned for being contrary to intra-community trade rules. Both publishers and bookstore owners abandoned their agreement on 30 June 2000. In response to a new complaint made in July 2000 by Libro over the boycott by German publishers and wholesalers who no longer supplied it, the Commission started a new investigation (*European Report*, 23 March 2002). It discovered, however, that the boycott was ultimately based on a mistaken interpretation and application of the new *Sammelsrevers* agreement, in particular its 'circumvention clause', which has now been corrected in the agreed undertaking.

In sum, the legitimacy for EU intervention was stronger when transborder effects could be deemed to be incompatible with EU competition rules, and private commercial actors therefore succeeded in securing policy reforms that they could not achieve through national channels.

The UK: EU intervention as an external legitimisation for internal reforms
The situation in the UK was very different from that in France and Germany. The British government shared the preferences of the European Commission and commercial actors. The inclination of EU institutions to apply free-market principles was in line with the political agenda of the UK government. Therefore, supranational intervention in this sector – initiated by the European Commission and especially DG Competition – only represented an additional incentive for the implementation of national policy reforms that were already being planned.

Retail price maintenance had existed in the UK and Ireland by means of the NBA since January 1900. The Commission adopted a decision on

12 December 1988 (89/44/EEC) stating that the NBA was affecting intra-community trade. Publishers' associations protested before the Court of First Instance, but the latter rejected the appeal in 1992 (ECJ 1992). Yet, upon further appeal, the ECJ annulled the judgement and the decision of the Commission (ECJ 1995), arguing that the judgement in the first instance did not take into account the existence of a common linguistic area between England and Ireland. The ECJ also insisted that the case differed from that of the VBBB/VBVB agreement (ECJ 1984), because the Dutch/Flemish system required publishers to set fixed retail prices for all Dutch-language books in the Netherlands and Belgium, while the NBA required only that a book be sold at the price fixed by the publisher providing the latter decided to publish the book as a 'net book'. However, the annulment of the Commission decision did not occur until 1995 and therefore the ECJ judgement upon further appeal should not be interpreted as an attempt to protect the NBA. The agreement was already dismantled and the ECJ might have chosen to adopt a *laissez-faire* attitude. Indeed, structural changes in the book market had taken place by that time. Most of the large publishing houses, such as Penguin, HarperCollins and Random House, had abandoned the application of the agreement (*The Times*, 27 September 1995).

This phenomenon was the logical outcome of a series of events which occurred from the end of the 1980s. Most significantly, the agreement came under attack from the Pentos and Waterstones (a subsidiary of WH Smith) bookstore chains. Nigel Newton, chairman of Bloomsbury Publishing, highlights the role of WH Smith as the party most closely associated with the demise of the NBA (*The Bookseller*, 20 February 1998). Moreover, the British Restrictive Practices Court declared the NBA void in 1997, thereby ending nearly a century of retail price maintenance for books in the UK. Pressure from large publishing houses heavily influenced the policy debate. The 'free market' coalition, which included commercial interest groups, the British Restrictive Practices Court and DG Competition was stronger than the proponents of a policy considering books as a special product. This can be explained by the more general dominance of a free market paradigm in the UK during this period. The book policy sector was as much subject to this strong tide as any other. The political debate was oriented towards a drive to deregulate the retail industry in general, and the decision taken concerning the book industry was part of this 'global' policy.[9]

Thus, the intervention from the Commission was paralleled by private actors' pressure to liberalise the book industry. Unlike in France, the liberal political agenda was also favoured by the British government, meaning that decisions from the British Court and DG Competition encountered no resistance – apart from the protests of publishers' associations. Without the support of their own national government, their chances of any side-payments at the European level were much less than for their French counterparts.

The role of private actors in stimulating the application of EU competition law to national policies via resort to the Commission and the Court as alternative policy venues was crucial in countries where policy and legislative traditions appeared embedded. The frequency of court decisions helped private actors put policy issues to the top of the political agenda and gradually eroded national policy frameworks which had previously appeared unchangeable. This phenomenon was particularly true in France and Germany, where the book policy sector is strongly regulated. Private actors therefore had a strong incentive to use European structures in order to challenge the prevailing *dirigiste* policy image in the book policy sector. By contrast, EU intervention only legitimised changes that were already under way in more liberal states.

Thus, EU-level developments in the book sector had a considerable impact on the choices of national governments. As in the audio-visual sector, states that had developed interventionist legislative and policy traditions felt particularly threatened by the *de facto* Europeanisation of book trade regulation, and attempted to resist the liberalisation process triggered by private actors and EU institutions. However, by portraying policy issues from a commercial perspective, EU institutions had been successful in shifting the venue of the policy-making process towards the EU level, as predicted in the 'image and venue' approach. Thus, although culture was initially considered to be the privileged domain of national sovereignty, governments recognised that their only chance to control the *de facto* intervention of EU institutions in the book sector was to try locking in at the EU level policy models that suited their preferences. With such hopes in mind, the French and the German governments attempted to shift the decision-making process back towards an intergovernmental mode, in which they though they would be better able to change the prevailing image of the policy problem at the EU level.

Competition between images

An institutionally diverse coalition of actors opposed the deregulation of the book industry and actively supported the development of an interventionist policy at the EU level. From the 1980s onwards, European publishers, the European Parliament, DG Education and Culture within the Commission, and isolated member governments such as France – and Germany in the late 1990s – prevented the book policy sector from being purely governed by competition rules and contributed to the creation of European support mechanisms in the book sector.

Dirigiste governments' strategies within the Council of Ministers
The Commission and the ECJ were not the most favourable venues for the *dirigiste* coalition to impose its policy preferences for the latter favoured economic actors with a strong stake in market liberalisation. Thus, as in the audio-visual sector, member governments which felt challenged by the supranational policy developments (in Scharpf's 'hierarchical decision' mode) attempted to shift the decision-making process back to a mode dominated by intergovernmental negotiations.

The 1980s: first attempts to impose a dirigiste *policy image*   In the face of the first wake of EU regulatory and judicial interventions in the 1980s, France was the most active opponent of the approach developed by DG Competition and the ECJ. The objective of the French government was to initiate the drafting of an EU directive implementing the principle of fixed book prices in the European Union, thereby locking in its own policy model at the EU level. In June 1985, 150 professionals met in Arles at the invitation of the French Ministry of Culture (Le Monde, 13 June 1985) in a possible attempt to create some kind of 'epistemic community' (Haas 1992). A text was adopted, laying the foundations for an EU directive on fixed book prices. Because of the opposition of other member states, the adoption of EU-level regulation related to book pricing was however obstructed. When the French delegation made a proposal for an EU directive on book prices during the Culture Council of December 1985, other states indeed opposed the measure.[10]

Further indications of the conflict between member states appeared when the Commission issued the 1989 Communication *Books and Reading: A Cultural Challenge for Europe* (European Commission 1989). The Direction du Livre et de la Lecture (DLL)[11] in France reacted vehemently against the Communication, which stated that fixed book prices have never proved to be the most suitable means for improving editorial production and promoting distribution. The French delegation had to insist strongly on attenuating the terms of a resolution on the promotion of books and reading (OJ C 183, 20.7.1989), prepared by the Ministers of Culture within the Council. As a result of French demands, instead of stating that ministers 'show their interest' in the Commission's 1989 Communication, the resolution stated that the ministers 'note the general thrust of the Commission Communication'.[12] The French obtained the alteration of the wording of the resolution, but this anecdote sheds light on the prevalence of liberal views in the Council. Member states were not at all united on this issue and most of them did not perceive the need for EU-level intervention, thus presenting huge problems to the French.

The 1990s: renewed attempts of the dirigiste *coalition in the new telecommunications age*　In the 1990s, technological developments raised new regulatory issues. Traditional regulations at the national – or even European – level revealed themselves as increasingly inefficient in the new telecommunications age. With the Internet, any European citizen can purchase books from all sorts of locations. For instance, the Belgian online bookshop Proxis.com tried to attract customers by lowering prices by up to 23 per cent from the price fixed by the publisher (*Le Monde*, 10 August 1999, *Libération*, 23 March 2000). International technological developments therefore represented a serious threat to national-level interventionist policies.

The DLL within the French Ministry of Culture believed that the Commission sought to take advantage of the 'window of opportunity' presented by the new technological environment in order to attack national systems of regulation in the book policy sector (*Livres Hebdo*, 15 September 2000). Thus, for the second time, the French government acted as a 'policy entrepreneur' in order to reorient the policy debate at the EU level. France sought to raise some support for book trade regulation during the period of the French presidency in 2000 (*Livres Hebdo*, 7 July 2000). As in the audio-visual sector, informal strategies – such as meetings outside the Community framework – were brought into play in order to influence the setting of the European agenda. During the Culture Council of July 2000, France selected the economics of the book industry in Europe as one of the priority issues for debate (*Agence Europe*, 20 July 2000). Furthermore, the French Ministry of Culture organised the Strasbourg Conference on the Economics of the Book Industry in Europe in September 2000. Placing the issue of book trade regulation at the top of the policy agenda was the immediate objective of the meeting. By actively interfering in the field of book policy, France aimed to impose *dirigiste* programmatic ideas as workable solutions in the policy discourse.

According to an adviser working for the Ministry of Culture (interviewed by *Livres Hebdo*, 15 September 2000), the purpose of the Strasbourg conference was also to measure the extent to which other states were concerned by the maintenance of fixed book price systems. Thus, the French government clearly demonstrated its ability to shift the venue of the decision-making process to the intergovernmental arena, hoping to lead the way towards the drafting of a common solution in the 'joint-decision' mode that would allow member states more participation in the EU decision-making process.

In the 1990s, the coalition-building potential for the French was stronger than in the previous decade. A greater number of states was in favour of such fixed price systems. Germany and Austria had had their own system challenged by the European Commission. As noted earlier,

Michael Naumann, then Minister of Culture in Germany, was a vehement supporter of fixed price systems and represented a strong ally for the French government (*Les Echos*, 17 November 1998). In 1997, the Austrian delegation had presented a short document entitled *The Vienna Memorandum on Cross Border Fixed Book Prices in European Linguistic Areas* to the Council of Ministers (*Council Press Release*, 28 May 1998). In Germany, professionals in the publishing sector were actively lobbying the government so that it would support the drafting of a European directive on book prices (*Le Monde*, 28 September 2000). German and Austrian MEPs adopted a resolution stating that it would be desirable to harmonise rules on the fixing of book prices on the basis of French law (OJ C 042, 17.2.1999). German MEP Willy Rothley prepared, in collaboration with a group of parliamentarians, a draft directive on book prices including sales on the Internet. The proposal proposed to take into account the existence of linguistic areas within the EU and put an end to any ongoing legal uncertainty (*Le Monde*, 12 October 2000).

Furthermore, other member states had adopted regulations on book prices in the 1990s. Since 1996, Portugal, Greece, and recently, Austria, had adopted a fixed price system for books. Italy and Belgium are also close to legislating in the same direction. In September 1997, member states adopted a decision on cross-border fixed book prices in European linguistic areas which recognised the dual character of books as the bearers of cultural values and as merchandise, and strongly emphasised the importance of a balanced assessment of the cultural and economic aspects of books. The decision states, in particular, that:

> some member states intend to authorise or draw up complementary cross-border fixed book-price regulations together with another member state within a homogeneous linguistic area, being of the opinion that such regulations should be possible provided that the fixed price is limited to that linguistic area and to editions published in the language concerned. (OJ C 305, 7.10.1997)

However, opposition from several states – such as the UK and Scandinavian countries – and the feeling that fixed price systems could be best preserved by respecting the subsidiarity principle, resulted in a lack of intergovernmental support for EU-level legislation.[13] The Council, in its resolution of 12 February 2001 (OJ C 073, 6.3.2001) on the application of national fixed book price systems, merely pointed out that member states are free to decide whether or not to apply a national statutory or contractual book price system. In practice, few member states felt really challenged by the Commission's attacks, which were directed mainly against cross-border agreements, and the incentive structures for policy actors were not favourable to either France or Germany.

Thus, it is clear that member states which felt that their national legislation was challenged by EU intervention reacted strongly against supranational entrepreneurship and subsequently behaved as 'first movers' in the fostering of a European-level legislative arrangement that would take into account their national interests. To do so, France and Germany attempted to portray books from a different perspective, i.e. as the bearers of cultural values that deserve special treatment. They shifted the venue of policy-making towards the intergovernmental venue, hoping that by reasserting member states' desire to participate in the decision-making process they would change the image of the policy problem at the EU level. However, the 'book case' shows that EU governments cannot impose an alternative image of a policy problem when their policy preferences do not converge. France and Germany were forced to lower their ambitions in the face of other member states' hostility or lack of interest for a European fixed price system. Interventionist governments could only obtain side-payments and, more significantly, be successful in securing national legislative arrangements against the intervention of other levels of governments.

The European Parliament as a favourable venue for the defence of the dirigiste *image*

If the Commission was impervious to publishers' appeals (*European Report*, 13 July 1991), the EP showed more sensitivity towards issues of fixed book prices. As in the audio-visual sector, the EP attracted lobbyists who did not enjoy such easy access to the Commission and national governments (Mazey and Richardson 2001). Furthermore, the EP always showed greater sensitivity for cultural concerns than the Commission or the ECJ.

As early as 1981 (OJ C 50, 9.3.1981), the EP adopted a resolution related to book prices, stating that the book policy sector should not be ruled by exclusively economic principles. In 1993, the EP adopted another resolution suggesting that the Commission should regulate price fixing in homogenous linguistic areas (OJ C 42, 15.2.1993). Finally in November 1998, the Parliament called upon the Commission to recognise national and regional measures aimed at promoting books (OJ C 379, 7.12.1998). The resolution also stated that the rules on the fixing of book prices should be harmonised on the basis of French law by means of a directive, and called for solutions to be found in order to deal with electronic commerce. Today, the EP has prepared a project for a directive which would allow member states to introduce or maintain price-fixing systems for books within their own territories (following an initiative from the German MEP Willy Rothley, as mentioned above). However, the system would refrain from imposing any additional obligations on the states that do not possess such systems. Thus, the EP was a more favourable institutional structure for the proponents of *dirigiste* policies and became the venue for 'cultural' lobbyists as a result.

Domestic interest groups also attempted to impose, in the face of EU institutions' intervention, an alternative policy image portraying books as a special commodity at the EU level. 'Cultural' interest groups, which were efficiently mobilised by *dirigiste* governments, developed active strategies aimed at reorienting the EU agenda (*Libération*, 30 September 2000). The Federation of European Publishers (FEP), which represents the national associations of book publishers of all member states, is the most powerful interest group defending national systems of fixed book prices against the application of EU competition rules. The FEP supported the idea of a European 'floor price' for books (*European Report*, 25 April 1992). As early as the beginning of the 1990s, the FEP initiated several meetings with European officials to convince them of the necessity to extend the national systems to the whole of the EU (*European Report*, 13 July 1991). The European Booksellers Federation and the European Writers Congress both support the FEP in pressing for the implementation of this policy (Federation of European Publishers 1995). In the Declaration of the European Writers Congress, the 'essential importance of not reducing the book to a commodity but of valuing it as a *cultural asset* [author's emphasis]' was reasserted (European Writers Congress 2000).

In sum, the policy actors which were supporting *dirigiste* policies in the book sector attempted to impose an alternative way of tackling book policy issues at the EU level. Member governments shifted the decision-making process back towards the intergovernmental mode, and interest groups in the book sector attempted to use the EP as a channel for the defence of their interests. However, the diversity of actors' preferences, combined with EU-level decisional constraints, has made the selection of a *dirigiste* policy option impossible.

Decisional constraints and the dominance of liberal preferences
EU-level intervention in the book sector has so far consisted of promoting a negative form of integration in the 'hierarchical' decision mode. Member governments did not agree upon any common solution. Essentially, in so far as EU institutions had been successful in shifting the decision-making process towards the supranational mode (by making use of their judicial and regulatory powers), the liberal image found a more favourable reception in the institutional context of the EU.

The only way to alter the prevailing image concerning the regulation of the book market would have been to gather sufficient intergovernmental support for an interventionist policy option. Most member states, however, did not feel that their policy traditions were challenged by EU institutions' use of their Treaty-based powers and were satisfied with the nature of the status quo. Moreover, the majority of EU states were in favour of the liberalisation of cultural markets. At the beginning of the

1980s, most European states were ruled by right-wing governments implementing liberal policies. For instance, there has been a shift in British economic policy from Keynesian-inspired principles to liberal or monetarist ones during the 1980s. Margaret Thatcher provided an ideological backing to free markets, resulting, as far as this study is concerned, in the UK being the most vehement objector to any positive harmonisation in the cultural sector. More generally, liberal ideas dominated the political agenda in Europe during the 1980s. In the same way that Keynesian ideas had an influence over policy-making in the 1970s, the liberals played a large political role during the 1980s (see for instance Hall 1992, 1993). In the 1990s, with the entrance of three Northern European states to the EU, the constellation of actors' interests became even more favourable to the selection of liberal options. Thus, book policy issues were perceived from an economic perspective by a majority of liberal governments within the Council of Ministers. Given that it was necessary to reach a consensual agreement within the Council, it was impossible for the *dirigistes* to impose their policy preferences.

However, the same coalition patterns conditioned the choice of policy options in the audio-visual and copyright sectors. What are the variables, therefore, which can account for the selection of different policy options from one sector to another? Why has no EU-level policy solution other than negative integration been implemented in the book policy sector, at least so far? In fact, in the two other policy sectors, if the majority of member governments in the Council seemed to favour the liberalisation of cultural markets, they also seemed to favour the delegation of policy sovereignty. The nature of the status quo, fundamentally, was too undesirable – as already demonstrated in the audio-visual case. On the contrary, most states were satisfied with the status quo in the book policy sector; in fact, most of them did not feel that their policy traditions were challenged by the EU institutions' use of their Treaty-based powers. Furthermore, EU institutions did not push for the design of a common solution concerning fixed price systems for books, as they did for the regulation of broadcasting. Therefore, only *dirigiste* states wanted a common solution drafted along interventionist principles, and they could not gather sufficient support for it.

Conclusion

The Europeanisation process of the book policy sector can be characterised, as in the audio-visual case, as the result of two interconnected and parallel processes. On the one hand, the ECJ, the European Commission and commercial private actors favoured an approach based on the application of economic principles to cultural policies. European institutions portrayed books from an economic perspective so as to make their intervention in this new policy area more legitimate, while private commercial actors, in typical losers' appeal strategies, used the European venue to ease the change of rhetoric, and thereby the change of policies, at the national level. The interaction between venue and image produced a self-reinforcing impetus, which resulted in the Europeanisation of the policy debate and further market liberalisation.

On the other hand, member states with the most salient policy preferences and 'cultural' interest groups entered the 'game' – at least partly in reaction to the Commission entrepreneurship – and aimed to reorient the debate in a direction that was more favourable to their interests. France, and Germany in the 1990s, opposed supranational entrepreneurship and attempted to lock in their preferred policy model at the EU level against potential attacks from the Commission and the Court. The French and the German governments, behaving as policy entrepreneurs, tried to change the decision mode at the EU level so as to ensure that member states would be involved in the process. This shows that member states favour the delegation of policy competence at the EU level essentially as a *reaction* against developments that they would not be able to control in any case. In most policy areas related to 'cultural affairs' the French government played a more active role than other EU governments. This was largely because French policy traditions were more often challenged by EU institutions' intervention those that of other EU states. Developments in the book policy sector demonstrate that a similar pattern can apply to other member states (i.e. Germany here) when the latter feel equally pressurised by EU-level policy developments (ECJ judgements and Commission decisions). This confirms that the use of rhetoric by a given jurisdiction as a way of controlling policy (or the search for different venues by policy actors as a way of changing the images of policy problems) *induces* other jurisdictions to react and enter the rhetoric contest as a way of preserving or regaining control over policy.

However, *dirigiste* member states failed to impose an interventionist policy image at the EU level. In fact, no common solution at all has been agreed upon so far. Most EU states were either in favour of the liberalisation of book trade or felt that their domestic legislative arrangements could be best preserved in the absence of any EU-level policy solution. The specific institutional features of the EU, which tend to favour negative integration, and the strength of the liberal coalition within the Council of Ministers coincided to make the selection of liberal policy solutions more likely.

Yet the dominance of the liberal coalition within the Council of Ministers could *also* be observed in the audio-visual sector and, as will be seen, in the field of copyright policy. Despite these cross-sector similarities, in the two other cases examined in the book, a common solution was implemented under the 'joint-decision mode', thus giving member states some influence in the formulation of EU-level policies. Essentially, the divergence in policy outcomes lies in the fact that most states did not feel challenged by European institutions' intervention, which was directed essentially against cross-border agreements, in the book policy sector. Put simply, European institutions did not sufficiently alter the nature of the default position so as to ensure that the venue of policy would change. The debate was not only about policy content but also about the level of policy intervention. This means that unless states' policy preferences converge (and they therefore agree to a common solution because it secures legislative arrangements that most of them favour), the nature of the status quo is a crucial determinant of member states' decisions to enact legislative arrangements at the EU level. In a context where member states disagree over the content of polity, a common solution is opted for only when the default solution is too unattractive.

Notes

1 Article 85 (now Article 81) prohibits as incompatible with the common market all agreements between undertakings, decisions by associations of undertakings and concerted practices which may affect trade between member states and which have as their object or effect the prevention, restriction or distortion of competition within the common market.

2 The example of the *Sammelsrevers* agreements will be discussed in further detail in the section on EU law and Germany below.

3 The example of the NBA will be discussed in further detail in the section on EU law and Britain below.

4 Note from the SAI on the Culture Council of 12–13 June 1986 in Amsterdam – Archives from the French Ministry of Culture.

5 Interview with Jack Lang, former Minister of Culture in France, Paris, 16 January 1999.

6 Case *Leclerc/Syndicat des libraires de Loire-Ocean* in 1985 (ECJ 1985c); Case *Ministère public* v. *Michel Cognet* in 1986 (ECJ 1986a), Case *Darras et Tostain* in 1986 (ECJ 1986b).

7 Minutes of the SGCI meeting on book policy issues of 9 June 1986 – Archives of the French Ministry of Culture.

8 Author's translation.

9 Interview with British official, DCMS, London, 18 May 2001.

10 Minutes of the SGCI meeting on book policy issues, 9 June 1986 – Archives of the French Ministry of Culture.

11 The DLL is the division in charge of the book policy sector within the French Ministry of Culture.

12 Confidential document – Archives of the French Ministry of Culture.

13 Interview with French official, Paris, 19 December 2001.

6

The Communitarisation of copyright policies

The copyright[1] sector presents another extremely interesting case of Europeanisation – and subsequently, Communitarisation – in the cultural field. In the 1970s, national level policies in the copyright sector were challenged by international technological developments and European institutions' policy entrepreneurship. In a similar fashion as in the book and audio-visual sectors, the ECJ and the European Commission intervened in a 'hierarchical decision' mode (Scharpf 2000), making use of their agenda-setting, regulatory and judicial powers. Five directives (three of which are examined in this chapter) were adopted as early as the 1980s and numerous judgements were passed by the ECJ long before the 1992 Treaty reform. In the copyright sector, if private subnational actors played a role in triggering the application of EU law in EU states, their influence in the Europeanisation process was less crucial than in the book policy sector. In the present case, it will be argued that European institutions *autonomously* developed a proactive integration agenda, justifying their intervention essentially with reference to the need to respond to new technological developments and ensure the functioning of the Single Market.

As happened in the audio-visual and book policy sectors, member states with salient policy preferences and 'cultural' interest groups[2] reacted against the liberal approach developed by the Commission and the ECJ and aimed to impose a different image of the policy problems at stake at the EU level. Thus, a *dirigiste* coalition, led by the French government and rights holders' groups, opposed a liberal coalition composed of Northern European states and consumers' groups. Each of these coalitions endeavoured to change the image of the policy problems at stake in order to control policy. The *dirigistes* attempted to define authors' rights as personal rights to be discussed on the level of human rights, while the liberals defended an economic definition of authors' rights, conceiving them primarily as property rights.

Two phases can be distinguished in the harmonisation of copyright legislation. In the early 1980s, the directives adopted implemented a high level of harmonisation, transposing at the EU level the 'Latin' conception of the *droit d'auteur* (in contrast to the Anglo-Saxon copyright system). The *dirigiste* coalition was successful in reorienting the policy debate at the EU level. Yet the 2001 Directive on copyright in the information society only initiated a 'minimal' level harmonisation within the EU, meant to cope with new technological challenges. During this second phase, the 'Information Society' image was used by liberal policy actors in order to promote a framework of regulation designed to generate competition. At the heart of current debates about copyright law and policy are some fundamentally different conceptions about the nature of intellectual property and its role in the information economy. What are the factors, then, that determined how policy options were chosen at the EU level? In other words, how can we explain the fact that different policy images came to dominate the policy debate at different periods of time?

In contrast to the situation in the book policy sector, where national policies could to some extent still be implemented, the contours of the policy debate in the copyright field made any common solution preferable to the status quo for member governments. Yet in a context where states' policy preferences strongly diverged, *dirigiste* states' room for manoeuvre was limited to the possibility of obtaining a satisfying political compromise at the EU level. The need for a common solution was perceived as even greater in the late 1990s than in the 1980s, thus exacerbating these dynamics. Furthermore, it will be demonstrated that alterations in the constellation of stakeholders involved in the decision-making process and in their ability to frame the debate, account for the selection of dissimilar policy options at different periods of time.

After presenting a brief sketch of member states' policy traditions in the copyright policy sector, the first supranational initiatives towards the harmonisation of EU copyright legislation, and the competition between images and venues which ensued from it, are scrutinised. The chapter then goes on to analyse EU-level policy outcomes, starting with the factors which led to a rather high level of harmonisation in the 1980s before looking at the limitations of EU harmonisation concerning resale rights and private copying legislation. The final section focuses on the 2001 Directive on copyright and related rights in the information society (2001/29/CE),[3] scrutinising the changes in the negotiating context which led to the selection of an entirely dissimilar type of policy options than in the 1980s.

Copyright v. *droit d'auteur*

Copyright regimes in EU countries are embedded in long-standing policy traditions. There are notable differences in outlook between member states, which are clearly illustrated by the contrast between the English usage of 'copyright' and the French usage of *'droit d'auteur'*. The French legislation on authors' rights, personified by the use of the *'droit d'auteur'* concept, is the most protective one for authors in the EU. In the French tradition, authors' rights are personal rights, to be discussed on the level of human rights. By contrast, the Anglo-Saxon tradition conceives 'copyright' as an economic right. The UK 1988 Copyright, Designs and Patents Act states that 'copyright is a property right'. With the exception of the UK and Ireland, all other EU states have copyright legislation, where *moral rights* – the right for authors to protect their good name, their reputation and their works – are central (Holderness 1998). These rights are inalienable, the only exception being the Dutch legislation, under which authors may contract to waive their rights.

Member states have also taken radically different attitudes on the issue of paternity – i.e. who is considered to be the creator of intellectual property. In the broadcasting sector, the status of 'author' is granted to the intellectual creator of a cinematographic work in countries where the 'continental' tradition applies. Those included in this category vary from country to country but include, for instance, the authors of pre-existing works and all those who have made contributions to the cinematographic work (Davies and Von Rauscher auf Weeg 1983). In Anglo-Saxon countries, by contrast, the legislation gives the status of 'author' of the cinematographic work to the *producer*. At the heart of these legal traditions are some fundamentally different conceptions about the nature of intellectual property and its role in the information economy. Intellectual property conceptualised as a universal human right differs in fundamental ways from its treatment as an economic interest under intellectual property law. A human rights approach is predicated on the centrality of protecting and nurturing human dignity and the common good. If intellectual property is conceptualised as an economic interest, intellectual property issues will be governed by economic goals such as improved competitiveness or profitability. Thus, attempts to harmonise copyright legislation at the EU level were hampered by the fundamental differences between EU legislative traditions (Davies 1981).

The role of European institutions

In 1974, the European Parliament had already issued a resolution on cultural issues mentioning the copyright sector. This was the first reference to European intervention in the field of intellectual property rights. The Parliament called upon the Commission to propose measures on 'the protection of the cultural heritage, royalties and other related intellectual property rights' (OJ C 62, 30.5.1974). The Commission published further official documents in the late 1970s and 1980s. As happened in the audio-visual and book policy sectors, the Court and the Commission intervened in the copyright policy sector when no competence in the field appeared in the Treaty – it was only in 1992 that article 128 of the Maastricht Treaty provided a potential legal basis for EU copyright policy, in the *dirigistes'* view. Consequently, the rationale for EU action in the area of copyright focused on the completion of the Single Market and on the need to deal with international technological developments. This approach provoked strong resistance in the states in which legislative regimes were favourable to authors.

Developing a rationale for Community action
Adapting to the new technological environment   Already preparing the ground for future action, the Commission mentioned the harmonisation of copyright legislation at the European level in the 1977 *Communication on Community Action in the Cultural Sector* (European Commission 1977).[4] Technical progress was presented as one of the key motives for supranational intervention. In particular, the multiplication of the means of reproduction of the written works, sounds and images was portrayed as a major policy problem. Addressing the issue of the reproduction of written works, the Commission suggested that 'a sum ... be included in the selling price of equipment and the material they [the consumers] use to guarantee the remuneration which authors, publishers, and performers are entitled to expect' (European Commission 1977: 13). In the 1982 *Communication on Stronger Community Action in the Cultural Sector* (European Commission 1982),[5] technological developments were once again presented as the most urgent motive for EU intervention. The Commission made it clear that the rights of authors were threatened by the 'anachronisms of legislation, which is trailing well behind technology' (European Commission 1982: 16), thereby paving the way for EU intervention.

In the first Commission publication which focused exclusively on copyright issues, the *Green Paper on Copyright and the Challenge of Technology* (European Commission 1988),[6] the Commission firmly stated that new technologies had entailed the *de facto* abolition of national frontiers, making the application of national copyright law obsolete. The Green Paper focused on the need for repressing piracy of sound and video recordings, audio-visual home copying, distribution rights and computer programs. However, the Green Paper did not tackle certain aspects of copyright law, such as authors' moral rights and artists' resale rights (for an extended discussion of how the 'economic' approach developed by the Commission influenced the selection of the themes discussed in the Green Paper, see Möller 1989). Proposals for supranational intervention were limited to technical matters and essentially promoted a negative form of integration.

Completing the Single Market

In order to justify the need for EU-level harmonisation of intellectual property law, the Commission also argued that disparities in national legislative traditions had a negative impact on the free movement of goods. In the field of intellectual property, it was difficult for the Commission to develop a copyright policy on the basis of the 'continental' model in the absence of treaty basis in this policy area. Developing an 'economic' approach towards copyright issues was therefore an efficient way to circumvent the absence of EU competence in this field.

In the 1977 Commission Communication, the harmonisation of resale rights legislation was presented as necessary in order to prevent 'a situation which, in so far as it distort[ed] competition, [was] inadmissible as regards the functioning of the common market' (European Commission 1977: 16). A similar argument was developed concerning the harmonisation of the length of copyright protection. The Commission stated that the diversity in the length of copyright protection in the EU had negative effects on the free movement of literary, musical and artistic works. The opposition expressed by the Commission to the 1978 Dietz Report (see Harris 1978), a study ordered by its own services as part of a more general concern for the development of an EU-level cultural policy, sheds light on the Commission's preference for a market-oriented approach. The content of the study was criticised for granting too much importance to the cultural aspects of copyright policy. This was made clear in 1985, when the copyright sector was identified by the *White Paper on the Completion of the Single Market* (European Commission 1985b)[7] as one of the areas in which harmonisation at the EU level was crucial.

The liberal approach developed by the Commission also appears in the documents issued in the 1980s that were specifically dedicated to copyright issues. When presenting its fundamental motives for addressing copyright issues in the 1988 Green Paper, the Commission stated that obstacles and legal differences that obstruct or distort cross-frontier trade had to be eliminated. The Commission stated that 'the effect of the provisions of the Treaty on free circulation of goods may be said to apply broadly, *mutatis mutandis*, to goods subject to copyright' (European Commission 1988: 19). The Commission also made it clear that it favoured the Anglo-Saxon model of copyright. As predicted by the 'image and venue' approach, the Commission attempted to impose a liberal policy image on copyright matters as a way of extending the remit of its competence. The Commission in fact paved the way for its preferred course of action, should an opportunity for policy intervention open up.

Concerning copyright legislation in the broadcasting sector, the guidelines contained in the proposal for the TWF Directive suggested what amounted to a dramatic liberalisation of the practice of copyright protection (European Commission 1984). In order to promote intra-community trade, the Commission recommended the granting by member states of a compulsory licence allowing trans-frontier distribution of intellectual works within Europe (Negrine and Papathanassopoulos 1990).[8]

Applying a liberal image to copyright policy issues allowed the Commission – and the ECJ – to apply the principles of the Treaty to this policy area. The next section examines how these institutions took concrete initiatives, by making use of their regulatory and legislative powers, in order to impose the principles of the Treaty in the copyright policy sector.

The ECJ as the target of losers' appeal strategies

Acting as a 'catalyst in the integration process' (Dehousse 1998: 71), the ECJ – and the Commission – extended the remit of their competence to the copyright sector even when the overall question of harmonising European copyright law was not discussed by member states. As has happened in the book and audio-visual sectors, ECJ judgements made it clear that copyright was within the control of the Treaty of Rome (for an analysis of the Court intervention in the copyright sector, see for instance McKnight 1992; Gotzen 1994). The approach developed by the Commission and the Court also suited the interests of private sub-national actors, who realised that they could use the legal sphere to achieve ends that could not be achieved through the ordinary policy process.

The theory of exhaustion of rights and the 'existence/exercise' dichotomy

Several doctrines developed by the ECJ were particularly challenging for national laws on copyright. To start with, the ECJ established the theory of exhaustion of rights, based on the principle that, where goods are lawfully placed on the market of a member state, copyright cannot be relied upon to restrict the free circulation of those goods. In principle, exhaustion of rights can arise in all cases where copies of a copyright work have been marketed by the copyright owner where the copyright protection does not or no longer exists (Dietz 1980). Thus, in *Musik-Vertrieb* v. *GEMA* (ECJ 1981a), the ECJ ruled that disparities between national legislative traditions did not justify practices that are not compatible with the Treaty. The ECJ case was initiated by two German record companies, which appealed against a ruling from a German Court. The German case had been raised in response to an initiative from the Gesellschaft für Musikalische Aufführungs (GEMA), the German copyright management society. GEMA wanted to require payment from the record companies of a fee reflecting the difference between the royalty applicable in one member state (i.e. Germany) and the lower royalty already paid in the member state where the records were already in circulation. The German Supreme Court stated that GEMA was entitled to invoke national legislation in order to claim payment of an additional royalty. The record companies realised that a Euro-litigation strategy could offer them additional means to pursue their objectives and appealed against the German judgement. Despite the intervention of the French, Belgian and Italian governments in support of GEMA, the ECJ ruled that what the German authors' society sought to achieve was absolutely prohibited by the Treaty and that European law had to be interpreted as precluding the application of such national legislation. In the 1988 Green Paper on copyright matters, the Commission explicitly asserted the primacy of the completion of the Single Market over the protection of copyright, explaining that 'as regards the free circulation of copyright goods, the developments of the exhaustion doctrine ... has ensured that national copyright laws will not have adverse or divergent effects on the functioning of the common market' (European Commission 1988: 161).

The ECJ developed a second doctrine, that of distinguishing between the *existence* and the *exercise* of intellectual property rights. The doctrine indubitably undermined the national protection afforded to intellectual property, since a right which cannot be exercised can only be deemed to exist in theory. Thus, in the case *Deutsche Grammophon* v. *Metro* (ECJ 1971) for instance, the ECJ ruled that although the Treaty does not affect the existence of rights recognised by the legislation of a member state, the exercise of such rights might fall within the prohibitions laid down by the Treaty.

European judges introduced notions that policy actors could not have imposed through national channels. The development of new doctrines specifically designed for the copyright sector shows the role of the ECJ as a favourable venue for the defence of the 'liberal image'. The Commission and the ECJ portrayed societies of authors as *undertakings* which, by controlling the main repertoire of copyrights in the territory of the member state in which they operate, were in a dominant position. Changing the 'image' of the policy problem also allowed for a shift in the venue of policy-making.

Private actors as proponents of the liberal image	The propensity of European institutions to extend the remit of their competence to new policy areas coincided with private actors' demands for more lenient legislative regimes.

The joined cases *Lucazeau* v. *Sacem* (ECJ 1989a) represented a serious challenge to French copyright policies.[9] Several discotheque owners accused the Société des Auteurs Compositeurs Editeurs de Musique (SACEM), the French authors' society, of charging excessively high rates and refusing to grant licenses for certain sections of its repertory. In response to their complaints, the Commission commenced a formal investigation into the compatibility of the level of royalty required by SACEM with Article 86 (now Article 82) of the Treaty. The ECJ ruled that the high royalties charged by SACEM to discotheques constituted unfair trading conditions prohibited by Article 86. Furthermore, the ECJ added that Article 85 (now Article 81) of the Treaty prohibits any concerted practice by copyright-management societies refusing to grant direct access to its repertoire to users established in another member state. Despite the inclination of Commission President Jacques Delors to give more credit to the demands of French 'cultural' groups,[10] the campaigns orchestrated by the creative community failed to prevent the ECJ from imposing EU competition law on the copyright sector. In fact, French private actors had recognised that resorting to the EU venue could help them change the image of the problem –copyright societies were portrayed as undertakings in a dominant position – and thus policies themselves.

In another ECJ judgement, *Coditel* v. *Ciné-Vog* (ECJ 1980b and ECJ 1981c), the cable television channel Coditel had invoked EU law in order to justify its right to broadcast the film *Le Boucher*. The producer of the film had granted the exclusive right to distribute the film to the channel Ciné-Vog, which claimed that its right had been violated. However, the ECJ chose to favour the protection of authors' rights and followed the opinions of Ciné-Vog and of the British, French and Dutch governments.

In a similar way, in the case *Warner Bros* v. *Christiansen* (ECJ 1988c), the ECJ ruled that the rights of the author – namely the exclusive right of performance and the exclusive right of reproduction – were not called into question by the rules of the Treaty. The ECJ was in this case dealing with the conflict between Danish authorities and a video-shop owner who wanted to eschew the rental rights legislation in Denmark and invoked European law. The ECJ supported the application of Danish copyright legislation.

In all the landmark cases examined, attacks against national copyright legislation were initiated by private actors, such as discotheque owners, the owner of a video-shop in the case of Danish legislation and record companies in Germany. Looking at the cases that were raised before the ECJ reveals that most preliminary rulings were related to the legislation of states where copyright law grants a high level of protection to authors, such as France and Germany.[11] As already observed in the audio-visual and in the book policy sectors, private actors had a higher incentive to use the European venue in order to change the prevailing image of copyright policy issues in states where constraining legislative systems were deeply embedded in national policy traditions. If the ECJ did not systematically rule in favour of EU competition law principles, it was always reluctant to recognise any general principle that could ensure the protection of copyright legislation against competition law, and thus represented a favourable venue for the defence of the liberal image.

Competition between venues and images: authors' rights as personal rights v. authors' rights as property rights

'Cultural' interest groups reacted with dismay to EU policy developments in the field of copyright. The 1988 Green Paper was strongly criticised by 'cultural' groups for focusing exclusively on economic and competition policy goals without addressing the specific concerns of authors' rights protection (*Le Monde Diplomatique*, July 1990). In September 1988, artistic personalities met in Delphes and drafted the European Charter for the Defence and the Future of Audio-visual Creation. The Delphes Charter, stating that 'cinematographic and audio-visual works are not a product like any others but an essential element of living culture' (cited in *Le Monde Radio-Television* 17 October 1988),[12] was intended to signify the concerns of the artistic community to national and EU policy-makers. In fact, authors attempted to portray authors' rights as personal rights that could not be assimilated to a simple property right.

National governments, and most notably France, where policy preferences in the cultural sector are the most salient, felt that their policy traditions were being questioned by the approach developed by EU institutions. Authors are powerful economic actors in France and the French government was also defending strong commercial interests by resisting any alteration of its legislation.[13] Thus, although it did not initially favour any delegation of competence to the EU level in the copyright sector, the French government had to reconsider its strategy.[14] After the publication of the 1988 Green Paper on copyright, the French felt that a 'defensive' position, which consisted of lobbying the Commission and the ECJ in order to 'secure' national arrangements, was no longer sustainable. Consequently, the most 'rational' option consisted of initiating a belligerent strategy aimed at locking in the French model at the EU level. Jack Lang, cited in *Le Monde*, made it clear that harmonisation of copyright law at the EU level had become a priority. Yet he favoured a high level of harmonisation for copyright law, arguing that 'lowering [the French] regime of copyright protection in order to conciliate different legislative approaches from the Anglo-Saxon tradition and from the Latin tradition would not be good for the Europe of Culture' and that 'on the contrary, for national identities to be preserved , it was necessary to rely on a strong level of protection for creators' (*Le Monde*, 5 July 1990).[15] For the French, the decision to transpose the policy debate at the EU level was the best strategy in a context that was defined by the *de facto* intervention of the Commission and the ECJ.

France, most Southern European countries, Germany, and 'cultural' interest groups formed an 'advocacy coalition' (Sabatier 1998) aimed at changing the way policy problems were framed at the EU level. Therefore, as in the book and audio-visual sectors, a *dirigiste* coalition of actors entered the 'game' in order to change the prevailing image of copyright policy issues at the EU level. As will be seen in the following section, the Commission documents which were issued after the 1988 Green paper – the 1989 *Communication on Books and Reading* (European Commission 1989) and the 1991 *Follow-up to the Green Paper* (European Commission 1991) – gave some weight to *dirigiste* concerns.

Thus, two parallel processes were in operation. On the one hand, the ECJ, the 'economic' DGs of the European Commission and private actors favoured an approach based on the application of economic principles to the copyright sector. Because their powers were more extended with regard to competition law, the ECJ and the Commission used the liberal image in order to assert the legitimacy of EU competence in the copyright sector – and successfully shifted the venue of decision-making towards the EU level. On the other hand, certain member states and 'cultural' interest groups entered the 'game' – at least partly in reaction to European insti-tutions' intervention – and aimed to reorient the debate towards a direction more favourable to their interests. In such a situation, what are the factors that determine which policy options are selected, when two coalitions of actors aim to impose their policy preferences and control policy?

The 1980s: explaining the success of the cultural coalition

The 1980s copyright directives ensured a high level of protection for European authors. The main victory for the *dirigistes* was the transposi-tion at the EU level of the 'Latin' tradition of authors' rights, in which the creator of an artistic work is considered to be its main author. An official from the French Ministry of Culture, who was in charge of the legislation on intellectual property from 1991 onwards, considers the influence of France to be crucial in determining the orientations of European legisla-tion in the copyright sector.[16] More generally, the positions defended by the 'cultural' lobby – and that were followed by the French government, in particular – were taken as a basis in the process of selecting EU policy options, at least when the latter dealt with matters that were of an essen-tially 'technical nature'.

The policy debate 'captured' by the cultural lobby
If the Commission had a propensity to act as a policy entrepreneur in the copyright sector, it was also amenable to the demands of 'cultural' inter-est groups. The opposition expressed against the 1988 Green Paper – and to the proposal for the TWF Directive – made it clear that European initiatives based solely on the extension of the Treaty principles to copy-right matters would face national level protests. As a result, the Commission followed a similar pattern to that for the renewal of the TWF

Directive, and sought to anticipate professionals' demands.

The Commission presented the need to regulate cable and satellite broadcasting as the most urgent matter to be dealt with at the EU level. Copyright issues were indeed considered to be the 'missing chapter' (Collins 1994) of the TWF Directive (89/552/EEC). Furthermore, the Commission pointed to the need for regulating new forms of broadcasting. During the preparatory phase of the Directive on satellite broadcasting and cable retransmission (93/83/EEC),[17] the Commission decided to enable the interested parties to participate in the policy debate (*European Report*, 29 September 1990). Martin Bangemann, then Internal Market Commissioner, and Jean Dondelinger, then Culture Commissioner, prepared a discussion paper designed to assess the views of the parties. When the Commission presented its proposals to the EU Ministers of Culture in November 1990, France spoke out again, with the support of Portugal, on the importance of copyright protection (*European Report*, 21 November 1990).

The final Directive on cable and satellite broadly satisfied the French delegation and 'cultural' interest groups (*Les Echos*, 7 April 1993). In April 1993, European Ministers responsible for the Internal Market portfolio managed to hammer out a political agreement on the substance of the common position on satellite and cable television copyright rules (*European Report*, 8 April 1993). The compromise rejected the system of compulsory licence (which would restrain authors' control over their works) initially proposed by the Commission. This solution had been strongly condemned by Catherine Tasca, then Minister for Communication in France, in her inauguration speech at the Eurovisioni International Cinema and Television Festival in October 1990 (*Le Monde*, 9 October 1990). Her position reflected the views of the rights holders, who had expressed almost unanimous resistance to the idea of a compulsory licence (Dreier 1991). The text of the Directive was actually similar to the proposals contained in the resolution adopted by professionals (authors, producers and public and private television channels) in Rome in October 1990.

Harmonising the term of copyright protection within the EU was another priority for the Commission. When it came to the stage, the Commission argued that disparities among member states' legislation on the term of protection of copyright formed an obstacle to freedom of movement and competition in the Single Market. Most member states allowed copyright protection for fifty years after the death of the author, apart from Spain where the length of protection was sixty years and France and Germany where copyright was protected for seventy years (*European Report*, 19 June 1991). In the same way as for the Directive on cable and satellite, the Commission sought to anticipate interest groups' demands concerning the term of copyright protection in order to avoid resistance at a later stage of the negotiation process (*Le Monde*, 13 November 1990). In a first stage, the Commission services drew up a questionnaire, that was to be sent to the actors interested by the issue (*European Report*, 13 March 1991). The questionnaire asked professionals whether they thought that harmonisation at the EU level was necessary and whether a harmonised term of protection should run for fifty years, seventy years or a different period after the death of the author. In a second stage, the Commission organised a round-table meeting for interested parties in June 1991. Those present at the hearing agreed that seventy years should elapse after an author's death before his/her work became public property (*European Report*, 19 June 1991). The opinions that were expressed served as the basis for the Commission proposals for a Directive harmonising the term of protection of copyright (93/98/EEC).[18] The use of proactive lobbying strategies allowed broadcasting circles to progressively construct a new image of the policy problem.

When it came to the stage of policy negotiations, conflicting views were expressed at the Internal Market Council meeting of November 1992 (*European Report*, 14 November 1992). The Netherlands, Luxembourg and Denmark, supported to a lesser extent by Ireland and Portugal, took the view that a seventy-year protection period was excessive. However, a political agreement favouring high-level harmonisation was reached in June 1993 (*European Report*, 16 June 1993). The states that were opposed to the seventy-year period voted against the text, but the latter was adopted with a qualified majority (*European Report*, 30 October 1993). The Directive on the term of copyright protection based itself on the highest existing level of protection in Europe – authors benefited from such a level of protection in Germany and in France for musical works. Philippe Lemaitre argued in *Le Monde* that 'in the interest of the French cultural lobby, the only way to harmonise legislation in this sensitive sector while respecting vested interests was to operate on the basis of the longest protection' (*Le Monde*, 16 June 1993). High-level harmonisation was implemented to the disadvantage of consumer organisations that were supporting the 'right to copy' for the public (Collins and Murroni 1996).

The same policy pattern applies to the proposals for the Directive on rental rights and lending rights in the field of intellectual property (92/100/EEC).[19] Already in the 1988 Green Paper, the Commission argued that the introduction of a rental rights in all EU member states should be considered a priority. Technological developments were mentioned as the main motive for promoting EU-level harmonisation of rental and lending rights. The Commission was especially worried about the new copying facilities that made it very easy to copy records and cassettes on a large scale without having to pay a copyright fee (*European*

Report, 5 December 1990). Moreover, legislation on rental and lending rights differed widely in the EU. For instance, while most EU countries had rental rights systems, Ireland and the Netherlands had no legislation for these matters (*Le Monde*, 8 January 1991). As for lending rights, they were covered neither by Irish nor by Italian copyright law.

In the 1988 Green Paper, the Commission had explained that a compromise would have to be found between 'the right to authorise rental' and 'the right to an equitable remuneration'. The protection of authors did not appear to be the main priority of the Commission. However, in the 1989 *Communication on Books and Reading* (European Commission 1989), the Commission's policy proposals were more substantial and highlighted the Commission's willingness to develop EU-level policies that would take into account authors' considerations. Thus, proposals concerning rental and lending rights followed the same pattern as other proposals for the harmonisation of copyright law. Although the initial approach as laid down in the 1988 Green Paper proposed that EU-level harmonisation should be aimed at facilitating the functioning of the Single Market, 'cultural' groups succeeded in taking control of the prevailing image of the policy problem and later proposals were made on the basis of the professionals' recommendations.

During policy negotiations, the definition of rights holders in relation to cinematographic or audio-visual works was the most strongly debated issue. The UK wanted legal persons (such as production companies) to be considered as possible authors, while France believed that only an individual should be regarded as such. The Commission had proposed that the director of a film be considered as its author and the producer as its co-author. Three delegations – Luxembourg, Ireland and the UK – expressed reservations on this point. The first two dropped their opposition and voted in favour of the common position and the UK abstained from the vote (*European Report*, 8 December 1990). Thus, the Directive stipulates that member states should consider the director of a film as its author, with the option of considering the producer as co-author (*European Report*, 8 December 1990). The Directive on rental rights was received positively by French interest groups representing creators, such as SACEM (*Le Monde*, 8 January 1991). The content of the Directive also pleased the International Federation of the Phonographic Industry (IFPI), which represents the interests of the European record industry.

By controlling the image of the policy issues at stake, the creative community succeeded in imposing its policy concerns at the EU level. Because cultural interest groups could make use of their high media profile – which had also played a role during the negotiations on the TWF Directive – they were successful in capturing the political debate and imposing an alternative policy image on copyright policy issues. The 'systemic openness' of the agenda-setting stage of the decision-making process (Peters 1996) also gave more opportunities for proactive policy actors to change the image of a policy problem in a direction which suited their interests. Thus, when the member governments debated the final selection of policy options within the Council of Ministers, the debate had already been 'captured' by cultural interest groups and *dirigiste* governments. At the policy negotiations stage, the QMV rule also played a role in avoiding 'lowest common denominator' policy outcomes.

In a situation where a common solution was in any case preferable to the status quo, 'cultural' lobbyists proved that they could still pull their weight on the selection of EU policy options by exercising purposive political activism. Does this mean that, contrarily to the hypotheses laid down earlier, *dirigiste* solutions can still be agreed upon when the default position (no EU-level solution) is not desirable? This is a premature conclusion if looked at in the light of the developments that took place in other sectors of copyright harmonisation. Indeed, the three directives discussed above were limited to 'technical' matters and did not fundamentally challenge the policy traditions of EU states. It will now be argued that EU-level negotiations concerning more 'politically sensitive' matters did not result in the forming of a political agreement among member states. Indeed, when fundamental dissimilarities in national policy traditions divided national delegations, the latter often recognised that preserving their sovereignty was the best option – unless, as will be discussed in the last part of this chapter, the status quo is viewed as the least desirable option.

The limits of European harmonisation: 'locking in national models at the EU level or defending national sovereignty?'

Various aspects of copyright legislation were not harmonised within the EU. This was the case, until 2001, for legislation on private copying and for artists' resale rights. It is still the case for authors' moral rights. EU-level harmonisation of resale rights and private copying, which was at the heart of extended political debates at the EU level, are examined here. It will be demonstrated that when 'politically sensitive' issues are at stake, harmonisation is much more problematical and tends to be limited to 'lowest common denominator' solutions.

From head-on clashes to the framing of a compromise: resale rights as a difficult case for EU harmonisation

Resale rights give artists and their heirs the right to receive a royalty on the selling price of works of art when such works are re-sold in the EU by an art market professional such as an auctioneer, gallery, or other art dealer. This allows artists and their beneficiaries to take a percentage of the seller's profit on the increased value of their works of art. This right was completely ignored by several EU states – including, most noticeably, the UK – until the drafting of an EU directive on these matters in 2001.

The need to harmonise national legislation on resale rights had already been underlined by the Commission in its 1977 Communication on *Community Action in the Cultural Sector*. Acting as a purposive agent, the Commission had already issued a proposal for a directive on resale rights in the wake of the 1977 Communication (Doutrelepont 1996). Although no further action was taken, the issue of resale rights was again mentioned in the 1982 Communication on *Stronger Community Action in the Cultural Field*, in which the Commission highlighted the difficulties caused by the disparities in national legislation. However, strong resistance from several states against the Commission entrepreneurship prevented the latter from pushing through any EU-level policy solution. The issue of resale rights harmonisation was not even mentioned in the 1987 Commission Communication entitled *A Fresh Boost for Culture in the European Community* (European Commission 1987).

In the 1990s, the Commission attempted to put forward new proposals for EU-level harmonisation of resale rights and decided to sound out the interested parties (*European Report*, 6 July 1991). The Commission was preparing the contours of the policy debate, waiting for the opening of a 'window of opportunity'. As had already been done for other copyright matters, the Commission invited the parties to fill in a questionnaire and organised a hearing where professionals could discuss controversial items. At this stage, only six EU member states had a domestic resale rights system: France, Italy, Belgium, Germany, Denmark and Spain. The constellation of actors' interests was still not favourable to the drafting of a common solution. The member states that did not have national legislation on resale rights for artists opposed the creation of a common system at the EU level. The UK expressed acute resistance to EU-level harmonisation attempts. The art sector in the UK is indeed regarded as one of the most dominant art markets in the EU. As a result, the introduction of resale rights was strongly opposed by auction houses such as Sotheby's and Christie's, which argued that the introduction of an EU resale right system would drive the art sales out of the European Union (*Courrier International*, 13 January 2000). Using their strong economic power, auction houses succeeded in capturing the political debate in the UK. The British government subsequently defended their interests in the face of both the Commission and other national delegations. The Netherlands, Ireland, Austria and Sweden did not have any domestic legislation on resale rights either (Doutrelepont 1996).

Thus, the Commission failed to pass its proposals for an EU-level resale rights system in the face of member states' resistance to EU policies that did not suit their policy traditions or their interests. In fact, unlike in the audio-visual and book policy sectors, the proposals of the Commission did not comprise an attempt to liberalise the policy sector. Implementing an EU-level resale rights system would have imposed an interventionist policy solution to all EU states. Any common solution required a consensual agreement within the Council of Ministers, and such support for resale rights harmonisation did not exist among member states. Fundamentally, in a policy area where the status quo suited most states' interests, a common solution could only have been implemented if most states had had similar policy preferences.

Seizing a new window of opportunity, the Commission drafted a new proposal for an EU directive in 1996 (Reinbothe 2001). At the time of the new Commission proposal, artists were entitled to resale rights in most EU countries. Artists and their representatives had indeed been successful in imposing the idea that they should be entitled to receive a royalty on the selling price of their works when re-sold by art market professionals. Only the UK, Ireland, Austria and the Netherlands had no legislation. The constellation of actors' preferences was therefore more favourable to the forming of a political agreement within the Council of Ministers. Mario Monti, then Competition Commissioner, argued that disparities among national systems were distorting trade within the Single Market, hence the need to establish a Euro-wide harmonised legal system (*European Report*, 1 June 1996). However, aware of the differences in the positions of EU states, the Commission seems to have adopted an attitude of 'self-restraint' and stated that harmonisation would be confined to national provisions that had a direct impact on the functioning of the Internal Market.

Predictably, London's auction houses reacted with dismay to news that the European Commission had finalised proposals for a levy on the sale of contemporary art works to be applied throughout the EU (*The Independent*, 16 March 1996). British Prime Minister Tony Blair personally intervened in the negotiation process by writing to EU Heads of Government, as well as the European Commission, in order to express his concerns (*Agence Europe*, 15 December 1999). Artist groups, on the other hand, welcomed the proposals. Janet Ibbotson, deputy chief executive of the Design and Artists Copyright Society, explained, in the name of artists, that 'we [the Design and Artists Copyright Society] are very much in favour of it. We have been campaigning for this since 1990. The art market is built on the back of artists. They should be entitled to money from subsequent sales which are often more lucrative. Artists don't benefit from copyright as other designers do' (cited in *Managing Intellectual Property*, April 1996). Four years of bitter negotiations were marked by an opposition between, on the one hand, artists, most member states and the European Commission and, on the other, the UK backed up by the Netherlands and Luxembourg and anti-resale rights groups. A political agreement was eventually accepted within the Council of Ministers in 2000.

The text of the final Directive (2001/84/EC) was a compromise between the various interests at stake, and goes a long way to meet the UK's concerns (Reinbothe 2001). The Groupement Européen de Sociétés d'Auteurs et de Compositeurs (GESAC), which represents European authors, deplored 'the successive alterations of the initial draft directive' (*Agence Europe*, 25 July 2001). 'Cultural' interest groups were opposed to the excessive transposition and transition period of the Directive as well as to several restrictions applied to the exercise of artists' resale rights. For instance, the Directive states that resale rights can only be claimed when the sales price exceeds 3000 euros. The limitation was opposed by the Commission and represents a concession to anti-resale rights groups (*Agence Europe*, 19 July 2001). The Directive contains an extended list of exemptions that make its constraining power very limited. Thus, if the QMV rule allowed the Directive to be adopted despite the fierce opposition of the UK, the British showed their ability to considerably alter the content of the Directive – this in a context where most other EU states, and the Commission, were supporting a higher level of harmonisation.

The resale rights Directive negotiations illustrate that when a member state has very salient interests in one policy area, and lobbies actively for their defence, its preferences are taken into account in the formulation of EU policies. In the audio-visual sector, France was the only delegation which defended so vehemently the introduction of television quotas in the TWF Directive. Despite the fact that the TWF Directive could have been adopted without the agreement of the French delegation and those countries which backed the French position – the QMV rule also applied – the French succeeded in imposing their policy concerns by making it clear that quotas were considered as vital for French national interests. A higher level of harmonisation was reached as a result of France's pressure in the audio-visual sector, whereas a lower level of harmonisation was implemented because of British demands in the copyright sector. However, the ability of one country to pull its weight on the choice of EU policy options should not be overstated. The UK was not able to oppose the enacting of the Directive in so far as a majority of states supported it; and the similarities with the audio-visual sector are again obvious.[20] No member state alone can fully control the game, especially in a negotiating context where the QMV rule applies.

The example of the resale rights Directive suggests that common solutions are agreed upon only when they suit the legislative and political traditions of a majority of states – unless, as shown in the audio-visual sector and as will be shown again below, the nature of the default position is too undesirable. This explains why harmonisation of resale rights for artists took place only in recent years, although proposals in this direction had already been put forward by the Commission in the 1980s.

Legislation on private copying: liberal states oppose EU-level harmonisation Most states' provisions allow performers some financial remuneration for sound or audio-visual works that are copied privately. In some cases the remuneration takes the form of a tax on audio or video-cassettes and in others the charge is made on recording equipment. Although the Commission laid out proposals for harmonising private copying legislation as early as the 1980s, private copying was not harmonised until 2001 in the new copyright Directive. As with resale rights, member states were in fact successful in blocking EU solutions that did not suit their policy preferences.

The first proposals for a 'Euro-wide' tape levy were put forward by the Commission in the late 1980s. An internal debate within the Commission over whether or not to propose an EU-wide levy on blank tapes held up the Commission's long-awaited plans. Peter Sutherland, then Competition Commissioner, and Lord Cockfield, in charge of the Internal Market, opposed any kind of levy. At the other end of the spectrum, Karl-Heinz Narjes, the Industry Commissioner, and Carlo Ripa di Meana, in charge of Culture, were pushing for an EU-wide tape levy (*Financial Times*, 2 June 1988). Yet, eventually, and in the same way as for resale rights legislation, the Commission proposals coincided with those of the most interventionist countries and with the positions of artists' lobbies. Proposals for an EU-wide tape levy had been put forward by the French government in the mid-1980s.[21] France was indeed disadvantaged by the interpretation of international conventions, which forced the French to return remuneration abroad without benefiting from the reciprocity of this principle. The Commission's 'cultural' approach towards private copying was evident in its line of argument. Jean-Francois Verstrynge, then Head of the Division for Intellectual Property, recalled Article 128 of the Treaty – which gives the EU a competence in the cultural sector – in order to justify the Commission proposals (*European Report*, 28 October 1992). As examined earlier in the book the Commission usually referred to Treaty provisions on the free circulation of goods and services in order to justify its intervention. In the present case, the Commission actually had an institutional interest in supporting the cultural coalition. The only proposals for EU-level intervention concerning private copying and resale rights emanated from *dirigiste* states and 'cultural' groups. Hence, the EU draft proposal upheld the continental notion of copyright which grants the author a 'moral right'.

However, the Commission could only be cautious in the face of member states' hostility towards EU harmonisation plans. In the late 1980s, only Germany and France applied tape levies in the EU. Spain and Portugal were about to enact laws, and a debate had been initiated in Belgium, Holland and Italy (*The Economist*, 9 July 1988). However, Denmark, Greece, Ireland and Luxembourg had no laws on tape levies.

The domestic systems and the rates of taxation therefore varied widely in the EU. The UK expressed its hostility to any form of EU-level harmonisation after having renounced the inclusion of remuneration for private copying in its own pending legislation.[22] Undoubtedly, the constellation of actors' preferences hindered the Commission from proposing an EU solution. As a result, the recommendations developed in the 1988 Green Paper on copyright issues stated that EU-level harmonisation was not justified in the analogue environment.

The Commission renewed its attempts to put forward policy proposals on the regulation of home copying when digital technologies seemed to change the parameters of the policy debate. Once again, the Commission appreciated the presence of a 'window of opportunity' which could allow for further supranational intervention. Technological developments were presented as the main justification for EU-level intervention. The Commission argued that compact digital cassettes and interactive compact disks, which began to arrive on the market in the early 1990s, would make the mass production of copies without loss of quality possible (*European Report*, 28 October 1992). In September 1992, the Commission informally submitted to the Internal Market Council a draft directive on home copying that planned to harmonise member states' laws (Vinje 1995).

However, the preferences of several states were still too salient; and the Commission's room for manoeuvre was restrained. Aware of the diversity between countries' preferences, the Commission sought to consult EU states before developing its proposals further (*European Report*, 26 September 1992). The reluctance of the UK, backed by Luxembourg, the Netherlands and Ireland, to agree to any common solution ultimately prevented the Commission from presenting a formal policy proposal.

Thus, EU-level harmonisation is particularly difficult when politically sensitive issues are at stake. By contrast, the first directives on copyright dealt with essentially 'technical' matters. Furthermore, in a context where the status quo is considered as a possible policy option, common solutions seem to be blocked when the opposition of several countries is too fundamental. In the resale rights and private copying cases, the status quo was a workable policy option. For private copying, this was at least true in the analogue environment (but not any more when digital technologies made the possibilities for 'copying' look even more uncontrollable). Therefore, in a context where member states were not too dissatisfied with the default position, a common solution was likely to be agreed upon only in a situation in which a majority of states would have a *mutual* interest in locking in at the EU level a common legislative arrangement. In the resale rights case, a political agreement at the EU level indeed became possible only after a sufficient number of states had implemented a system of resale rights at home. In the private copying case, no common solution could be been agreed upon for years – but private copying legislation is part of the 2001 framework Directive on copyright (2001/29/CE) discussed in the following section.

The new Copyright Directive: dominance of the 'information society image'

The Directive on copyright in the information society is presented by EU officials as part of 'a new generation of copyright harmonisation'.[23] It harmonises several essential rights of authors and neighbouring rights holders, such as limitations and exceptions thereto, the protection of technological measures and the protection of rights management information. The framework Directive has the most horizontal impact of all *acquis communautaire* directives. It is portrayed as the European Union's response to the challenge of structuring copyright protection in the new environment of digital services. It will be argued here that the selection of 'liberal' policy options during the framework Directive negotiations can be accounted for by referring to the proactive role of the Commission in the new technological environment, the increasingly undesirable nature of the default position, and changes in the constellation of actors' interests.

EU-level regulation as a technical necessity?
The development of digital technologies in the 1990s revived pre-existing pressures for supranational intervention. Mario Monti, then Internal Market Commissioner, made it clear that in the field of copyright, 'the agenda is often set by technological developments, and increasingly by developments at the international level' (Vienna Conference on Intellectual Property Rights, July 1998). According to him, a new legislative framework capable of responding to new technological challenges was needed. The digital revolution indeed signified that the medium could gradually be 'liberated' from the message. For instance, telephone networks can carry full motion video-programs and traditional print media are giving way to electronic delivery systems as the preferred platform for disseminating text and data (Hugenholtz 1996). The convergence of platforms was seen as a direct challenge to the copyright systems that were in force in EU member states. National laws were indeed becoming less efficient in controlling piracy and private copying. These developments, captured by terms such as the 'digital revolution' and the 'Information Society', represented a window of opportunity which allowed the Commission to push through its policy proposals, as had already happened, for instance, for the resale rights Directive.

The Commission referred to the 'Information Society' for the first time in the *White Paper on Growth, Competitiveness, Employment: the Challenges and Ways Forward into the 21st Century* (European

Commission 1993). In 1994, a task force on 'Europe and the Information Society' was set up. The task force presented a report to the Corfu European Council in June 1994, which pointed out that 'technological progress now enables us to process, store, retrieve and communicate information in whatever form it may take – oral, written or visual – unconstrained by distance, time and volume' (High Level Group on the Information Society 1994). Acting as a purposive agent, the Commission subsequently issued a Communication entitled *Europe's Way to the Information Society* (European Commission 1994b), which opened the way for more specific initiatives on key areas like intellectual property. It is in this context that the Commission adopted the *Green Paper on Copyright and Related Rights in the Information Society* (European Commission 1995b),[24] intended to stimulate the debate with all the interested parties (Vandoren 1996). The risk that the information society would increase the number of situations in which differences between the laws of the member states might obstruct trade in goods and services was presented as the main justification for EU-level intervention.[25] Viviane Reding, then Commissioner for Culture, explained in her speech at the European Summit of Madrid in 2000 that:

> In this context [i.e. the information society], self-regulation is set to play an increasing role. When preparing and applying the 'ground rules', self-regulation is an approach particularly well suited to the intrinsic features of the Internet, particularly the proliferation of players involved. This was one of the conclusions of the recent debate on the Commission's Green Paper on technological convergence. (Reding 2000b)

Thus, the information society provided the Commission with the opportunity to respond purposively and maximise the likelihood of the success of its proposals. The Commission undoubtedly showed its propensity to act as a supranational entrepreneur, as had also happened in the audiovisual and in the book policy sectors. New technologies and their impact on the functioning of the Single Market were again used as the main rationale for EU intervention.

Or a political decision?

In fact, the drafting of the framework Directive was as much a political decision as a technical necessity. EU developments need to be relocated within the broader framework of international copyright negotiations.

In the field of trade policy, the European Commission shares its competencies with member states. Therefore, DG Trade within the Commission was pressing for Article 113 (now Article 133) of the Treaty, the clause which gives the EU sole authority to conclude multilateral trade pacts in goods, to include services and intellectual property as areas covered by the WTO. DG Trade wanted, indeed, to extend its negotiating rights in intellectual property and services – such as telecommunications and software.

DG Internal Market, which does not have any negotiating rights within the WTO, favoured another strategy. Essentially, DG Internal Market sought to extend the remit of its competence by becoming part of the World Intellectual Property Organization (WIPO).[26] In December 1996, the WIPO had signed two new treaties: on the protection of authors ('WIPO Copyright Treaty') and on the protection of performers and phonogram producers ('WIPO Performances and Phonograms Treaty'),[27] which provides additional protections for copyright deemed necessary in the modern information era. The treaties provide authors with some further control over the rental and distribution of their work, which they did not have under the Berne Convention alone. They also prohibit the circumvention of technological measures for the protection of works and the unauthorised modification of rights management information contained in works.

Yet the European Community was not a member of the WIPO Treaty, meaning that it could not vote at the WIPO assemblies – although it could attend as an observer. The only way for the Community to become a contracting party to the WIPO Treaty in its own right, and thereby obtain a right of representation within the assembly, was to implement the WIPO Treaties in the EU. The European Community had to bring the laws on copyright and related rights in the EU in line with the WIPO Treaties, in order to set the stage for joint ratification of the Treaties by the member states and the European Community (Hugenholtz 2000). Thus, Mario Monti warmly welcomed the WIPO treaties for filling 'existing gaps in international intellectual property protection in the field of new technological applications', as well as providing 'a stable legal framework which will promote international trade in Information Society services and will give consumers access to a wide variety of new products, while at the same time facilitating the fight against piracy in all of its forms'.[28] Favouring the implementation of the WIPO treaties was also a way for DG Single Market to assert its competence over DG Trade. Thus, an internal conflict of competence between the Trade DG and the Internal Market DG was also at the origin of the Internal Market Commissioner's proposals for the 2001 framework Directive.

Thus, the contours of the policy debate were more favourable to the implementation of a common solution than in the 1980s. On the one hand, the Commission, if also motivated by institutional considerations, could use the context of the digital revolution as a 'window of opportunity' to further its policy proposals. On the other, member states' sovereignty was challenged by the impact of technological developments. If this had, to a lesser extent, already been the case in the 1980s, the cultural lobby had then been successful in imposing an alternative image, conceiving authors' rights as personal rights to be discussed on the level of human rights, upon the policy problems at stake. This did not happen during the negotiations on the framework copyright Directive. What were, then, the factors that resulted in the choice of a different type of policy option?

New policy actors enter the game: a constellation of interests less favourable to dirigiste *solutions*
With the development of digital technologies, new stakeholders started influencing the policy-making process. Telecommunication companies, the telecommunication and electronics industry and business software groups were fighting to guarantee the functioning of the networks. From an industrial point of view, it is indeed important that the possibility of making private copies is not too strongly restricted (Wikström 1998). Thus, network operators were successful in forming a liberal coalition encompassing consumer organisations, disabled associations, industry groups and broadcasters, which concentrated its lobbying strategy towards the Commission – and the Internal Market DG in particular. Various actors with different interests allied themselves in order to promote the liberalisation of the copyright sector. Economic actors, who had very strong commercial interests to defend, were successful in 'framing' the debate in a way that would allow them to gain the support of consumer groups. In the event consumer associations' fears were indeed instrumentalised by network operators both as a justification for their lobbying campaigns and as a source of political support (interview with French official, Ministry of Culture, 22 April 2002). As Lewinsky argues, 'it seems that the idea of an incontestable information society, to which authors' rights and neighbouring rights would be obstacles is beginning to gain influence in Europe' (1998: 139). The liberal coalition was successful in imposing a new policy image, the 'Information Society' policy image, which determined the way copyright issues were portrayed and in the event allowed for further liberalisation of the sector.

Thus, not only was the status quo not a desirable option, but the constellation of actors' interests was also in favour of liberal stakeholders. Member states and 'cultural' lobbies had therefore little room for manoeuvre in resisting supranational intervention.

The cultural coalition: attempts to reorient the EU-level policy debate
The cultural coalition, composed essentially of interventionist states, the artistic community and music industry representatives, reacted strongly against supranational initiatives. Yet, the *dirigistes* failed in locking in their favoured regulatory model at the EU level. As in the audio-visual sector, however, the cultural coalition was successful in preserving national legislative systems by ensuring a loose wording of the final Directive.

'*Alliance between the industry and the creative community: when* '*cultural*' *and* '*economic*' *interests get along* Throughout the negotiations, reactions from the various lobbies were robust. Bernard Miyet, President of SACEM, argued that the legitimacy of authors' rights was being threatened 'in the name of technological progress, free trade and the so-called new philosophy of free culture' (Miyet 2001). Both creators and entertainment companies opposed this drive. In the wake of the publication of the 1995 Green Paper on copyright in the information society, European entertainment companies mounted a strong lobby, active both at the national and at the international level, in order to secure legal protection for works distributed over the Internet (Financial Times, 23 May 1997). The IFPI played a particularly strong role during the negotiation process. Industry representatives were lobbying the Commission directly (European Report, 18 October 1997, European Report, 11 July 1998), in an attempt to impose their concerns at the earliest stage of the policy-making process. After the unveiling of the first draft directive, the IFPI pursued its lobbying strategies against a text that would 'facilitate the sale of devices to record encrypted digital music signals' and which failed to harmonise home copying legislation (Financial Times, 11 December 1997). Developing a 'multi-track approach' (Mazey and Richardson 2001), its lobbying efforts were also directed towards the UK government. Commercial interests were obviously the key concern of the IFPI; Europe's music industry was worth nearly 12 billion euros in 2000 (European Report, 15 July 2000). In the view of the European Association for Telecommunications Networks (ETNO), the IFPI uses the piracy argument as a 'smokescreen to strengthen its grip on music and film distribution over the Internet'. Their real worry is, according to ETNO, that artists will be 'tempted to bypass big record companies and market their works directly over the web' (cited in Financial Times, 20 January 1999).

A similar stance was defended by the GESAC, which represents European authors and composers' societies, and the International Association of Audiovisual Writers and Directors (AIDAA), which represents authors worldwide. Specific concern was expressed over the loose wording of Article 5 of the Directive, which deals with exemptions from the reproduction right for temporary copies (*European Report*, 24 December 1997). The FERA, which represents European film directors, shared this view. In a letter to Jacques Santer, then Commission president, the FERA emphasised 'the dangers of any blind policy of convergence' between the audio-visual and telecommunications sectors (*European Report*, 24 May 1997).

Among European states, France gave the strongest support to rights holders' considerations. Spain, Italy and Belgium backed the French position during the negotiation process. By contrast, Northern European countries, followed by the UK, Luxembourg and the Netherlands favoured a compromise that would give more weight to consumers' interests (*Le Figaro*, 10 December 2001). The cultural coalition engaged in virulent lobbying campaigns, hoping to change the prevailing image of the policy problem and redesign the framing of the political compromise at the EU level.

The European Parliament as a key actor in the policy-making process
In a similar manner as in the audio-visual sector, 'cultural' lobbies and industry representatives perceived the co-decision procedure as a new opportunity structure and directed their lobbying strategies towards the EP.

In January 1999, more than 350 European artists signed a petition calling on the EP to increase protection of intellectual property rights in the new digital environment (*European Report*, 20 January 1999). The initiative was actually orchestrated by the IFPI; illustrating the propensity of industry representatives to mobilise the artistic community and build an 'ad hoc coalition' around a specific policy issue. Lobbying campaigns were successful in pushing through some of the major concerns of the music industry. During the first reading, the EP supported the arguments put forward by copyright owners and the creative community, while arguments from Internet access providers were voted down by the Legal Affairs Committee (*Music and Media*, 20 February 1999).

The EP was however confronted with the Commission's institutional interests; indeed a political game between the two institutions characterised the last stage of the decision-making process and determined the selection of final policy options. The IFPI and 'cultural' lobbies such as the AIDAA expressed their dissatisfaction with the text adopted by the Commission after the first reading of the EP. The AIDAA urged the Council of Ministers and the EP to 'spurn measures taken under pressure from the Bangemann Cabinet' (cited in *European Report*, 17 July 1999) and lamented that the Commission refused to countenance some of the Parliament's amendments.

The lobbying campaigns of the cultural coalition before the EP were renewed during the second reading in October 2000. In a 'soft' lobbying exercise, the IFPI held a 'Friends of Music' evening in Strasbourg, which allowed prominent artists to meet with MEPs in an informal setting (*Billboard*, 4 November 2000). However, the EP did not change the essence of the Council common position and approved a text that was perceived as satisfactory by Internet network operators (*Agence Europe*, 15 February 2001). ETNO welcomed the Parliament's vote, adding that 'an unjustified increase in costs for European Internet users would have seriously undermined EU plans to exploit the development of the information society as an engine for growth and employment' (cited in *World*

Intellectual Property Report, 15 March 2001). New powerful stakeholders had succeeded in imposing a policy image that was favourable to their interests upon copyright matters. As argued by President of SACEM Bernard Miyet:

> The struggle for the defence of authors' rights and copyright is a constantly renewed struggle. The only difference is, today the interests at stake are much more powerful than they were then. It is no longer about unruly clients or difficult partners. Telecommunications giants have joined in the dance with considerable means of influence. They cannot be overlooked, especially since vertical integration strategies are in the making. These newcomers must be persuaded that any destabilisation of the culture/entertainment industries would have highly negative repercussions for them. (Miyet 2001)

'A common solution legitimising the status quo?'
EU Ministers for External Affairs agreed to endorse the version of the text approved by the EP in April 2001 (*European Report*, 12 April 2001). The final text does not create a genuinely harmonised framework at the EU level. A consensus was reached on the definition of the rights that were to be protected by copyright (reproduction rights, public communication rights, and distribution rights). Concerning the controversial issue of the 'exceptions' to copyright, a long list of optional exemptions to copyright ensures that member states are able to retain their legal traditions in this area. The list is exhaustive only in the sense that no other exceptions can be applied. However, member states are free to apply only part of the exceptions, meaning that they can pick and choose at will only those exceptions they need or find expedient. The GESAC, which defended a stricter definition, considers that it failed to impose its views (*Le Monde*, 11 April 2001). The IFPI regretted that the final draft left open the possibility for EU governments to intervene in an 'ad-hoc manner' (*European Report*, 15 July 2000).

Although the Commission was in favour of a stricter definition of the exceptions to copyright, member states were not able to reach a political agreement on a precise list of authorised exceptions.[29] National traditions were too divergent to allow for the design of a compromise solution. Again, it is evident that when member states cannot further their interests at the EU level, they are tempted to opt for the status quo. In the present case however, pressures for 'some form of common solution' were too strong for member states to oppose the drafting of an EU-level solution. Most member states realised that even a minimal level of harmonisation would be in their interest in the face of digital technologies. As a result, the formulation of the final text was extremely loose (for an opinion on the lack of harmonisation of exceptions, see Haart 1998), thereby allowing the states to preserve their legislative systems. One could say that the

Commission was successful in extending the remit of its competence by pushing through its proposals for the framework Directive, while member states were successful in preventing EU legislation from having any constraining power on them. 'A common solution legitimising the status quo' could ironically describe the political outcomes of the negotiations on the 2001 copyright Directive.

Another issue, that of the legal protection for anti-copying mechanisms, provoked heated debate (*European Report*, 12 April 2001). The aim of the measure is to ensure that an exception, for example reproduction on copying for the purposes of illustration or as a teaching aid, can be applied even when rights-holders have put in place mechanisms preventing copying, such as digital traces intended to prevent piracy. Here again, a compromise was found between rights holders' and consumers' interests. The Directive rules that rights holders, either voluntarily or through agreements with other parties, should make copying processes available to beneficiaries of specific exemptions such as schools and libraries (Doherty and Griffiths 2000: 19). However, rights holders have total control over the manufacture and distribution of know-how provisions for neutralising anti-copying mechanisms.

Finally, one of the most crucial subjects of controversy was the right of authors to be 'compensated' for the copying of their works (*Agence Europe*, 9 June 2000, *European Report*, 17 February 2001). France and Germany favoured the use of the words 'fair remuneration' to ensure better protection of rights holders (*European Report*, 26 April 2000). Yet, the advocates of the right for fair remuneration (*Le Monde*, 31 May 2000) failed to impose their concerns in the face of other states' opposition. Denmark, Luxembourg, the UK, Ireland, Sweden and the Netherlands expressed objections to the principle itself. Member states were also divided over the definition of the conditions in which compensation should be granted to rights holders. In the final Directive, the principle of fair compensation applies to three of the exceptions, namely reprography, private copies and the reproduction of programmes for transmission in certain social institutions. However, here again member states are allowed some scope in the interpretation of the provision (*European Report*, 12 April 2001). The way they decide to compensate authors is left to their discretion. They also can decide on their treatment of time-shifting practices, that is, private copies made from radio or television for the purpose of viewing or listening to the broadcast at a later and more convenient time.

On more 'technical' aspects of private copying harmonisation, a compromise was reached between the various interests at stake. For instance, in order to balance the needs of the copyright holders and those of the Internet service providers and telecommunications operators who transmit and carry the copyright-protected materials, the Directive included a mandatory exception for the reproduction of technical copies. To qualify for this exception, the reproduction activity must be transient or incidental by nature and must constitute an essential part of a technological process. In addition, the sole purpose of the reproduction activity must be to enable transmission in a third-party network or to facilitate the lawful use of a copyrighted work that has no significant economic impact on the copyright holder (Doherty and Griffiths 2000: 18).

Member states' reluctance to agree to a text that would challenge their national laws and traditions resulted in a vague formulation of the final Directive. The same phenomenon had resulted in the failure of the negotiations on private copying in the early 1990s. Why, then, were the policy options retained for the framework Directive different? To start with, the Commission could take advantage of the 'window of opportunity' created by the 'digitalisation' of the society in the late 1990s. The combination of the proactive role of the Commission and of the unfavourable location of the status quo in member states' decision set resulted in the drafting of a common solution. Promoting a loose wording of the final text was a rational option for member states. In France, for instance, most officials thought that too much harmonisation would have challenged the level of protection granted to authors by French legislation (*Le Figaro*, 10 December 2001). In so far as the status quo was not a possible policy option, the only way for states to preserve their policy traditions was to design a lenient EU-level solution.

Conclusion

As in the audio-visual sector, and, to a lesser extent, the book sector, the Communitarisation of copyright policies was initiated by the ECJ and the Commission. EU institutions successfully extended their remit to new policy areas by portraying policy issues from an economic perspective, thus confirming that policy-makers from another venue can attack existing policy arrangements in order to expand their own policy jurisdictions. In the copyright case, *dirigiste* policy actors reacted in the same manner as in the two other cases examined here: using the *dirigiste* policy image, they attempted to reorient the focus of the policy debate at the EU level in order to further their policy preferences through the European medium. Thus, conflicting policy images which conveyed different conceptions about the nature of intellectual property and its role in the information economy were used by policy actors as weapons to further their interests. Furthermore, it becomes evident, when looking at the attitude of the French government, that member states' choice to design EU common solutions was at least partly a reactive strategy, developed in a context constrained by the *de facto* intervention of the ECJ and the Commission and the impact of technological developments. Again, the use by the

European jurisdiction of the liberal image as a tool for controlling policy, associated with commercial actors' 'venue-shopping' strategies at the EU level induced other jurisdictions to react and enter the rhetoric contest as a way of preserving or regaining control over policy. These dynamics ensured that governance of the policy sector was increasingly taking place at the European level.

Two phases can be distinguished in the harmonisation of copyright legislation. In the early 1980s, the directives adopted by member states implemented a high level of harmonisation, transposing at the EU level the 'Latin' conception of the *droit d'auteur* (in contrast to the Anglo-Saxon copyright system). Yet, the 2001 Directive on copyright in the information society only formulated vague guidelines meant to create a 'minimal' level of harmonisation within the European Union in order to cope with new technological challenges. The contours of the policy debate were however the same during the two successive phases of the Europeanisation of copyright legislation. First, decision rules – the QMV rule – required consensual agreement within the Council (but increased the chances of avoiding lowest common denominator solutions). Second, the undesirable nature of the status quo should have pushed member states towards some form of harmonisation, but quite likely on the basis of a lowest common denominator solution insofar as states held conflicting preferences. We could therefore have expected similar policy solutions to be selected during the two successive harmonisation phases– whatever the latter would comprise. The analysis carried out in this chapter pointed out several factors that explain why divergent policy options were in fact chosen.

In the 1980s, what allowed for the transposition of the most protective legislation for authors at the EU level was the ability of 'cultural' interest groups, supported by France and Southern European countries, to change the prevailing image of the policy problem at the EU level. This outcome runs counter to the prediction that when the venue of policy moves towards the European level, a liberal image should prevail. As far as European legislation only dealt with 'technical matters' – as opposed to more politically sensitive areas such as private copying for instance – the proactive role of the cultural coalition allowed for the *dirigiste* policy image to prevail. *Dirigiste* actors were successful in blocking European solutions that did not suit their interests. This demonstrates that using proactive strategies can allow certain policy actors to dominate the policy debate. But why, then, have they not been able to do so in recent years?

In the 1990s, the constellation of actors' interests was much less favourable to creators. New powerful economic actors, such as telecommunication network operators, had entered the 'game' and benefited from a strong lobbying capacity. Whereas authors' groups and *dirigiste* governments benefited from the absence of a strong 'counter-lobbying power' in the 1980s, the constellation of actors in the late 1990s was more likely to force the drafting of a 'political' compromise at the EU level. Indeed, the interests of the new actors involved in the policy-making process were in line with the Commission's approach towards copyright issues. In the new digital environment, the Commission wanted to promote the development of the 'Information Society', which meant that further liberalisation was to be implemented. In so far as the status quo was considered the least desirable policy option, the cultural coalition had no choice but to accept a political compromise that would fail to transpose its policy concerns at the EU level.

Whereas in the book policy sector most member states felt that their national legislative systems could be best preserved by maintaining the status quo, a majority of them were convinced that harmonisation was necessary in the copyright sector. Technological developments, along with the liberalisation strategies that were initiated by EU institutions, made the control of national policy choices increasingly difficult. Again, the nature of the status quo was a crucial factor in the explanation of both Communitarisation dynamics and EU policy formation, thus showing that these two stages are interconnected. In the second phase of harmonisation of copyright policies, the undesirable nature of the default position induced member states to opt for a common solution, thereby restricting, in a second stage, the room for manoeuvre of the *dirigiste* coalition.

Notes

1 The term 'copyright', by contrast to 'authors' rights' is used in this chapter to refer to the policy sector examined here, as it is the one that has been retained in the English-speaking community. However, the meaning of the two terms is not identical. In the US and in the UK, laws define 'copyright' as a 'property right'. European laws, in general, define authors' rights as human rights that are inalienable.

2 By using the term 'cultural' groups, I refer in this chapter to interest groups which represent the creative community, i.e. such as representatives of authors of written and audio-visual works.

3 Thereafter referred to as the 'framework Directive'.

4 Hereafter referred to as 'the 1977 Communication'.

5 Hereafter referred as 'the 1982 Communication'.

6 Hereafter referred to as 'the 1988 Green Paper'.

7 Hereafter referred to as 'the 1985 White Paper'.

8 The Commission had already laid down this proposal in the 1984 Green Paper on the *Establishment of a Common Market for Broadcasting* (European Commission 1984).

9 Letter from Commission President Jacques Delors to President of SACEM M. Delanoe, 5 October 1989 – Archives of the French Ministry of Culture.

10 Confidential document – Archives of the French Ministry of Culture.

11 For instance, the cases *Basset* v. *SACEM* (ECJ 1987), *Lucazeau* v. *SACEM* (ECJ 1989a), *Ministère Public* v. *Tournier* (ECJ 1989b), *Cholay and société 'Bizon's Club'* v. *SACEM* (ECJ 1990) were related to the excessive and alleged discriminatory nature of the royalties charged by SACEM, the French copyright society.

12 Author's translation.

13 Handwritten notes on a meeting of EU Ministers of Culture in 1989 in Brussels (no date) – Archives of the French Ministry of Culture.

14 Notes from the SAI between 1986 and 1989 -Archives of the French Ministry of Culture.

15 Author's translation.

16 Interview with Marc Nicolas, advisor for the French Ministry of Culture, Paris, 9 January 2001.

17 Hereafter referred to as 'the cable and satellite Directive'.

18 Hereafter referred to as 'the Directive on the term of copyright protection'.

19 Hereafter referred to as 'the rental rights Directive'.

20 *The Economist* points out that: '[W]hile the British government can commission reports on *droit de suite*'s malign effects ['droit de suite' meaning 'resale rights'], it is powerless to stop it being imposed. The decision will be taken by a qualified majority vote within the EU. Eight other European countries already have *droit de suite*. Bild Kunst, the German national collecting agency, has lobbied hard for *droit de suite* to be introduced throughout Europe and now that Germany holds the EU presidency, it is determined to push through *droit de suite*' (*The Economist*, 13 February 1999).

21 Minutes of the SGCI meeting on the Culture Council of 28 November 1983 in Athens – Archives of the French Ministry of Culture.

22 Minutes of the SGCI meeting on the 1988 Green Paper on Copyright, 2 November 1988 – Archives of the French Ministry of Culture.

23 Europa website: http://europa.eu.int/comm/internal_market/en/intprop/news /reinbothe04–04–02.htm.

24 Hereafter referred to as 'the 1995 Green Paper'.

25 The Commission therefore concluded that it had an 'obligation to take measures in respect of copyright and related rights in order to guarantee the free movement of goods and the freedom of services' (European Commission 1995b: 10).

26 Interview with a French official, Ministry of Culture, 2002.

27 Based on existing international treaties, namely the Berne Convention for the Protection of Literary and Artistic Works as revised in Paris on 24 July, 1971, and the Rome Convention for the Protection of Performers, Producers of Phonograms and Broadcasting Organizations of 26 October 1961, a WIPO conference in Geneva adopted the WIPO Copyright Treaty and the WIPO Performances and Phonograms Treaty on 20 December 1996.

28 European Commission Press release, 'WIPO Diplomatic Conference concludes its work: two new Treaties on intellectual property adopted in Geneva on 20 December 1996', IP/96/1244, Brussels, 20 December 1996.

29 Interview with Christian Auinger, EU official, Internal Market DG, 21 September 2001.

7

Conclusion

Communitarisation as an interactive process

In the three issue areas examined comprehensively in the book, European intervention began with the application of the Rome Treaty principles. In the three cases, the ECJ and the 'economic' DGs of the Commission plainly attempted to portray cultural matters from an economic perspective, so that their intervention in new policy areas would become justifiable. Using the liberal image was in fact an efficient way to attack other policy jurisdictions and change the venue of decision-making. Private actors, at the subnational level, developed a similar strategy: they provoked the Europeanisation of the policy debate, the European venue being considered as more favourable to the consideration of their issues, with the objective of promoting the liberalisation of cultural markets. The interactions between images and venues produced a self-reinforcing system characterised by positive feedback mechanisms which provoked policy change. The proactive role of the Commission was particularly visible in the copyright and audio-visual sectors, where EU intervention could be justified not only with reference to the requirements of the Single Market, but also with regards to world-wide technological changes. Private actors played an important role in the three policy areas examined, but were particularly proactive in the book policy sector, prompting EU institutions' examination of book trade legislation in the EU. Thus, the Europeanisation of national policies in the book, audio-visual and copyright fields (in the sense that national level policy choices were constrained by EU-level policy developments) was essentially the result of European institutions' *de facto* intervention, which benefited from the support of private commercial actors, in policy areas where they intervened through the 'economic back door'.

In a second stage, member states that felt that their national legislative and policy traditions were challenged by EU institutions' intervention responded by trying to initiate the development of a positive European cultural policy that would take into account their policy preferences and impose a more *dirigiste* policy agenda. Interventionist states and professionals from the cultural sector attempted to impose an alternative image of the policy issues that were being considered at the EU level. French policy-makers were presenting policy matters from a cultural or *dirigiste* perspective – which also suited less obviously trumpeted commercial motives along with preserving their competence. France distinguished itself by the strength of its response to supranational entrepreneurship. In the audio-visual sector, it succeeded in imposing content quotas despite the opposition of a majority of governments. In the book policy sector, France was the first member state to suggest the drafting of a *dirigiste* policy solution at the EU level: the French government proposed, as early as the 1980s, the setting up of a European fixed price system for books. Finally, in the copyright sector, France was the most vehement backer of the 'Latin' tradition of the *droit d'auteur*. In the book policy sector, the German government also played a proactive role in EU policy negotiations when the cross-border agreement between Germany and Austria was under threat. Like France, Germany had an interest in reorienting the policy debate in directions that were more favourable to its own policy traditions. Thus, similar dynamics can be observed in the three case studies that were examined here. When states have played a proactive role in the cultural sector, it was because their own legislative arrangements were threatened and a defensive strategy was no longer sustainable.

Not only does this show that it is essential to focus on the interaction between developments that take place at various levels of governance, but it also highlights that developments initiated by supranational actors can induce other national or subnational actors to enter the policy-making process. In the three cases examined, it is possible to distinguish two phases in states' attitudes. Initially, all EU governments preferred to safeguard their policy sovereignty in the cultural sector. It is only after certain states (France, Germany and certain Southern European states) felt that their policy traditions were threatened (either by technological developments or European institutions' intervention on economic rationales) that they decided to delegate some policy competencies to the supranational level. This dynamic interaction between different levels of governance resulted in a 'locus of governance shift' from the national towards the EU level. Put differently, the Communitarisation of the sectors examined can be seen as a story of 'reversed intergovernmentalism': EU institutions' competence-maximising strategies triggered member states' attempts to reorient the EU policy-making process into their favoured directions. Using the 'image and venue' approach allows us to capture the interaction between different institutional venues *over time* and brings two new dimensions to the 'multi-level governance' model. First, rather than picturing the static 'multi-actorness' of the EU decision-making process, a dynamic model can shed light on how action by one institutional venue can induce action by another one. Second, it becomes clear that these interactions do not only characterise the EU decision-making system once in place, but are at the very heart of the dynamics of integration. Jachtenfuchs and Kohler-Koch (1996) have already charaterised the EU as a 'dynamic multi-level system', where 'dynamic' refers to the permanent process of institutional change and 'multi-level system' to the multi-actorness nature of the EU decision-making process. Yet they do not explain how multi-level interactions between actors provoke the very process of institutional change. A possible model of these dynamics was revealed here, whereby in sectors where no Treaty competence allowed for EC intervention, the ECJ and the Commission tend to 'Europeanise' the policy area by applying economic principles, thus provoking reactions form *dirigiste* actors who then try to lock in their own policy models at the EU level. How generalisable these finding are, and where future research should look, will be dealt with below. For now, let us look at the book's findings concerning the selection of EU-level policy solutions, once the dynamics of Communitarisation were activated.

Explaining the selection of EU policy options

EU-level policy solutions leaned towards liberal concerns. In the audio-visual sector, the TWF Directive contributed to liberalising the broadcasting sector. France was successful in imposing content quotas, but the latter were enforced only 'where practicable'. France was also successful in obtaining 'side-payments', such as support mechanisms for the European audio-visual industry – Audiovisual Eureka or the Media Programme – but such schemes had a marginal impact on audio-visual policies in Europe. The legislative developments gave way to liberal demands and France was only successful in obtaining concessions in a limited number of sectors – the advertising ceiling, for instance, was a compromise between liberal and *dirigiste* states. This tendency was exacerbated with the renewal of the Directive in 1997. Thus, EU intervention in the audio-visual sector initiated the liberalisation of the sector in Europe and no *dirigiste* model was adopted on the basis of French preferences at the European level. In the copyright sector, two distinct phases can be distinguished. The 1980s directives implemented a relatively high level of harmonisation, transposing on to the EU level the 'Latin' conception of the *droit d'auteur* (in contrast to the Anglo-Saxon copyright system). Yet the 2001 Directive on copyright in the information society only formulated vague guidelines meant to create a 'minimal' level of harmonisation in order to cope with new technological challenges. In the book sector, states with interventionist policy traditions did not succeed in imposing a positive type of integration. In contrast to the two other cases, interventionist states were the only ones that favoured the drafting of a common solution at the EU level. France and Germany attempted to set up a European fixed price system for books, but faced fundamental opposition from other EU states. Governments that defended the setting up of a *dirigiste* policy option at the EU level failed to further their policy preferences through the European medium, and book markets have, until today, been subject to a negative form of integration. Thus, the evidence presented in the book illustrates that EU-level policies in the cultural sector were drafted along liberal lines. Why has this been the case?

Whereas negative integration can be implemented by the Commission and the ECJ, which make use of their judicial and regulatory powers, positive integration requires the *consensual agreement* of member states within the Council (Scharpf 1996). Yet, in a decision-making context characterised by its 'multi-actorness' and the diverging preferences of the actors involved, it was difficult for the *dirigistes* to obtain sufficient support for their favoured models. Thus, the impact of decision rules must be examined in conjunction with the constellation of actors' interests. In the event the majority of member governments within the Council consistently favoured – or did not oppose – the liberalisation of cultural markets. This means that even when *dirigiste* states were successful in pulling the decision mode back towards the intergovernmental mode in order to exploit a venue more likely to be favourable to their interests, they failed to change the dominant image of cultural policy issues at the EU level. In the audio-visual and in the copyright sectors, *dirigiste* states did not obtain the support of the necessary qualified majority and had to accept a 'political compromise'. In the audio-visual sector, France was virtually isolated in its demands for *dirigiste* policies, both during the 1980s negotiations and during the renewal of the TWF Directive negotiations. In the copyright sector, the alteration of the constellation of actors involved in the policy-making process had an evident influence on the selection of policy options. In the 1990s, the constellation of actors' interests was much less favourable to the *dirigistes* than in the 1980s. New powerful economic actors had entered the 'game' and the constellation of actors was more likely to force the drafting of a 'political' compromise. This was reinforced by the fact that the interests of the new actors involved in the policy-making process were in line with the Commission's approach towards copyright issues. In the book policy sector, the minority that strongly favoured a positive type of integration could not secure enough support within the Council. The fundamental opposition from several states and the feeling that fixed price systems could best be preserved by respecting the subsidiarity principle resulted in a lack of intergovernmental support for EU-level legislation. Thus, EU decision rules favoured deregulatory policies.

Furthermore, because *dirigiste* states decided to draft EU-level solutions as a reaction against developments that they could not control, their negotiating power was more constrained than that of liberal states. Interventionist states aimed to reorient the policy orientations formulated at the EU level in order not to be subject to the *de facto* intervention of EU institutions. As a result, they were extremely unlikely to use their right of veto to oppose a compromise which, in any case, would be more favourable to their interests than the default situation. In so far as EU institutions had extended their competence to the cultural sector by using their legislative and regulatory powers, upon which member states have no leverage, it was impossible to change the *venue* of the policy-making process and thereby the image of the policy itself. Once supranational actors, with the complicity of subnational actors which felt disadvantaged by domestic policies, had succeeded in shifting the locus of decision-making towards the EU level, they could also control the image of the policy problems at stake. Therefore, if state actors aimed to maximise their interests and preferences, an intergovernmentalist approach cannot account for essential aspects of the Communitarisation of cultural policies. Essentially, it would not explain why states could *not* choose the status quo in the audio-visual and copyright sectors.

Yet, how generalisable are these findings? EU institutions (the ECJ and the Commission) instigated a high level of harmonisation in areas such as environmental policy, social policy or gender equality. The developments that have taken place in the cultural sector illustrate the opposite, i.e. that when EU institutions intervene in a new policy area by making use of their judicial and regulatory powers, they tend to favour liberal policy solutions. How can this divergence in outcomes be accounted for? One element of explanation lies in that domestic groups which supported the Europeanisation of policies in the environmental and gender equality sectors were in favour of *interventionist* policies. EU institutions therefore had to satisfy the demands of 'anti-liberal' constituencies. For instance, Sbragia explains how 'green-minded governments and environmentalist groups were the leaders, pulling the "laggards" towards accepting higher standards of environmental regulation than many could have agreed at the national level' (2000: 293). By contrast, in the cultural policy sector, the groups which favoured the Europeanisation of the policy debate had a strong stake in market liberalisation. Furthermore, the high level of harmonisation reached in the environmental and the social sectors for instance was in fact due to greater intergovernmental support for higher standards. The ECJ and the Commission were as suspicious towards interventionist policies in these sectors as they were in the cultural sector. Concerning environmental policy, the ECJ delineated these instances in which the principles of the Internal Market can be constrained by environmental protection and restricted the access of environmental groups to the ECJ (Sbragia 2000). Within the Commission, many 'environmental' problems were dealt with by DGs that were in fact not sympathetic to environmental considerations. And finally, the propensity of the Commission and the Court to implement positive policies in these areas was considerably slowed down in the new economic climate of the 1980s. Mazey (1998) explains that the gender implications of various policies ceased being considered as a priority in the 1980s. In the context of the economic recession, the policy debate focused on the necessity to restore economic competitiveness and market deregulation acquired the status of a new orthodoxy.

Forgotten variables?

Another aspect of the policy-making process has possibly been neglected in the book: the nature of the policy problem itself. As argued by Rittberger and Richardson (2001), 'in terms of regulatory tools, different problems might require different tools'. Thus, it is perfectly possible to introduce different types of policies for the regulation of different policy problems: solely because 'it makes sense' for most of the decision-makers in a given policy area. In the case of gender equality for instance, it is widely accepted – especially among EU policy-making elites – that employment legislation should ensure equality between men and women. The case of cultural policy, by contrast, is much more divisive. Whether culture deserves a special status exempting it from the rules of free trade is subject to far more subjective appraisal. Yet it is precisely this aspect of the policy-making process that was at the heart of the dynamics of Europeanisation examined in this book – which focused on the way policy actors attempted to *portray* issues of cultural policy in very different ways. Thus, the nature of the policy problem – i.e. whether culture 'objectively' needs a certain type of regulation – has not been treated as an explanatory variable here precisely because, as just mentioned, it is extremely difficult to evaluate in an objective manner whether the policy problem at stake did require interventionist policies, as argued by French cultural lobbyists in particular, or if indeed further market liberalisation was justified.

Furthermore, the role of personalities has been discussed only marginally in the book. This might represent a caveat to providing a comprehensive explanation of both Communitarisation and EU policy formation. The role of Jacques Delors and of strong-minded French politicians, such as President François Mitterrand or the Minister of Culture Jack Lang, was crucial in giving weight to the policy entrepreneurship strategies of the cultural coalition. For instance, the scheme Audiovisual Eureka would never have been founded without the personal involvement of François Mitterrand. In the book sector, Jack Lang was particularly efficient as a defender of the 'Lang regulation' on book prices. Without his intervention and support to the 'interventionist' lobby, French legislation might have been further endangered. In the same manner, the presence of Leon Brittan and Lord Cockfield in the Commission in the 1980s contributed to impose a liberal hue to broadcasting regulation harmonisation plans. Yet it seems that strong-minded individuals act either as 'dampeners' or 'stimulators' in the policy-making process. In other words, they might succeed in obtaining more advantageous 'side-payments' or more efficiently securing national legislative arrangements that they believe are essential. Yet the theoretical model used here works without including the role of personalities as an independent variable. The influence of personalities can only exacerbate certain tendencies that would have appeared in the decision-making process regardless.

Also worthy of note, if the wideness of the book topic contained the risk of overlooking certain facets of the policy-making process, this caveat was offset by the clear advantages of being able to provide a more comprehensive explanation of the EU policy-making process in the cultural sector. By focusing on both Communitarisation dynamics and EU policy formation, it was possible to provide a more inclusive understanding of both processes and highlight the connection between the two variables. If Europeanisation/Communitarisation takes place as a result of the *de facto* intervention of European institutions in new policy areas where they do not have any competence, the room for manoeuvre for the proponents of *dirigiste* solutions is likely to be restrained at the stage of policy negotiations. If EU institutions are successful in switching the venue of decision-making towards the EU level, liberal solutions are more likely to be put in place. This is especially the case in policy sectors where the only legal basis that could be exploited to justify EU intervention is to be found in the economic principles of the Treaty.

Agenda for future research

Further research in other policy sectors has yet to be carried out. In the cultural policy sector, research on fiscal harmonisation for book sales – there is an EU-level debate on the harmonisation of the value added tax in the book policy sector – have not been undertaken by political scientists. Other under-researched sectors, such as education policy, could represent another fruitful field of research. The European Commission has also applied an economic definition to the education sector in order to justify its intervention in this policy area. For instance, in the *White Paper on Education and Training* (European Commission 1995c), the need to foster further cooperation between European countries in the field of higher education is measured against the need to develop qualifications responding to the 'skill needs of the Single Market'. It would be particularly interesting to look at other sectors where integration was *'not obvious*', given the lack of Treaty competence and/or the clashing policy and regulatory traditions of the member states, so as to test the conclusions reached here in sectors where initial conditions were similar.

At the theoretical level, more systematic proposals are needed as to how agenda definition (the definition of policy problems) strategies play a role in the Communitarisation process (locus of governance displacement) of public policies. In particular, more research is required in order to find out in which conditions 'agenda definition' strategies do/do not play a role in the Communitarisation process of public policies, and in which conditions they are/are not successful. Another possible path for future research is to study the interaction between ideas and interests in the policy-making process. When actors attempt to define the agenda, do they always further underlying objective interests? Or do ideas define actors' interests? I concentrated here on the way actors used policy ideas in order to further their – perceived – interests and control policy, as proposed by the 'image and venue' approach. I argued that ideas can shape actors' perceptions of their interests, at the stage of preference formation, and be used to further these perceived interests, at the stage of policy formulation. Yet, 'sequencing' the policy-making process has its inherent limitations. First, preferences can change during the policy formulation process. Socialisation processes can occur while actors get involved in the decision-making process. Second, this approach does not inform us on how preferences are shaped and the relative significance of ideas and interests at this stage. Delimiting the respective impact of each is one of the most difficult endeavours faced by social scientists to date. Arguably, this is an impossible endeavour given the interpenetrability of idea and interests. Yet research techniques have been proposed by social scientists (see Checkel and Moravcsik 2001) in order to test the explanatory power of ideas versus interests in shaping actors' preferences. Double-interviews with the actors under consideration at different moments of time could for example provide researchers with reliable data as to the stability/volatility of actors' preferences, which would then need to be analysed in connection with possible explanatory variables.

Future policy developments

Are the dynamics revealed here likely to characterise future negotiations in the cultural sector, and on European policies more generally? It is highly probable that this will indeed be the case. The fundamental technological changes that are taking place will increase the reactive position of EU states. This is particularly true in the cultural sector, which continues to be affected by dramatic changes in the way information is delivered and accessed. The European Commission seems to be using the current transformations as a 'window of opportunity' to further the remit of its action and the liberalisation of markets. Already in the 1994 Bangemann Report (High Level Group on the Information Society 1994), technological advances were presented as the cause of 'profound changes in the way we view our societies and also in their organisation and control'. Technological change is presented as unavoidable, and as a justification for further reliance on self-regulatory markets. Again in the Bangemann Report, it is argued that 'the market will decide winners and losers' and that 'given the power and pervasiveness of technology, this market is global'.

The impact of the 'Information Society' and the 'media revolution' was evident in the three case studies examined here. The Commission justified the extension of its competence to new policy areas by referring to the need to cope with new technological challenges. This phenomenon is not necessarily novel; such arguments were already raised in the early 1980s when the spread of blank tapes made the protection of authors' rights more uncertain. However, current technological developments take place on a global scale and impact upon media policies in all countries, provoking a new form of commercial competition that ignores borders. This means that regulatory institutions with global impact will perhaps lead the way for future policy changes. Yet, in so far as both the WTO and the European Union (for all the reasons discussed in the book) are institutions with essentially economic and commercial objectives, it is unlikely that states with interventionist policy traditions will be in a strong negotiating position to impose their views and policy preferences.

Appendix 1: Article 151 of the Treaty of the European Union

TITLE XII

CULTURE

Article 151

1. The Community shall contribute to the flowering of the cultures of the Member States, while respecting their national and regional diversity and at the same time bringing the common cultural heritage to the fore.

2. Action by the Community shall be aimed at encouraging cooperation between Member States and, if necessary, supporting and supplementing their action in the following areas:

   - improvement of the knowledge and dissemination of the culture and history of the European peoples,
   - conservation and safeguarding of cultural heritage of European significance,
   - non-commercial cultural exchanges,
   - artistic and literary creation, including in the audiovisual sector.

3. The Community and the Member States shall foster cooperation with third countries and the competent international organisations in the sphere of culture, in particular the Council of Europe.

4. The Community shall take cultural aspects into account in its action under other provisions of this Treaty, in particular in order to respect and to promote the diversity of its cultures.

5. In order to contribute to the achievement of the objectives referred to in this Article, the Council:

- acting in accordance with the procedure referred to in Article 251 and after consulting the Committee of the Regions, shall adopt incentive measures, excluding any harmonisation of the laws and regulations of the Member States. The Council shall act unanimously throughout the procedure referred to in Article 251,
- acting unanimously on a proposal from the Commission, shall adopt recommendations.

Appendix 2: Decision 508/2000/EC of the European Parliament and of the Council of 14 February 2000 establishing the Culture 2000 programme

Article 1 'Duration and Objectives'

The Culture 2000 programme shall contribute to the promotion of a cultural area common to the European peoples. In this context, it shall support cooperation between creative artists, cultural operators, private and public promoters, the activities of the cultural networks, and other partners as well as the cultural institutions of the Member States and of the other participant States in order to attain the following objectives:

> – 'promotion of cultural dialogue and of mutual knowledge of the culture and history of the European peoples;
> – promotion of creativity and the transnational dissemination of culture and the movement of artists, creators and other cultural operators and professionals and their works, with a strong emphasis on young and socially disadvantaged people and on cultural diversity;
> – the highlighting of cultural diversity and the development of new forms of cultural expression;
> – sharing and highlighting, at the European level, the common cultural heritage of European significance; disseminating know-how and promoting good practices
> concerning its conservation and safeguarding;
> – taking into account the role of culture in socioeconomic development;
> – the fostering of intercultural dialogue and mutual exchange between European and non-European cultures;
> – explicit recognition of culture as an economic factor and as a factor in social integration and citizenship;
> – improved access to and participation in culture in the European Union for as many citizens as possible'.

The Culture 2000 programme shall further an effective linkage with measures implemented under other Community policies which have cultural implications.

Appendix 3: Articles of the 1989 TWF Directive (89/552/EEC) on the distribution and production of European works

Article 4
1. Member States shall ensure where practicable and by appropriate means, that broadcasters reserve for European works, within the meaning of Article 6, a majority proportion of their transmission time, excluding the time appointed to news, sports events, games, advertising and teletext services. This proportion, having regard to the broadcaster's informational, educational, cultural and entertainment responsibilities to its viewing public, should be achieved progressively, on the basis of suitable criteria.
2. Where the proportion laid down in paragraph 1 cannot be attained, it must not be lower than the average for 1988 in the Member State concerned.
However, in respect of the Hellenic Republic and the Portuguese Republic, the year 1988 shall be replaced by the year 1990. 3. From 3 October 1991, the Member States shall provide the Commission every two years with a report on the application of this Article and Article 5. That report shall in particular include a statistical statement on the achievement of the proportion referred to in this Article and Article 5 for each of the television programmes falling within the jurisdiction of the Member State concerned, the reasons, in each case, for the failure to attain that proportion and the measures adopted or envisaged in order to achieve it.
The Commission shall inform the other Member States and the European Parliament of the reports, which shall be accompanied, where appropriate, by an opinion. The Commission shall ensure the application of this Article and Article 5 in accordance with the provisions of the Treaty. The

Commission may take account in its opinion, in particular, of progress achieved in relation to previous years, the share of first broadcast works in the programming, the particular circumstances of new television broadcasters and the specific situation of countries with a low audiovisual production capacity or restricted language area.

4. The Council shall review the implementation of this Article on the basis of a report from the Commission accompanied by any proposals for revision that it may deem appropriate no later than the end of the fifth year from the adoption of the Directive.

To that end, the Commission report shall, on the basis of the information provided by Member States under paragraph 3, take account in particular of developments in the Community market and of the international context.

Article 5

Member States shall ensure, where practicable and by appropriate means, that broadcasters reserve at least 10 % of their transmission time, excluding the time appointed to news, sports events, games, advertising and teletext services, or alternately, at the discretion of the Member State, at least 10 % of their programming budget, for European works created by producers who are independent of broadcasters. This proportion, having regard to broadcasters' informational, educational, cultural and entertainment responsibilities to its viewing public, should be achieved progressively, on the basis of suitable criteria; it must be achieved by earmarking an adequate proportion for recent works, that is to say works transmitted within five years of their production.

Bibliography

Archives from the French Ministry of Culture – Fontainebleau, France

Fonds Francis Beck 1981–1984
Fonds Richard Boidin 1988–1990
Fonds Denis Delbourg 1982–1986
Fonds Marie-Anne Duhar 1984–1986
Fonds Christian Dupavillon 1981–1985
Fonds Didier Hamon 1987–1992
Fonds Sylvie Hubac 1990–1993
Fonds Dominique Meyer 1984–1986
Fonds Marc Nicolas 1988–1992

ECJ cases

ECJ (1968a). *Commission* v. *Italy*, Case 7/68, ECR 1968: 423.
ECJ (1968b). *Parke Davis* v. *Centrafarm*, Case 24/67, ECR 1968: 55.
ECJ (1971). *Deutsche Grammophon* v. *Metro*, Case 78/70, ECR 1971: 487.
ECJ (1974). *Giuseppe Sacchi* v. *The State*, Case 155/73, ECR 1974: 409.
ECJ (1979). *Rewe-Zentral* v. *Bundesmonopolverwaltung fur Brantwein* ('*Cassis de Dijon*'), Case 120/78, ECR 1979: 649.
ECJ (1980a). *Procureur Du Roi* v. *Debauve*, Case 52/79, ECR 1980: 833.
ECJ (1980b). *Coditel* v. *Ciné-Vog Films*, Case 62/79, ECR 1981: 881.
ECJ (1981a). *Music Vertrieb Membran GmbH and K-Tel International* v. *GEMA*, Cases 55/80 and 57/80, ECR 1981: 147.
ECJ (1981b). *Commission* v. *France*, Case 90/79, ECR 1981: 283.
ECJ (1981c). *Coditel* v. *Ciné-Vog Films*, Case 262/81, ECR 1982: 3381.
ECJ (1984). *VBBB and VBVB* v. *Commission*, Cases 43 and 63/82, ECR 1984: 29.
ECJ (1985a). *Cinéthèque SA and others* v. *Fédération Nationale des Cinémas Francais*, Cases 60 and 61/84, ECR 1985: 2605.
ECJ (1985b). *Association des Centres distributeurs E. Leclerc and others* v. *Au Blé Vert*, Case 229/83, ECR 1985: 1.

ECJ (1985c). *Saint-Herblain Distribution* v. *Syndicat des Libraires de Loire-Ocean*, Case 299/83, ECR 1985: 2515.

ECJ (1986a). *Ministère Public* v. *Michel Cognet*, Case 355/85, ECR 1986: 3231.

ECJ (1986b). *Boriello* v. *Alain Darras and Dominique Tostain*, Case 95/84, ECR 1986: 2253.

ECJ (1987). *G. Basset* v. *SACEM*, Case 402/85, ECR 1987: 1747.

ECJ (1988a). *Bond van Adverteerders* v. *Netherlands*, Case 352/85, ECR 1988: 2085.

(ECJ 1988b). *Syndicat des libraires de Normandie* v. *L'aigle distribution*, Case 254/87, ECR 1988: 4457.

ECJ (1988c). *Warner Brothers Inc.* v. *Christiansen*, Case 158/86, ECR 1988: 2605.

ECJ (1989a). *Lucazeau* v. *SACEM*, joined cases 110/88 and 241/88 and 242/88, ECR 1989: 2811.

ECJ (1989b). *Ministère Public* v. *Tournier*, Case 395/87, ECR 1989: 2521.

ECJ (1990). *J. Cholay and société 'Bizon's Club'* v. *SACEM*, Case C-270/86, ECR 1990: 4607.

ECJ (1991a). *Commission* v. *France ('Tourist Guide' Case)*, Case 154/89, ECR 1991: 659.

ECJ (1991b). *Commission* v. *Italy ('Tourist Guide' Case)*, Case 180/89, ECR 1991: 709.

ECJ (1991c). *Commission* v. *Greece ('Tourist Guide' Case)*, Case 198/89, ECR 1991: 727.

ECJ (1991d). *Commission* v. *Netherlands*, Case 353/89, ECR 1991: I-4069.

ECJ (1992). *Publishers Association* v. *Commission*, Case T-66/89, ECR 1992: 1995.

ECJ (1995). *Publishers Association* v. *Commission*, Case 360/92P, ECR 1995: 23.

Legislation

Commission Decision 78/516/EEC of 26 May 1978 relating to a proceeding under Article 85 of the EEC Treaty (IV/29.559 – RAI/UNITEL), OJ L 157, 15.6.1978.

Commission Decision 81/1030/EEC of 29 October 1981 relating to a proceeding under Article 86 of the EEC Treaty (IV/29.839 – GVL), OJ L 370, 28.12.1981.

Commission Decision 82/123/EEC of 25 November 1981 relating to a proceeding under Article 85 of the EEC Treaty (IV/428 – VBBB/VBVB), OJ L 054, 25.2.1982.

Commission Decision 89/44/EEC of 12 December 1988 relating to a proceeding under Article 85 of the EEC Treaty (IV/27.393 and IV/27.394, Publishers Association – Net Book Agreements), OJ L 022, 26.1.1989.

Commission Decision 89/441/EEC of 21 December 1988 on aid granted by the Greek Government to the film industry for the production of Greek films, OJ L 208, 20.7.1989.

Conclusions of the Ministers of Culture meeting within the Council of 18 May 1990 on future eligibility for the 'European City of Culture' and on a special European Cultural Month event, OJ C 162 , 3.7.1990.

Decision 93/424/EEC of the Council of 22 July 1993 on an action plan for the introduction of advanced television services in Europe, OJ L 196, 5.8.1993.

Decision 719/96/EC of the European Parliament and of the Council of 29 March 1996 establishing a programme to support artistic and cultural activities having a European dimension (Kaleidoscope), OJ L 99, 20.4.1996.

Decision 97/C 305/02 of the Council of 22 September 1997 on cross-border fixed book prices in European linguistic areas, OJ C 305, 7.10.1997.

Decision 2085/97/EC of the European Parliament and of the Council of 6 October 1997 establishing a programme of support, including translation, in the fields of books and reading (Ariane), OJ L 292, 24.10.1997.

Decision 2228/97/EC of the European Parliament and of the Council of 13 October 1997 establishing a Community action programme in the field of cultural heritage (the Raphael Programme), OJ L 305, 8.11.1997.

Decision 508/2000/EC of the European Parliament and of the Council of 14 February 2000 establishing the Culture 2000 programme, OJ L 063, 10.3.2000.

Decision 2000/821/EC of the Council of 20 December 2000 on the implementation of a programme to encourage the development, distribution and promotion of European audiovisual works (MEDIA Plus – Development, Distribution and Promotion 2001–2005), OJ L 13, 17.1.2001.

Directive 87/54/EEC of the Council of 16 December 1986 on the legal protection of topographies of semiconductor products, OJ L 024, 27.1.1987.

Directive 89/552/EEC of the Council of 3 October 1989 on the coordination of certain provisions laid down by Law, Regulation or Administrative Action in Member States concerning the pursuit of broadcasting activities, OJ L 298, 17.10.1989.

Directive 91/250/EEC of the Council of 14 May 1991 on the legal protection of computer programs, OJ L 122, 17.5.1991.

Directive 92/38/EEC of the Council of 11 May 1992 on the adoption of standards for satellite broadcasting of television signals, OJ L 137, 20.5.1992.

Directive 92/100/EEC of the Council of 19 November 1992 on rental right and lending right and on certain rights related to copyright in the field of intellectual property, OJ L 346, 27.11.1992.

Directive 93/7/EEC of the Council of 15 March 1993 on the return of cultural objects unlawfully removed from the territory of a Member State, OJ L 074, 27.3.1993.

Directive 93/83/EEC of the Council of 27 September 1993 on the coordination of certain rules concerning copyright and rights related to copyright applicable to satellite broadcasting and cable retransmission, OJ L 248, 6.10.1993.

Directive 93/98/EEC of the Council of 29 October 1993 harmonizing the term of protection of copyright and certain related rights, OJ L 290, 24.11.1993.

Directive 95/47/EC of the European Parliament and of the Council of 24 October 1995 on the use of standards for the transmission of television signals, OJ L 281, 23.11.1995.

Directive 96/9/EC of the European Parliament and of the Council of 11 March 1996 on the legal protection of databases, OJ L 077, 27.3.1996.

Directive 97/36/EC of the European Parliament and of the Council of 30 June 1997 amending Council Directive 89/552/EEC on the coordination of certain provisions laid down by law, regulation or administrative action in Member States concerning the pursuit of broadcasting activities, OJ L 202, 30.7.1997.

Directive 2001/29/CE of the European Parliament and of the Council of 22 May 2001 on the harmonization of certain aspects of copyright and related rights in the information society, OJ L 167, 22.6.2001.

Directive 2001/84/EC of the European Parliament and of the Council of 27 September 2001 on the resale right for the benefit of the author of an original work of art, OJ L 272, 13.10.2001.

Regulation 3911/92 of the Council of 9 December 1992 on the export of cultural goods, OJ L 395, 13.12.1992.

Resolution from the European Parliament on measures to protect the European cultural heritage of 13 May 1974, OJ C 62, 30.5.1974.

Resolution from the European Parliament on Community action in the cultural sector of 8 March 1976, OJ C 79, 5.4.1976.

Resolution from the European Parliament on literary translation in the Community of 18 January 1979, OJ C 39, 12.2.1979.

Resolution from the European Parliament on the fixing of book prices of 13 February 1981, OJ C 50, 9.3.1981.

Resolution from the European Parliament on radio and television broadcasting in the European Community of 12 March 1982 ('The Hahn Resolution'), OJ C 87, 5.4.1982.

Resolution from the European Parliament on stronger Community action in the cultural sector of 18 November 1983, OJ C 342, 19.12.1983.

Resolution from the European Parliament on literary translation in the Community of 18 November 1983, OJ C 342, 19.12.1983.

Resolution from the European Parliament on International Youth Year of 10 July 1985, OJ C 229, 9.9.1985.

Resolution from the European Parliament on the European Foundation of 12 December 1985, OJ C 352, 31.12.1985.

Resolution from the European Parliament on the promotion of books and reading in Europe of 21 January 1993, OJ C 42, 15.2.1993.

Resolution from the European Parliament on common book price-fixing across borders of 20 November 1998, OJ C 379, 7.12.1998.

Resolution of the representatives of the Governments of the Member States of 24 July 1984 on measures to combat audio-visual pirating, OJ C 204, 24.7.1984.

Resolution of the representatives of the Governments of the Member States of 24 July 1984 on measures to ensure that an appropriate place is given to audio-visual programmes of European origin, OJ C 204, 3.8.1984.

Resolution of the Ministers responsible for Cultural Affairs, meeting within the Council, of 13 June 1985 concerning the annual event 'European City of Culture', OJ C 153, 22.6.1985.

Resolution of the Ministers responsible for Cultural Affairs, meeting within the Council, of 13 June 1985 concerning a European sculpture competition, OJ C 153, 22.6.1985.

Resolution of the Council and the ministers with responsibility for Cultural Affairs, meeting within the Council, of 27 September 1985 on collaboration between libraries in the field of data processing, OJ C 271, 23.10.1985.

Resolution of the Ministers responsible for Cultural Affairs, meeting within the

Council, of 20 December 1985 on special conditions of admission for young people to museums and cultural events, OJ C 348, 31.12.1985.

Resolution of the Ministers responsible for Cultural Affairs, meeting within the Council, of 17 February 1986 on the establishment of transnational cultural itineraries, OJ C 044, 26.2.1986.

Resolution of the Ministers with responsibility for Cultural Affairs, meeting within the Council, of 13 November 1986 on the protection of Europe's architectural heritage, OJ C 320, 13.12.1986.

Resolution of the Ministers with responsibility for Cultural Affairs, meeting within the Council, of 13 November 1986 on business sponsorship of cultural activities, OJ C 320, 13.12.1986.

Resolution of the Council and of the Ministers responsible for Cultural Affairs, meeting within the Council of 13 November 1986 on the European cinema and television year (1988), OJ C 320, 13.12.1986.

Resolution of the Council and of the Ministers responsible for Cultural Affairs, meeting within the Council of 9 November 1987 on the promotion of translation of important works of European culture, OJ C 309, 19.11.1987.

Resolution of the Council and of the Ministers responsible for Cultural Affairs, meeting within the Council of 27 May 1988 on the future organisation of their work, OJ C 197, 27.7.1988.

Resolution of the Council and the Ministers responsible for Cultural Affairs, meeting within the Council of 18 May 1989 concerning the promotion of books and reading, OJ C 183, 20.7.1989.

Resolution of the Council of 8 February 1999 on fixed book prices in homogeneous cross-border linguistic areas, OJ C 042, 17.2.1999.

Resolution of the Council of 12 February 2001 on the application of national fixed book-price systems, OJ C 073, 6.3.2001.

Treaty of Nice amending Treaty on European Union, the treaties establishing the European Communities and certain related acts, OJ C 80, 10.3.2001.

Official documents

Adonnino, P. (1985). *Reports from the ad hoc Committee on a People's Europe* ('The Adonnino Reports'), *EC Bulletin* Supplement 7/85.

Assemblée Nationale française (1995a). Rapport d'information No. 2188 sur la proposition de directive [COM(95) 86 final], déposé par la délégation de l'Assemblée Nationale pour l'Union européenne et présenté par M. François Guillaume, 27 July 1995.

Assemblée Nationale française (1995b). Compte-rendu des débats de l'Assemblée Nationale sur la Directive 'Télévision Sans Frontières', 16 November 1995.

Cannes Declaration of European Culture Ministers (2003), Cannes Festival, 15 May 2003.

Comité de Vigilance pour la Diversité Culturelle (2003). Appel des artistes et des créateurs pour la diversité culturelle, January: www.sacem.fr.

Conference on *The Economics of the Book Industry in Europe*, 29–30 September 2000, Ministère de la Culture et de la Communication, Strasbourg.

Conference proceedings of the Florence Conference on culture and its relations with technology and the economy, 25–28 March 1987, EC Bulletin 3–1987.

Council Press Release of the Audiovisual/Cultural Affairs Council of 28 May 1998, Brussels.

Council of Europe (1989). *European Convention on Transfrontier Television*, 5 May 1989, European Treaty Series, No. 132.

Culture Council (1982). Culture Ministers informal meeting in Naples of 17 and 18 September 1982, EC Bulletin 9–1982.

Culture Council (1984). Culture Ministers meeting of 22 November 1984, EC Bulletin 11–1984.

Culture Council (1987). Culture Ministers informal meeting in Copenhagen on 10 and 11 December 1987, EC Bulletin 12–1987.

European Commission (1977). *Commission Communication on Community Action in the Cultural Sector* [COM(77) final].

European Commission (1982). *Commission Communication on Stronger Community Action in the Cultural Sector* [COM(82) 590 final)].

European Commission (1983). *Interim Report Realities and Tendencies in European Television: perspectives and options* [COM(83) 229 final].

European Commission (1984). *Television Without Frontiers. Green Paper on the Establishment of the Common Market for Broadcasting Especially by Satellite and Cable* [COM(84) 300 final].

European Commission (1985a). *Commission Communication on the Creation of a Community Framework System for Book Prices* [COM(85) 258 final].

European Commission (1985b). *The Completion of the Internal Market – White Paper of the Commission to the Attention of the European Council* [COM(85) 310 final].

European Commission (1986). *Proposal for a Council Directive Concerning Broadcasting Activities* [COM(86) 146 final].

European Commission (1987). *Commission Communication. A Fresh Boost for Culture in the European Community* [COM(87) 603 final].

European Commission (1988). *Green Paper on Author's Right and the Technological Challenge* [COM(88) 172 final].

European Commission (1989). *Commission Communication on Books and Reading: a Cultural Challenge for Europe* [COM (89) 258 final].

European Commission (1990). *Commission Communication on Audiovisual Policy* [COM(90) 78 final].

European Commission (1991). Follow-up to the Green Paper. Working Programme of the Commission in the Field of Copyright and Neighbouring Rights [COM(90) 584 final].

European Commission (1993). *White Paper: Growth, Competitiveness, Employment – the Challenges and Ways Forward into the Twenty-first Century* [COM(93) 700 final].

European Commission (1994a). *Green Paper on Strategy Options to Strengthen the European Programme Industry in the Context of the Audiovisual Policy of the European Union* [COM(94) 96 final].

European Commission (1994b). *Communication on Europe's Way to the Information Society: an Action Plan* [COM(94) 347 final].

European Commission (1995a). *Proposal for a Directive Amending Directive 89/552/EEC on the Coordination of Certain Provisions Laid Down by Law,*

Regulation or Administrative Action in Member States Concerning the Pursuit of Broadcasting Activities [COM(95) 86 final].

European Commission (1995b). *Green Paper on Copyright and Related Rights in the Information Society* [COM(95) 382 final].

European Commission (1995c). *White Paper on Education and Training – Teaching and Learning Towards the Learning Society* [COM(95) 590 final].

European Commission (1996), *First report on the Consideration of Cultural Aspects in European Community Action* [COM(96) 160 final].

European Commission (2005). *Proposal for a Directive Amending Council Directive 89/552/EEC on the Coordination of Certain Provisions Laid Down by Law, Regulation or Administrative Action in Member States Concerning the Pursuit of Television Broadcasting Activities* [COM(2005) 646 final].

European Council (1969). Final Communiqué of the Hague Summit of 1 and 2 December 1969, EC Bulletin 1–1970.

European Council (1972). Conference proceedings of the Paris Summit, 19 and 20 October 1972, EC Bulletin 10–1972.

European Council (1973a). Conference proceedings of the Copenhagen Summit, 14 and 15 October 1973, EC Bulletin 12–1973.

European Council (1973b). *The Declaration on European Identity*, Copenhagen Summit of 14 and 15 October 1973, EC Bulletin 12–1973.

European Council (1983). *The Solemn Declaration on European Union of 19 June 1983*, EC Bulletin 6–1983.

European Parliament (1990). Report concerning the implementation of an action programme to promote the development of the European audiovisual industry (1992–1995) ('The Barzanti Report'), PE 144.275/fin. PE A 3–0293, 3 November.

European Parliament (2002). Working Paper *Cultural Policies in EU Member States*, EDUC 107A, May 2002.

French Government (1987). *Livre Bleu pour une Europe de l'Education et de la Culture*, 24 March.

Genscher, H.D. and Colombo, E. (1981). *Genscher-Colombo Plan*, EC Bulletin 11–1981.

High Level Group on the Information Society (1994). *Europe and the Global Information Society. Recommendations of the High-level Group on the Information Society to the Corfu European Council* ('The Bangemann Report'), Brussels, 26 May 1994.

Tindemans, L. (1976). *Tindemans Report on European Union*, EC Bulletin, Supplement 1/76.

Vienna Conference on Intellectual Property Rights, Opening speech from Commissioner Mario Monti, July 1998, http://europa.eu.int/comm /internal_market/copyright/conferences/1998–07–conference-vienna-opening_en.htm.

WTO (1998). Background note to the audiovisual services, S/C/W/40, WTO, Geneva.

Books and articles

Ahearne, J. (2003). 'Cultural policy in the Old Europe: France and Germany', *International Journal of Culture Policy* 9(2): 127–131.

Baumgartner, F. and Jones, B. (1991). 'Agenda dynamics and instability in American politics', *The Journal of Politics* 53: 1044–1073.

Baumgartner, Frank R. and D. Jones, Bryan (1993). *Agendas and Instability in American Politics*, Chicago: The University of Chicago Press.

Baumgartner, Frank R. and D. Jones, Bryan (1994). 'Attention, boundary effects, and large-scale policy change in air transportation policy', in D.A. Rochefort and R.W. Cobb (eds), *The Politics of Problem Definition. Shaping the Policy Agenda*, Lawrence: University Press of Kansas.

Börzel, T. (1999). 'Towards convergence in Europe? Institutional adaptation to Europeanization in Germany and Spain', *Journal of Common Market Studies* 39, 4: 573–596.

Bosso, Christopher J. (1994), 'The contextual bases of problem definition', in D.A. Rochefort and R.W. Cobb (eds), *The Politics of Problem Definition. Shaping the Policy Agenda*, Lawrence: University Press of Kansas.

Brossat, C. (1999). *La culture européenne: définitions et enjeux*, Brussels: Bruylant.

Burns, R. and Van der Will, W. (2003). 'German cultural policy: an overview', *International Journal of Cultural Policy* 9 (2): 133–152.

Campbell, J.L. (1998). 'Institutional analysis and the role of ideas in political economy', *Theory and Society* 27: 377–409.

Caudron, G. (1992). 'La Télévision à Haute Définition (TVHD): des enjeux culturels et industriels majeurs pour l'Europe', *Revue du Marché Commun et de l'Union Européenne* 355: 152–154.

Caust, Jo (2003). 'Putting the "art" back into arts policy-making: how arts policy has been "captured" by the economists and the marketers', *The International Journal of Cultural Policy* 9 (1): 51–63.

Checkel, Jeffrey and Moravcsit, Andrew (2001). 'A constructivist research programme in EU studies?', *European Union Politics* 2(2): 219–249.

Chirac, J. (2005). Speech on the occasion of the symposium for a Europe of culture, Paris, 2 May.

Collins, R. (1994). *Broadcasting and Audiovisual Policy in the European Single Market*, London: John Libbey and Company Ltd.

Collins, R. and Murroni, C. (1996). *New Media, New Policies: Media and Communications Strategies for the Future*, Cambridge: Polity Press.

Cornil, C. (1996). 'Bilan sur la directive Télévision sans frontières du 3 octobre 1989', *Les Petites Affiches* 68: 13–16.

Cram, L. (1997). *Policy-making in the EU. Conceptual Lenses and the Integration Process*, London: Routledge.

Craufurd Smith, Rachael (2004). 'European Community intervention in the cultural field: continuity or change?', in Rachael Craufurd Smith (ed.), *Culture and European Union Law*, Oxford: Oxford University Press.

Davies, G. (1981). 'Harmonization of copyright legislations in the European Communities', *European Intellectual Property Review* 3, 3: 67–71.

Davies, G. and Von Rauscher auf Weeg, H. (1983). *Challenges to Copyright and*

Related Rights in the EC, Oxford: ESC Publishing Limited.

Dehousse, R. (1998). *The European Court of Justice*, Basingstoke: Macmillan.

Delcourt, J. and Papini, R. (eds) (1987). *Pour une politique Européenne de la culture*, Paris: Economica.

Delors, J. (1985), *Address to the Opening of the European Parliament of 12 March 1985*, Introduction to the Programme of the Commission for 1985 in Debates of the European Parliament, OJ 2–234.

De Witte, B. (1995), 'The European content requirement in the EC Television Directive – five years after', in E.M. Barendt (ed.), *The Yearbook of Media and Entertainment Law 1995*, Oxford: Clarendon Press: 101–127.

De Witte, B. (2001), 'Trade in culture: international legal regimes and EU constitutional values', in G. De Burca and J. Scott (eds), *The EU and the WTO. Legal and Constitutional Issues,* Oxford: Hart Publishing: 237–255.

Dietz, A. (1980). 'Copyright and the EEC – harmonization of national laws', *European Intellectual Property Review*, June 1980: 189–193.

Doherty, M. and Griffiths, I. (2000). 'The harmonization of European Union copyright law for the digital age', *European Intellectual Property Review* 22, 1: 17–21.

Doutrelepont, C. (1996). *Le droit et l'objet d'art: le droit de suite des artistes plasticiens dans l'Union Européenne*, Bruxelles: Bruylant.

Dreier, T. (1991). 'Broadcasting and copyright in the Internal Market: the new proposal by the EC Commission concerning cable and satellite broadcasts', *European Intellectual Property Review* 13, 2: 43–47.

Dumont, H. (1992). 'Les compétences culturelles de la Communauté Européenne. Bilan critique et perspectives', *Revue Interdisciplinaire d'Etudes Juridiques* 29: 1–47.

Earnshaw, D. and Judge, D. (1996). 'From cooperation to codecision: the European Parliament's path to legislative power', in J.J. Richarsdon (ed.), *European Union: Power and Policy-Making*, London: Routledge: 96–127.

Esmein, B. (1999). 'Les politiques de l'Union Européenne dans le domaine de la culture, de l'éducation et des langues', *Journal of European Integration History* 5, 2: 75–105.

European Writers Congress (2000). Declaration on the fixed book price in the European Union, Conference on the Book Economy in the European Area, Strasbourg, 29–30 September.

Federation of European Publishers (1995). *Policy statement of the Federation of European Publishers*, 19 May 1995: http://europa.eu.int/en/agenda/igc-home/instdoc/industry/feppolic.html.

Fraser, M. W. (1996). 'Television', in H. Kassim and A. Menon (eds), *The European Union and National Industrial Policy*, London: Routledge: 204–225.

Frediani, C.M. (1992). 'La politique de la communauté européenne en matière d'éducation et de culture', *Europe en Formation* 284: 51–64.

Freedman, D. (2003). 'Cultural policy-making in the free trade era: an evaluation of the impact of current World Trade Organization negotiations on audio-visual industries', *International Journal of Cultural Policy*, 9(3): 305–318

Gamson, W.A. and Modigliani, A. (1989). 'Media discourse and public opinion on nuclear power: a constructionist approach,' *American Journal of Sociology* 95 (1): 1–37.

Garett, G. (1992). 'International cooperation and institutional choice: the European Communities Internal Market', *International Organization* 46, 2: 533–558.

Goldberg, D., Prosser, T. and Verhulst, S. (1998). *EC Media Law and Policy*. London: Longman.

Goldstein, J. (1993). *Ideas, Interests and American Trade Policy*, Ithaca: Cornell University Press.

Gotzen, F. (1994). *L'harmonisation du droit d'auteur au sein de l'Union Européenne*, Colloque Mondial de l'OMPI sur l'Avenir du Droit d'Auteur et des Droits Voisins, Paris, 1–3 June, WIPO Publications.

Granturco, T. (1999). 'La genèse de l'intégration de la culture au sein des compétences communautaires', *Journal of European Integration History* 5, 2: 109–126.

Haart, M. (1998). 'The proposed Directive for Copyright in the Information Society: nice rights, shame about the exceptions', *European Intellectual Property Review* 20, 5: 169–171.

Haas, E.B. (1964). *Beyond the Nation-state: Functionalism and International Organization*, Stanford: Stanford University Press.

Haas, P. (1992). 'Epistemic communities and international policy coordination', *International Organization* 46, 1: 1–35.

Hall, P. (1992). 'The Movement from Keynesianism to monetarism: institutional analysis and British economic policy in the 1970s', in S. Steinmo, K. Thelen and F. Longstreth (eds), *Structuring Politics*, New York: Cambridge University Press: 90–113.

Hall, P. (ed.) (1993). *The Political Power of Economic Ideas: Keynesisnism across Nations*, Princeton: Princeton University Press.

Harcourt, A. (2002). 'Engineering Europeanisation: the role of the European institutions in shaping national broadcasting regulation', *Journal of European Public Policy* 9, 5: 736–755.

Harcourt, A.J. (2005). *The European Union and the Regulation of Media Markets*, Manchester: Manchester University Press.

Harris, B. (1978). 'Copyright in the EEC – the Dietz Report', *European Intellectual Property Review*, November 1978: 2–7.

Harrison, J. and Woods, L. (2000). 'European citizenship: can audio-visual policy make a difference?', *Journal of Common Market Studies* 38, 3: 471–495.

Hayes-Renshaw, F. and Wallace, H. (1997). *The Council of Ministers*, London: Macmillan Press.

Hesmondhalgh, D. (2002). *The Cultural Industries*, London: Sage.

Hoffman, S. (1966). 'Obstinate or obsolete? The fate of the nation state and the case of Western Europe', *Daedalus* 95: 892–908.

Holderness, M. (1998). 'Moral rights and authors' rights: The keys to the information age', *The Journal of Information, Law and Technology*: http://elij.warwick.ac.uk/jilt/infosoc/98_1hold/holder.htm.

Hooghe, L. and Marks, G. (1997). 'The making of a policy: the struggle over European integration', European Integration Online Papers 1, 4: http://eiop.or.at/eiop/texte/1997-004a.htm.

Hooghe, L. and Marks, G. (2001). *Multi-level Governance and European Integration*, Oxford: Rowman and Littlefield.

Hugenholtz, P.B. (ed.) (1996). *The Future of Copyright in a Digital Environment*, London: Kluwer Law International.

Hugenholtz, B. (2000). 'Why the Copyright Directive is unimportant', *European Intellectual Property Review* 11: 501–502.

Humphreys, P. (1994). *Media and Media Policy in Germany. The Press and Broadcasting Since 1945*, Oxford/Providence, USA: Berg Publishers.

Humphreys, P. (1996). *Mass Media and Media Policy in Western Europe*, Manchester: Manchester University Press.

Jachtenfuchs, M. and Kohler-Koch, B. (1996). 'Regieren in dynamischen Mehrebenensystem', in M. Jachtenfuchs and B. Kohler-Koch (eds), *Europäische Integration*, Opladen: Leske & Budrich: 15–44.

Jacobsen, J.K. (1995). 'Much ado about ideas. The cognitive factor in economic policy', *World Politics* 47: 283–310.

Jaumain, M. (1997) 'Some features of cultural policies applied in Belgium, particularly in the French-speaking community', *Journal of Arts Management, Law and Society*, 27 (3).

Kangas, A. (2001). 'Cultural policy in Finland', *Journal of Arts Management, Law and Society* 31(1).

Keller, P. (1997). 'The New Television Without Frontiers Directive', in E.M. Barendt (ed.), *The Yearbook of the Media and Entertainment Law*, Oxford: Clarendon Press: 45–73.

Kennet, W. (1996). 'The European Community and the General Agreement on Trade in Services', in N. Emiliou and D. O'Keefe (eds), *The European Union and World Trade Law*, Chichester: John Wiley: 136–148.

Krebber, D. (2002). *Europeanisation of Regulatory Television Policy: The Decision-Making Process of the Television Without Frontiers Directives from 1987 & 1997*, Baden-Baden: Nomos Verlagsgesellschaft.

Kruse, J. (1994). 'The EC–US conflict over film and television software', *Intereconomics* 29: 284–291.

Lane, R. (1993). 'New Community competences under the Maastricht Treaty', *Common Market Law Review* 5: 939–979.

Lange, A. and Renaud, J.L. (1989). *The Future of the European Audiovisual Industry*, Media Monograph no.10, European Institute for the Media.

Larsson, T. and Svenson, P. (2001). 'Cultural policy in Sweden', *Journal of Arts Management, Law & Society* 31 (1) 79–96.

Lequesne, C. (1993). *Paris-Bruxelles: Comment se fait la politique européenne de la France*, Paris: Presses de la Fondation Nationale de Sciences Politiques.

Levy, D.A. (1999). *Europe's Digital Revolution. Broadcasting Regulation, the EU and the Nation State*, London: Routledge.

Lewinsky, S. (1998). 'A successful step towards copyright and related rights in the information age: the new E.C. proposal for a Harmonisation Directive', *European Intellectual Property Review* 20, 4: 135–139.

Lipgens, W. (1982). *A History of European Integration*, Vol. 1, Oxford: Clarendon Press.

Littoz-Monnet, A. (2003). 'European cultural policy: a French creation?', *French Politics*, 1: 255–278.

Littoz-Monnet, A. (2005). 'The European politics of book pricing', *West European Politics* 28 (1): 159–181.

Looseley, D.L. (1995). The *Politics of Fun: Cultural Policy and Debate in Contemporary France*, Oxford: Berg Publishers.

Looseley, D.L. (2001). 'Cultural policy in France since 1959: arm's length, or "up close and personal"', Nordic Cultural Institute.

Looseley, D.L. (2003). 'Back to the future: rethinking French cultural policy, 1997–2002', *International Journal of Cultural Policy* 9(2): 227–234.

Ludlow, P. (2001) 'The Treaty of Nice: neither triumph nor disaster', *ECSA Review*, 14(2): 1–11.

Machet, E. and Robillard, S. (1998). *Television and Culture: Policies and Regulations in Europe*, Düsseldorf: The European Institute for the Media.

Maggiore, M. (1990). *Audiovisual Production in the Single Market*, Luxembourg: Office for Official Publications of the European Communities.

Massart-Piérard, F. (1986). 'Limites et enjeux d'une politique culturelle pour la Communauté européenne', *Revue du Marché Commun* 293: 34–40.

Mazey, S. (1998). 'The EU and women's rights: from the Europeanisation of national agendas to the nationalisation of a European agenda?', *Journal of European Public Policy*, 5, 1: 131–152.

Mazey, S. and Richardson, J. (2001). 'Interest groups and EU policy-making: organizational logic and venue shopping', in J. Richardson (ed.), *European Union: Power and Policy-Making*, London: Routledge: 217–234.

McKnight, E. (1992). 'Copyright in a Single Market in broadcasting', *European Intellectual Property Review* 14, 10: 343–350.

McMahon, J. (1995). *Education and Culture in Community Law*, London: Athlone Press.

Menon, A. (1996). 'France and the IGC of 1996', *Journal of European Public Policy* 2, 3: 231–252.

Miyet, B. (2001). 'The Internet disrupts the stage', Chairman's message on the web site of the French authors' society (SACEM), July 2001: www.sacem.fr/english/index.html.

Möller, M. (1989). 'Author's right or copyright', in F. Gotzen (ed.), *Copyright and the European Community. The Green Paper on Copyright and the Challenge of New Technology*, Brussels: E. Story-Scientia: 11–20.

Monti, M. (1998). *Opening Speech for the International Conference on Intellectual Property Rights*, Vienna, 12–14 July 1998: http://europa.eu.int /comm/internal_market/en/wwwvienn/en/speech.htm.

Moravcsik, A. (1993). 'Preferences and power in the European Community: a liberal intergovernmentalist approach', *Journal of Common Market Studies* 31, 4: 473–524.

Moravscik, A. (1999). *The Choice for Europe: Social Purpose and State Power from Messina to Maastricht*, London: UCL Press.

Moussis, N. (2001). *Access to European Union: Law, Economics, Policies*, Rixensart: European Study Service.

Negrine, R. and Papathanassopoulos, S. (1990). *The Internationalization of Television*, London: Pinter Publishers.

Nugent, N. (1999). *The Government and Politics of the European Union*, 4th edn, London: Macmillan Press.

Obaton, V. (1997). *La promotion de l'identité européenne depuis 1946*, Genève: Institut Européen de l'Université de Genève.

Papathanassopoulos, S. (1990). 'Broadcasting and the European Community: the Commission's audiovisual policy', in K. Dyson and P. Humphreys (eds), *The Political Economy of Communications*, London: Routledge: 107–123.

Parrish, R. (2003). *Sports Law and Policy in the European Union*, Manchester: Manchester University Press.

Pauwels, C. and Loisen, J. (2003). 'The WTO and the audiovisual sector. Economic free trade vs cultural horse trading', *European Journal of Communication* 18(3): 291–313.

Peters, G. (1996). 'Agenda-setting in the European Union', in J. Richardson (ed.), *European Union. Power and Policy-Making*, London: Routledge: 61–76.

Pollack, M.A. (1997). 'Delegation, agency, and agenda setting in the European Community', *International Organization* 51, 1: 99–134.

Pollack, M. (2000). 'The end of creeping competence? EU policy-making since Maastricht', *Journal of Common Market Studies* 38, 3: 519–538.

Pongy, M. (1996). 'L'action culturelle de l'union Européenne entre logiques politique et professionnelle', in *The European Yearbook of Comparative Government and Public Administration*, volume III, Baden-Baden: Nomos Verlagsgesellschaft: 243–255.

Pongy, M. (1997). 'Entres modèles nationaux et eurogroupes d'intérêts professionnels: l'action de l'Union dans la culture', *Cultures et Conflits* 28: 129–145.

Puchala, D.J. (1999). 'Institutionalism, intergovernmentalism and European integration: a review article', *Journal of Common Market Studies* 37, 2: 317–331.

Putnam, R.D. (1988). 'Diplomacy and domestic politics. The logic of two-level games', *International Organization* 42: 427–460.

Reding, V. (2000a). Speech on 'Which cultural policy for the European Union', *Conference of the World Association of Newspapers*, Hanover, 1 June 2000. http://europa.eu.int/comm/avpolicy/legis/speech_en.htm.

Reding, V. (2000b). Speech on 'Europe's competitive position in the Internet-based economy', *European Summit*, Madrid, 11 January 2000. http://europa.eu.int/comm/avpolicy/legis/key_doc/Madrid_en.htm.

Rein, M. and Schön, D. (1991). 'Frame-reflective policy discourse', in P. Wagner, C. Hirschon Weiss, B. Wittrock and H. Wollman (eds), *Social Sciences and Modern States, National Experiences and Theoretical Crossroads*, Cambridge: Cambridge University Press.

Reinbothe, J. (2001). 'Recent intellectual property legislative developments in the European Union: copyright and related rights', 9th Annual Conference on International Intellectual Property Law and Policy, Fordham University, 19 April.

Riou, A. (1996). 'Le prix du livre et la jurisprudence de la Cour de Justice des Communautés européennes', *Les Petites Affiches* 143: 19–23.

Rittberger, B. and Richardson, J. (2001). '(Mis-)Matching declarations and actions? Commission proposals in the light of the Fifth Environmental Action Programme', Paper presented to the Seventh Biennial International Conference of the European Community Studies Association (ECSA), May 31–June 2, 2001, Madison, Wisconsin.

Rochefort, David A. and Cobb, Roger W. (1994). 'Problem definition: an emerging perspective', in D. Rochefort and R. Cobb (eds), *The Politics of Problem Definition: Shaping the Policy Agenda*, Lawrence: University Press of Kansas.

Sabatier, P.A. (1998). 'An advocacy coalition framework of policy change and the role of policy-oriented learning therein', *Policy Sciences* 21: 129–168.

Sallois, J., Wangermée, R. and Wallon, R. (1993). 'Administrer la culture?', *Revue française d'administration publique* 65: 1–178.

Sbragia, A.M. (2000). 'Environmental policy. Economic constraints and external pressures', in H. Wallace and W. Wallace (eds), *Policy-Making in the European Union*, Oxford: Oxford University Press: 293–316.

Scharpf, F.W. (1996). 'Negative and positive integration in the political economy of European welfare states', in G. Marks, F.W. Scharpf, P.C. Schmitter and W. Streeck (eds), *Governance in the European Union*, London: Sage: 15–39.

Scharpf, F.W. (1997). *Games Real Actors Play: Actor-Centered Institutionalism in Policy Research*, Oxford: Westview Press.

Scharpf, F.W. (1999). Contribution to 'Approaches to the study of European politics': www.eustudies.org/ratioanlchoice.html. (First published in the ECSA Review 12, 2: 2–9.)

Scharpf, F.W. (2000). 'Notes toward a theory of multilevel governance in Europe', MPIfG Discussion Paper 00/5.

Schuster, J.M. (2002). 'Informing cultural policy. Data, statistics, and meaning', International Symposium on Culture Statistics, 21–23 October, Montréal.

Shore, C. (2000). *Building Europe: the Cultural Politics of European Integration*, London: Routledge.

Soriano, M.C. (1999). 'Le Traité CE et la fixation des prix dans le secteur du livre', *Revue du Marché Unique Européen* 2: 361–390.

Standholtz, W. and Stone Sweet, A. (1997). 'European integration and supranational governance', *Journal of European Public Policy* 4, 3: 297–317.

Standholtz, W. and Stone Sweet, A. (eds) (1998). *European Integration and Supranational Governance*, New York: Oxford University Press.

Standholtz, W. and Zysman, J. (1989). '1992: Recasting the European bargain', *World Politics* 42: 95–128.

Sticht, P. (2000). *Culture européenne ou Europe des cultures? Les enjeux actuels de la politique culturelle en Europe*, Paris: L'Harmattan.

Stone, D.A. (1989). 'Causal stories and the formation of policy agendas', *Political Science Quaterly* 104: 281–300.

Stone Sweet, A. and Brunell, T. (1998). 'The European Court and the national courts: a statistical analysis of preliminary references, 1961–95', *Journal of European Public Policy* 5, 1: 69–97.

Stone Sweet, A. (2000). *Governing with Judges: Constitutional Politics in Europe*, Oxford: Oxford University Press.

Surel, Y. (1997). 'Quand la politique change les politiques. La loi Lang du 10 Août 1981 et les politiques du livre', *Revue française de science politique* 47: 147–172.

Valéry, P. (1919). *La Crise de l'esprit*, Paris: Nouvelle Revue Française.

Vandoren, P. (1996). 'Copyright and related rights in the Information Society', in B. Hugenholtz (ed.), *The Future of Copyright in a Digital Environment*, London: Kluwer Law International: 153–169.

Venturelli, S. (1998). *Liberalizing the European Media: Politics, Regulation, and the Public Sphere*, Oxford: Oxford University Press.

Vinje, T.C. (1995). 'Harmonizing intellectual property laws in the European

Union: past, present and future', *European Intellectual Property Review* 8: 361–377.

Weiler, J.H.H. (1993). 'Journey to an unknown destination: a retrospective and prospective of the European Court of Justice in the arena of political integration', *Journal of Common Market Studies* 31: 417–446.

Wheeler, M. (2000). 'Research note: The "undeclared war" Part II. The European Union's consultation process for the new round of the General Agreement on Trading Services/World Trade Organization on Audiovisual Services', *European Journal of Communication* 15 (2): 253–262.

Wiesand, A.J. (1995). *Handbook for Cultural Affairs*, Baden-Baden: Namos Verlagsgesellschaft.

Wikström, P. (1998). *Internet, Copyright and Freedom of Information: Problems of the EU Directive and MAI International Roundtable*, 9 October 1998, Finnish Institute, London.

Williams, R. (1989). *The Politics of Modernism*, London: Verso.

Wincott, D. (1996). 'The Court of Justice and the European policy process', in J. Richardson (ed.), *The European Union: power and policymaking*, London: Routledge,

Zandvliet, C.E. (1997/98). 'Fixed book prices in the Netherlands and the European Union: a challenge for Community competition law', *The Columbia Journal of European Law* 3: 413–451.

Zetterholm, S. (ed.) (1994). *National Cultures and European Integration: Exploratory Essays on Cultural Diversity and Common Policies*, Oxford /Providence, USA: Berg Publishers.

Internet sources

www.attac.org.
www.cnc.fr.
www.culture.fr.
www.europa.eu.int.
www.culturalpolicies.net.
www.culturelink.orh/culpol/index.html.

Index